AF580046

May 13, 2015

For Roby and Larry & Jeremy.

I hope you enjoy the history and paintings of the town "Where Time Stood Still."

Best Wishes

[illegible]

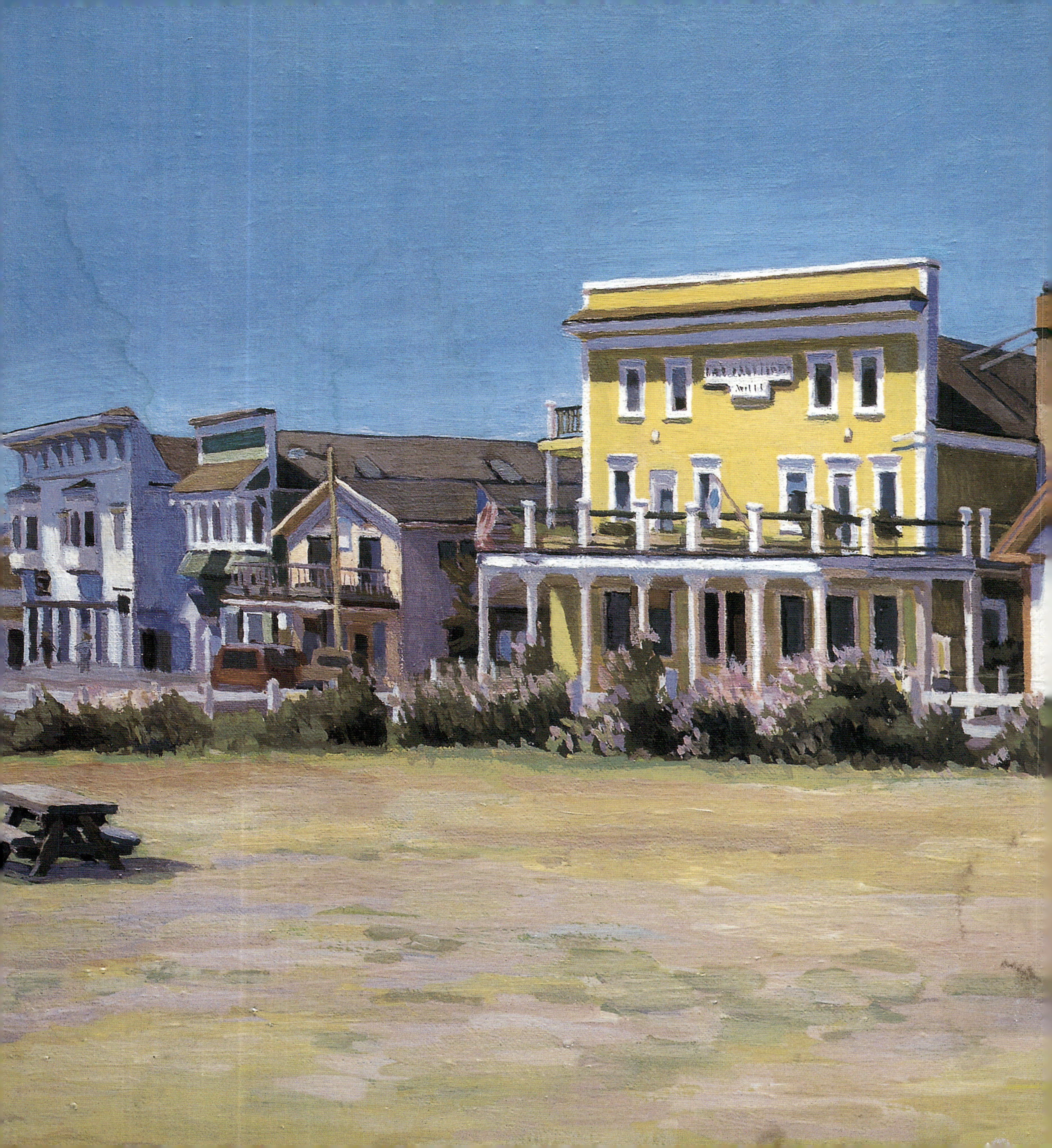

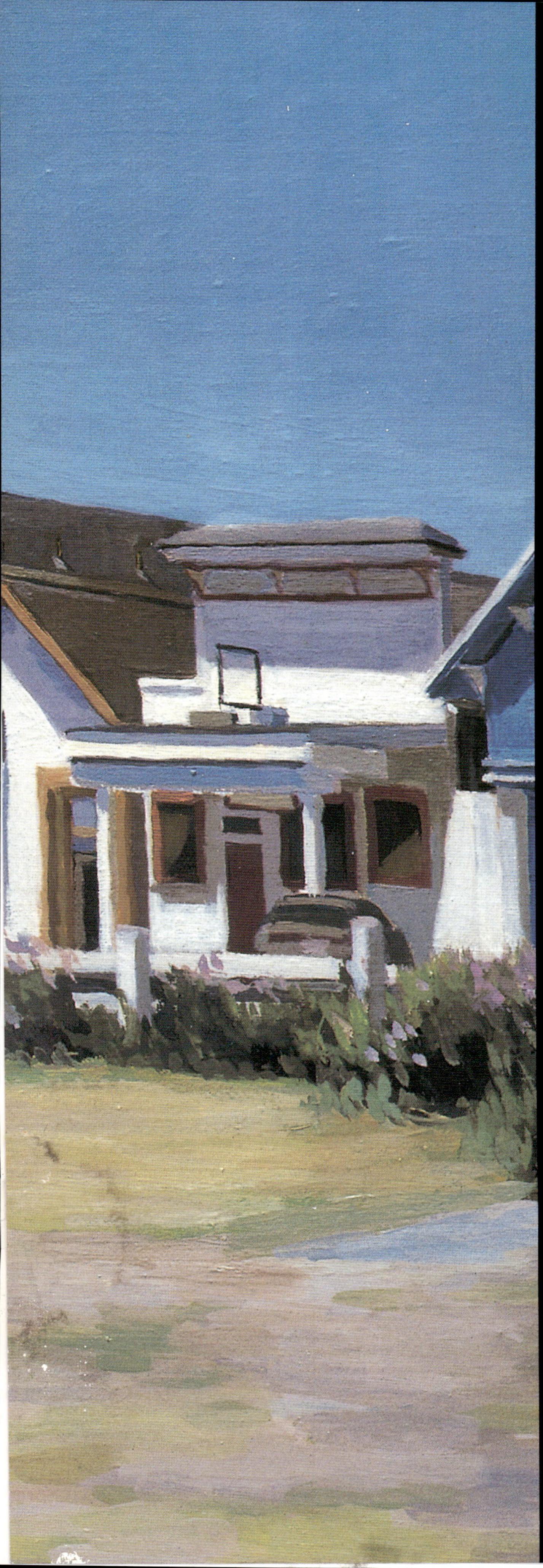

Mendocino: A *Painted Pictorial*

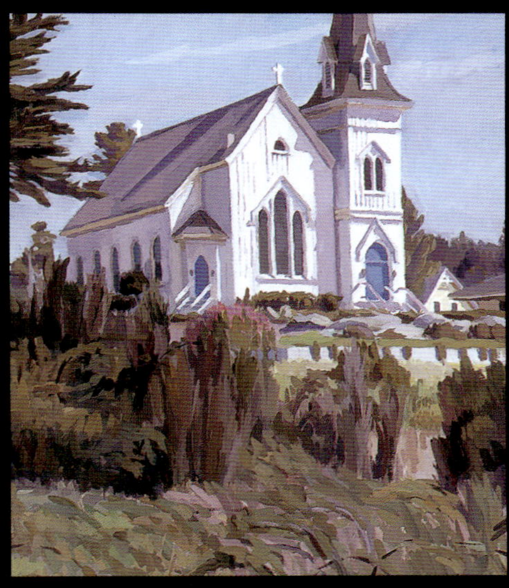

The Art of Kevin Milligan
with
A Comprehensive History
of Mendocino City

A Publication from
Coastside Graphics

Acknowledgments

I am grateful for the continuing support of Patricia Dillon. It was first her idea for me to found my own gallery in Mendocino, and her belief in my work helped me accomplish this—a significant step toward creating *Mendocino: A Painted Pictorial.*

When I was a child my mother Jacquelyn Milligan encouraged me to draw whenever I had a spare moment and to become whatever I wanted to be. While I was growing up, I observed my father Guy Milligan paint, and I learned how to view the world through his eyes. His paintings taught me to take notice of the beauty in everyday life around me and showed me how to see composition in nature. I am also blessed by the lifelong love and support of my sister Lisa, my brothers Kris and Gary, and their families.

Wilbur Niewald provided me with exceptional painting and drawing instruction while I studied at the Kansas City Art Institute. His lessons centered on how to perceive color in nature while painting and drawing from observation. Focused on working in oils, his training has been instrumental in my development as a painter. While at the Kansas City Art Institute, I became a friend of fellow student painters Rodney Franko and Dean Shaffer. For more than 27 years we have shared artistic criticism, encouragement, and humor in friendship, helping me through difficult times.

Donald A. Gazzaniga, who served as both publisher and book designer, made the production of this book possible. I appreciate how beautifully he has designed and formatted the material to best display my work and thereby express my vision. He also took the photographs for the book jacket and served as a liaison to the printer, Ever Best Printing Company of Hong Kong, where this book was printed on wood-free paper.

John Birchard Photography produced 74 of the 76 color transparencies used to make the color plates.

Vicki Hessel Werkley has been an extraordinary editor. Her writing ability and knowledge of Mendocino history made a powerful contribution to this work. We met at the Kelley House research library when we were both looking into details of local history for our respective books. She brought so much of her own creative force and understanding of Mendocino's history to this project, and was equally willing to lend her original research, that we ended up writing the text together. Her love of Mendocino history and attention to detail will also be found in her novel *Taking the Redwoods*, the story of a young woman becoming an artist—a photographer—in 1885 Mendocino. Vicki is also the editor of more than 14 fiction and non-fiction books and author of the historical novel *Girl-On-Fire*. Regrettably, due to illness and the passing of her mother, Vicki was unable to participate in the final draft of this book.

We are both eternally grateful to Mendocino Historical Research, Inc. at the Kelley House Museum and especially to the Directors, first Marjorie Eseppi and then Charlie West, for providing invaluable assistance and access to important documents as well as permission to reprint from their numerous publications. The extent of our research could not have been completed without MHR, Inc., which continues to serve anyone interested in the history and genealogy of the region (*www.mendocinohistory.org*). We wish Dorothy Bear and Beth Stebbins were still around so we could thank them personally for beginning the organized collection and preservation of Mendocino's history.

Thanks also to the Mendocino Community Library and the Mendocino County Historical Society, Inc., to Nancy Brauer for help with the maps, and to the following, who contributed as historical consultants and/or proofreaders: Evelyn Abernethy-Hansen, Chet Boddy, Terrance Carthy, Lorraine Hee Chorley, Daniel Dickson, Maureen Gazzaniga, Gretchen Imlay, Jean Laidig, Dee Lemos, Jack Lemos, Rich Lemos, Loretta Hee McCoard, Jim Meacham, Alvin Mendosa, Dorothy Morrison, Hilda Pertha, Dr. Madge Peirsol, Miriam Rice, Rosamond Rodrigues, Kevin Silva, Wally Smith, Charles Stevenson, Charlie West, Trisha West, Glenné Zaslowsky, and Jennie and Lucia Zacha.

The Mendocino community has welcomed me and supported my new endeavors with Coastside Gallery and the book *Mendocino: A Painted Pictorial.*

Thank you all!

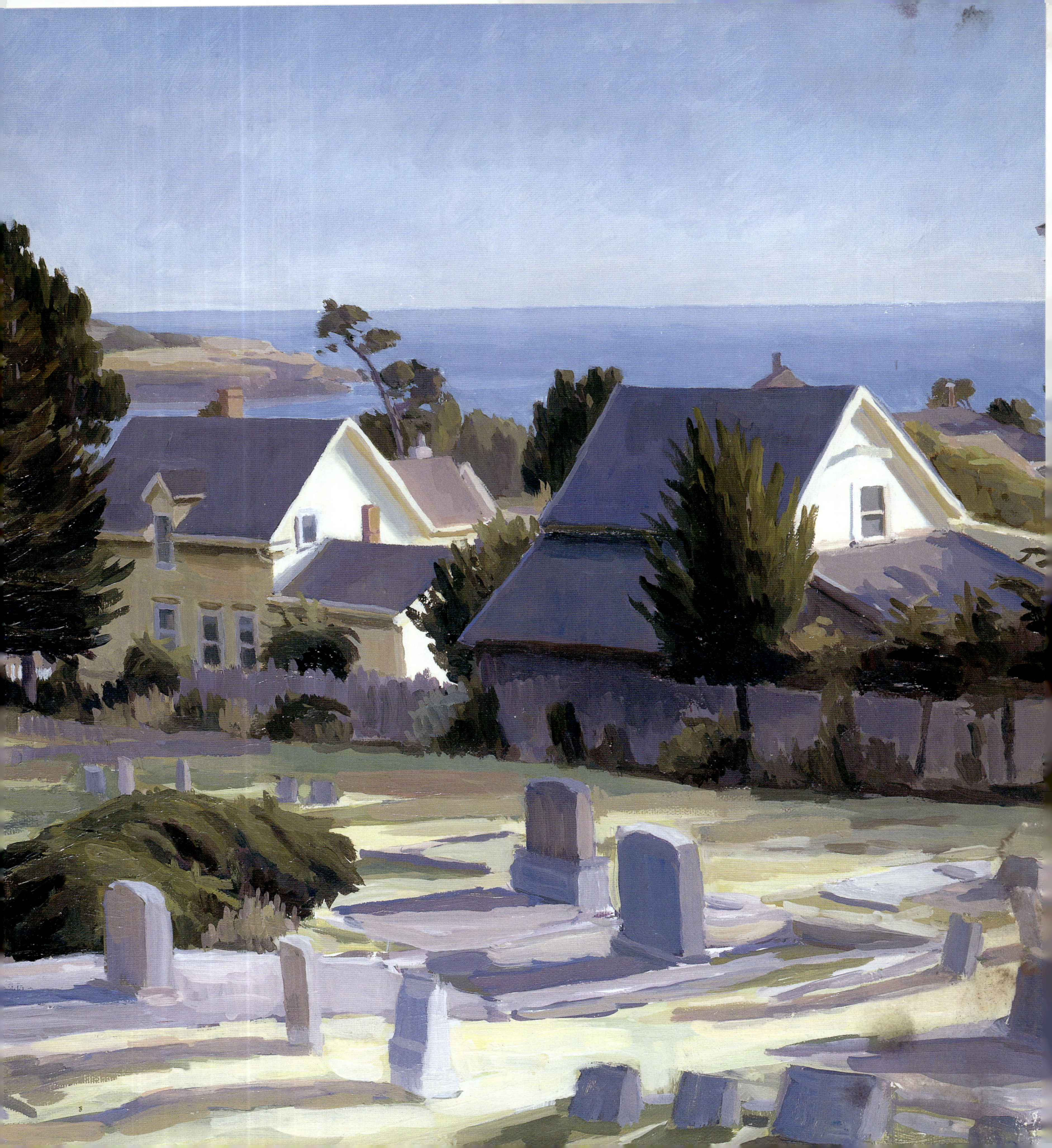

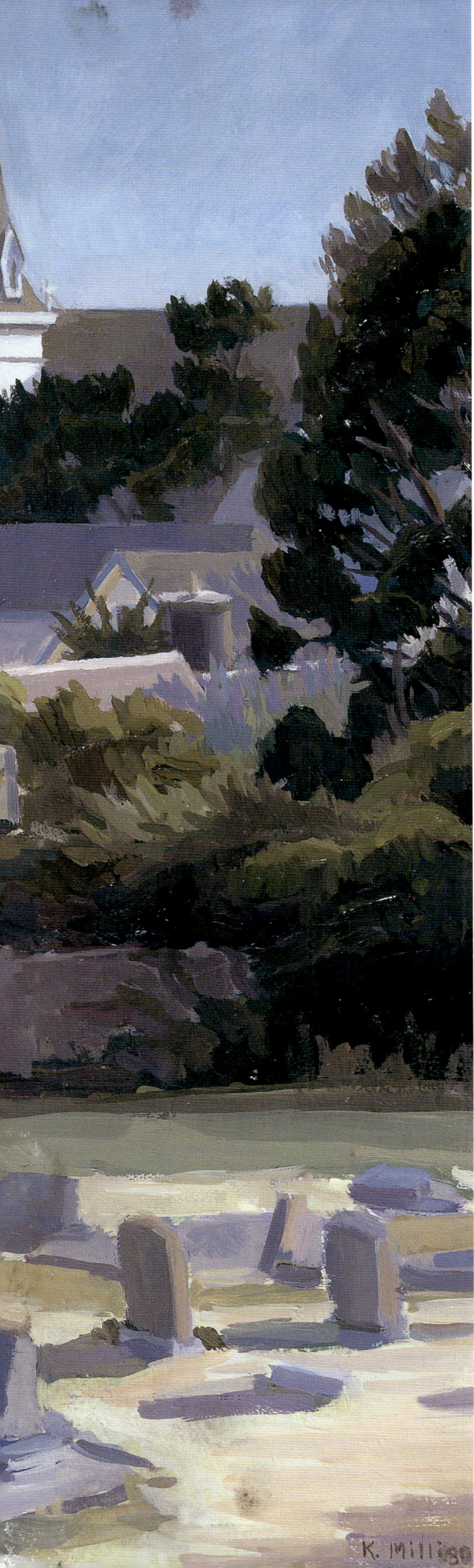

Foreword

The California town of Mendocino is like no other. Situated on a tiny peninsula jutting into the Pacific Ocean, it is bounded by Agate Cove to the north and Big River flowing into Mendocino Bay on the south. The land is nearly flat where the western Headlands drop abruptly into the sea. Four-story bluffs reveal coves, natural bridges, sea caves and secluded beaches—each taking on different aspects depending on the height of the tide and waves. During the winter months, fierce storms batter the cliffs while twenty-foot waves crash with a thunder that resonates in the caves beneath, and can be heard miles away. The terrain gradually rises to the hills of the central and eastern sections. From the higher elevations beautiful panoramas look down on wooden rooftops of quaint New England-style buildings and trademark water towers, all with the bay and ocean beyond.

In June of 1997, I made my first trip to Mendocino as a needed break from the rigors of a busy season working in the San Francisco Bay Area. In addition to seeking a quiet get-away, I'd hoped to find a subject to begin a painting for eventual publication as a lithograph in a series called "The California Coast." My previous travels had taken me along the Central Coast from San Francisco to Carmel, painting subjects that became the basis for this California Coast lithograph series. I wanted to expand the series to subjects north of San Francisco and had tried to imagine what the town of Mendocino might look like. When I arrived and first took in the setting of the village, it was a complete surprise. Old wooden buildings next to open fields and the ocean were reminiscent of Cape Cod, Martha`s Vineyard and Nantucket Island of Massachusetts. It became apparent that Mendocino contained numerous subjects suited to my art.

That initial day I arrived in town, I began my first Mendocino painting from the elevated field of Evergreen Cemetery. I looked over rooftops and across to the church steeple set against the bay and ocean. Headstones in the foreground cast long shadows from the evening summer light. It was a timeless scene and revealed much about the town. I continued on this painting during the next three years (1997–1999).

In August, I returned to Mendocino as a tourist for a second time to continue work on the Evergreen Cemetery picture. In addition, I began a second painting of the Captain Lansing home and water tower from the field between the White Gate and Nicholson House Inns. Then, in October I came back to continue work on the first two paintings and began a third—another view of the Captain Lansing complex from nearer the White Gate Inn on Howard Street and in the afternoon light. My appreciation for the Mendocino landscape continued to grow, and I began thinking of opening my own gallery in order to effectively exhibit the new paintings and the many more I was sure would follow.

On June 5, 1998 I opened Coastside Gallery on the ground floor of a water tower at 10540 Lansing Street at the corner of Calpella Street. Living, working, painting and exhibiting in the coastal village enabled me to develop a productive momentum. As a resident working in the town, I became familiar with different back-street views I might have otherwise missed. Using a portable easel outdoors, I developed the method of operation I still practice today; working as weather permits some mornings or afternoons, and evenings when the days are longer in the middle of the year. As I continued to paint and discover new views in different sections of the town, my appreciation of the landscape deepened as I saw more of it.

After making numerous paintings of Mendocino (more than eighty in two years), it became apparent that they could serve as a pictorial documentation and be shared with others in the form of a book. Structures built in the nineteenth century were still standing in the twenty-first. Most of them were showing signs of age. Many wooden water towers and houses were leaning, had holes in their roofs and walls, and needed major repair. In such cases, my paintings of the weathered buildings could document the old look before restoration took place.

The paintings that appear in this book were reworked many times. Noting my easel's location with rocks, golf tees, paint marks or wooden stakes, I returned to the same site to work on a painting. The process sometimes takes weeks, months and occasionally a few years. Studying nature and the challenge of capturing a particular quality of light and space demand such a protracted process. During the course of the multiple sessions, the painting is modified many times, allowing me the chance for new insights and to see the subject with more understanding. Thus, nature ends up a source of information, providing a never-ending challenge. It's difficult for me to consider a picture "finished." I just stop working on it!
— Kevin Milligan

Preface

You can't go home again," said Thomas Wolfe. Factually, of course, he was right. Yet, in the mind's eye all things are possible—even going home again—if one makes that journey back by memory lane. For deep within the soul of every man is the firm conviction that his particular home was never a place that must eventually succumb to the inevitable changes a relentless world demands of less favored communities. Good and bad, happy and sad, his home was the place his life began and it would always remain the ultimate end he was forever seeking as year after year he traveled fitfully down the highways and byways of his life.

My home was a town where time stood still. It was a town in which the new Twentieth Century obsession with growth and progress had strangely failed to gain a foothold—a place where many of America's halcyon yesterdays were still today's. For a few brief years, a decade or two at most, the tempo of life in that isolated village had failed to keep pace with the faster moving turn-of-the-century outside world. It was, in truth, a town where, briefly, time stood still.

And so, of course, it was also a town where a boy could dream life's golden dreams and live and grow and learn, not only from his strait-laced elders but also from the fields and streams and forests and ocean coves and beaches by which he was completely surrounded.

Yes, that was Mendocino in the early Nineteen Hundreds—a little mill town far up the Northern California coast—a "dog-hole" lumber shipping port clinging to a rocky point, which jutted out into the boiling surf of the Pacific—a town where the dark green forest crept down to the edge of towering ocean cliffs.

At times I count them over and over, every one apart—my rosary of days lived long ago in that land where, for a few short years, time had stood still—days that merge and blend and weave themselves into a colorful tapestry of months and years as I journey back down the half-forgotten road to yesterday—a journey that leads to a golden land of dreams and memories, a sanctuary filled with hopes and dreams and aspirations that will never die.

Preface from James K. Peirsol's *My Boyhood in Mendocino, 1905-1917*
Mendocino Historical Review (Volume VII, Number 1) Winter, 1982

James Kinsey Peirsol was born on Main Street in Mendocino City, California on December 28, 1898
and lived in the town until 1917. A newspaperman for 47 years, he died in Orange County, California on December 5, 1996.

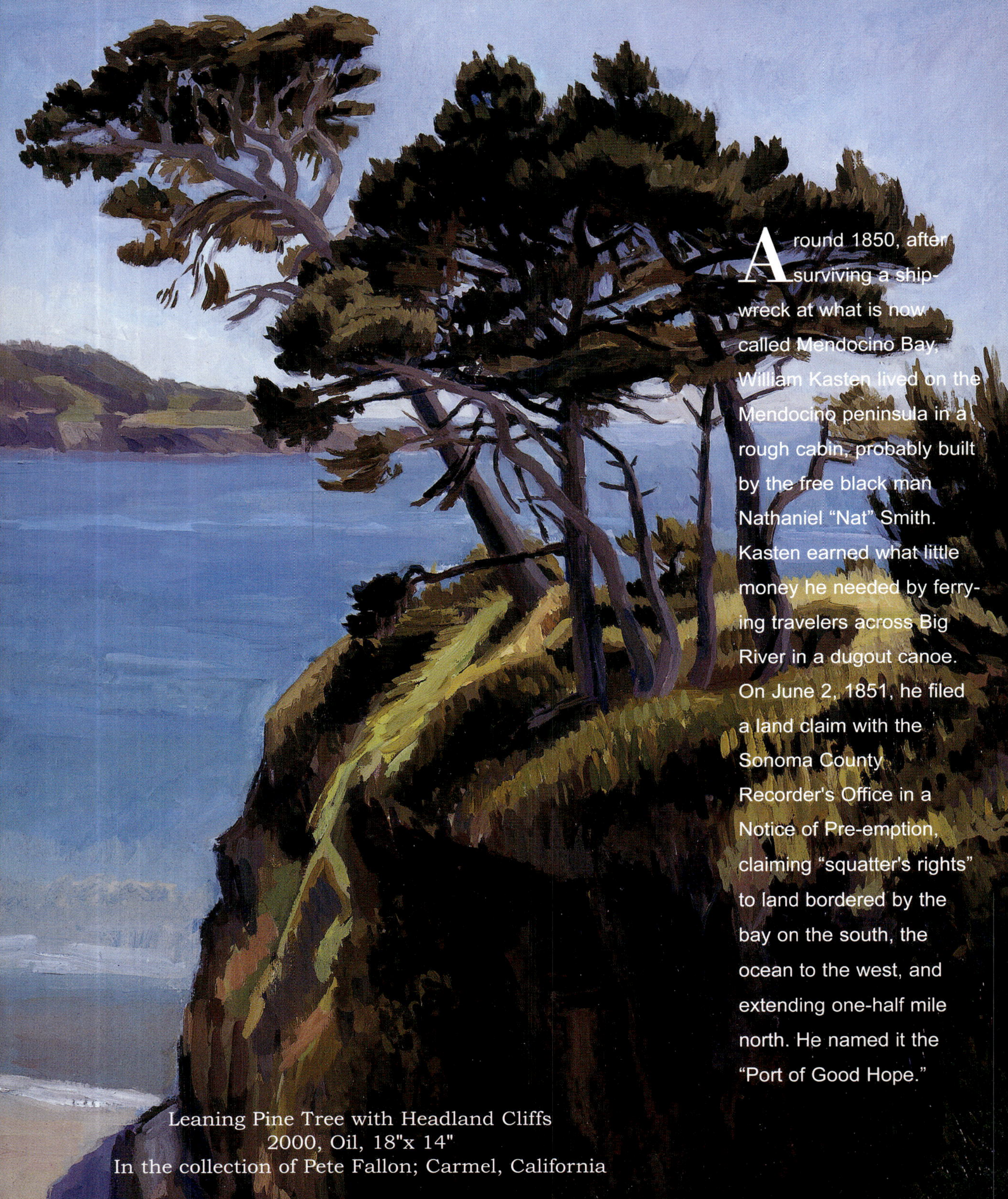

Around 1850, after surviving a shipwreck at what is now called Mendocino Bay, William Kasten lived on the Mendocino peninsula in a rough cabin, probably built by the free black man Nathaniel "Nat" Smith. Kasten earned what little money he needed by ferrying travelers across Big River in a dugout canoe. On June 2, 1851, he filed a land claim with the Sonoma County Recorder's Office in a Notice of Pre-emption, claiming "squatter's rights" to land bordered by the bay on the south, the ocean to the west, and extending one-half mile north. He named it the "Port of Good Hope."

Leaning Pine Tree with Headland Cliffs
2000, Oil, 18"x 14"
In the collection of Pete Fallon; Carmel, California

Early History

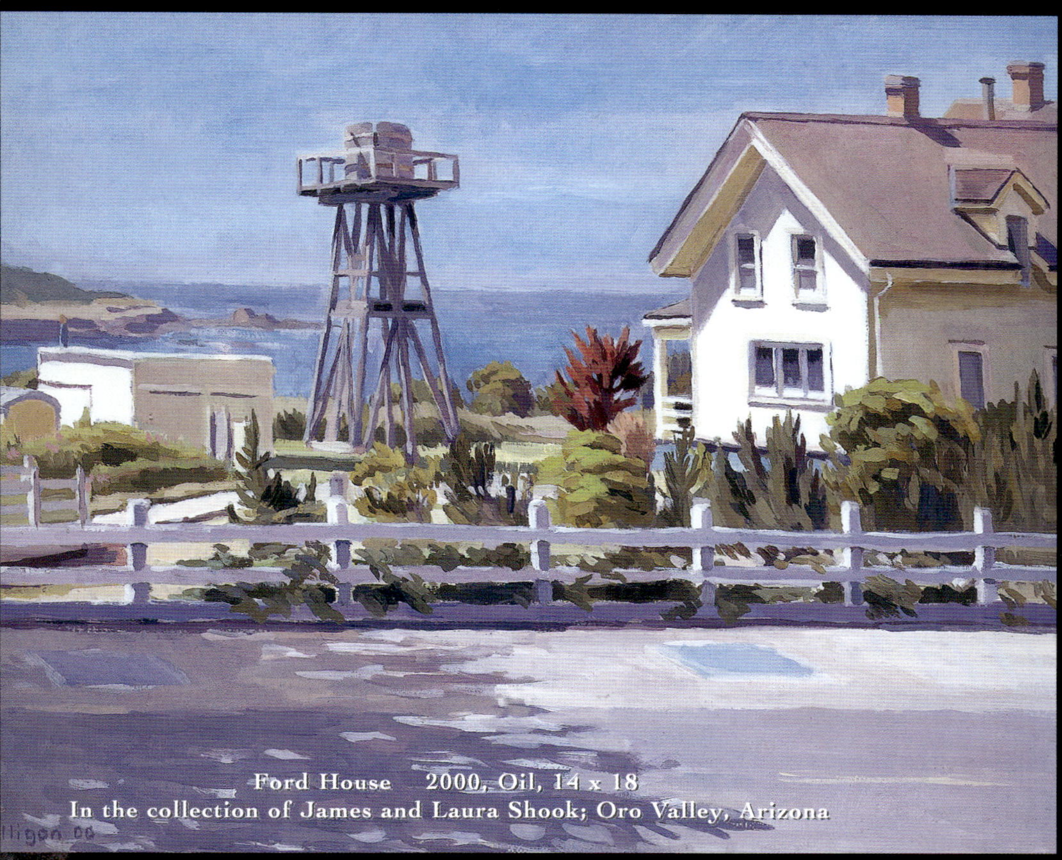

Ford House 2000, Oil, 14 x 18
In the collection of James and Laura Shook; Oro Valley, Arizona

One year ago today we were married. We left home and all friends to seek another home in this land to henceforth share each other's joys—and sorrows. May we as we journey on through life find each successive year the happiest we have ever spent as I now feel this to have been, and we indeed become "one heart and mind" and may we so live that when the fleeting years of time have passed away—our Heavenly Father will welcome us to our Eternal Home.

Diary of Martha Ford; Thursday, May 3, 1855; Mendocino California

It was Jerome Bursley Ford who first realized the potential of the Mendocino Coast. He went there in 1851 hoping to salvage cargo from China lost on the *Frolic*, a clipper ship that had wrecked near present-day Point Cabrillo. After finding the ship's surviving contents had already been taken by others includng the Pomo Indians, Ford made an important connection a few miles south. He met a shipwrecked German named William Kasten living on the bluffs overlooking the mouth of Big River, now called Mendocino Bay. Kasten ferried travelers across the watercourse in a dugout canoe, but he also took Ford a few miles upriver where the taller trees grew. Ford had been working at Bodega with other east coast lumbermen, Captain Stephen Smith and Henry Meiggs. Smith and Meiggs had interests in San Francisco, including a wharf at North Beach where sawn lumber could be shipped. When Ford returned with stories of the giant redwoods and Douglas-fir trees, Meiggs arranged two reconnaissance trips up the coast by schooner. Weather prevented the first from landing at Mendocino Bay, but the second was successful. It included Edwards C. Williams, who sixty years later wrote of his dugout journey up Big River:

> *The winter rains had not wholly ceased and the river bank full, its slight ripples meeting the verdure of the shore, the tall redwoods with their great symmetrical trunks traveling toward the skies, with the bright colors of the rhododendrons profusely scattered over the hills forming the background, the clear blue sky above reflected in the placid river and over the hush and solitude of the primeval forest — all combining to impress upon our minds the beauty and the truth of the opening of Bryant's Thanatopsis, "The groves were God's first temples," and as I recall the beauty of the picture, I cannot but regret the part it appeared necessary for me to enact in what now looks like a desecration.*

Still, there was no denying the opportunity before them. Reports from his scouts convinced Meiggs to start a sawmill and lumber business on the little peninsula inhabited by only William Kasten. Meiggs assembled a small group of men to execute the project, including J. B. Ford, E. C. Williams and another associate working in Bodega, John Edward Carlson. By 1852 Meiggs needed a ship to carry mill machinery from San Francisco to the mouth of Big River. He hired Captain David Lansing and ship's carpenter William H. Kelly (also known as Kelley), to command the brig *Ontario*. Though it appears Meiggs never set foot there, these six men are the true pioneers of the Mendocino timber industry and the town that grew up around it.

While Ford went ahead overland to build and run the mill, the other founders, plus some forty laborers and mechanics, embarked on the *Ontario* to join him, a trip that proved to be arduous. As E. C. Williams recorded in his diary:

> *We were not out of sight of land before our troubles began. The ship, which had been at anchor a long time, had become very dry above the water line, and as soon as put upon the wind and headed up the coast, the motion began to loosen the oakum in the seams and let in the water.*

The crew became anxious as the ship took in water, but with the leadership of Lansing and Williams a mutiny was averted. The water, he notes, did not come in very badly at first, but:

> *. . .was increasing from day to day, until the workmen became alarmed and insisted upon going back to San Francisco. The Captain said that with good weather there was no danger, and the workmen agreed that if they were put on pay, they would man the pumps and keep the ship free of water. This was arranged for, and, the weather favoring us, we made port without mishap.*

When the town's pioneers arrived in 1852 looking for property to establish a sawmill, Kasten traded land for $100 and a promise of the first run of lumber sawn at the new mill. It was from this first redwood that the house in the painting was built on Albion Street. Kasten lived there until 1854, when he sold it and the rest of his holdings to William Kelly for $2650, saying Mendocino was becoming too crowded. He departed for Mexico, never to be heard from again. The Kellys lived in the house until 1861 while their own home was being constructed on Main Street, and their first child Emma Shirley, known as Daisy, was born there. The House was later purchased by William Heeser and remained in his family for 105 years.

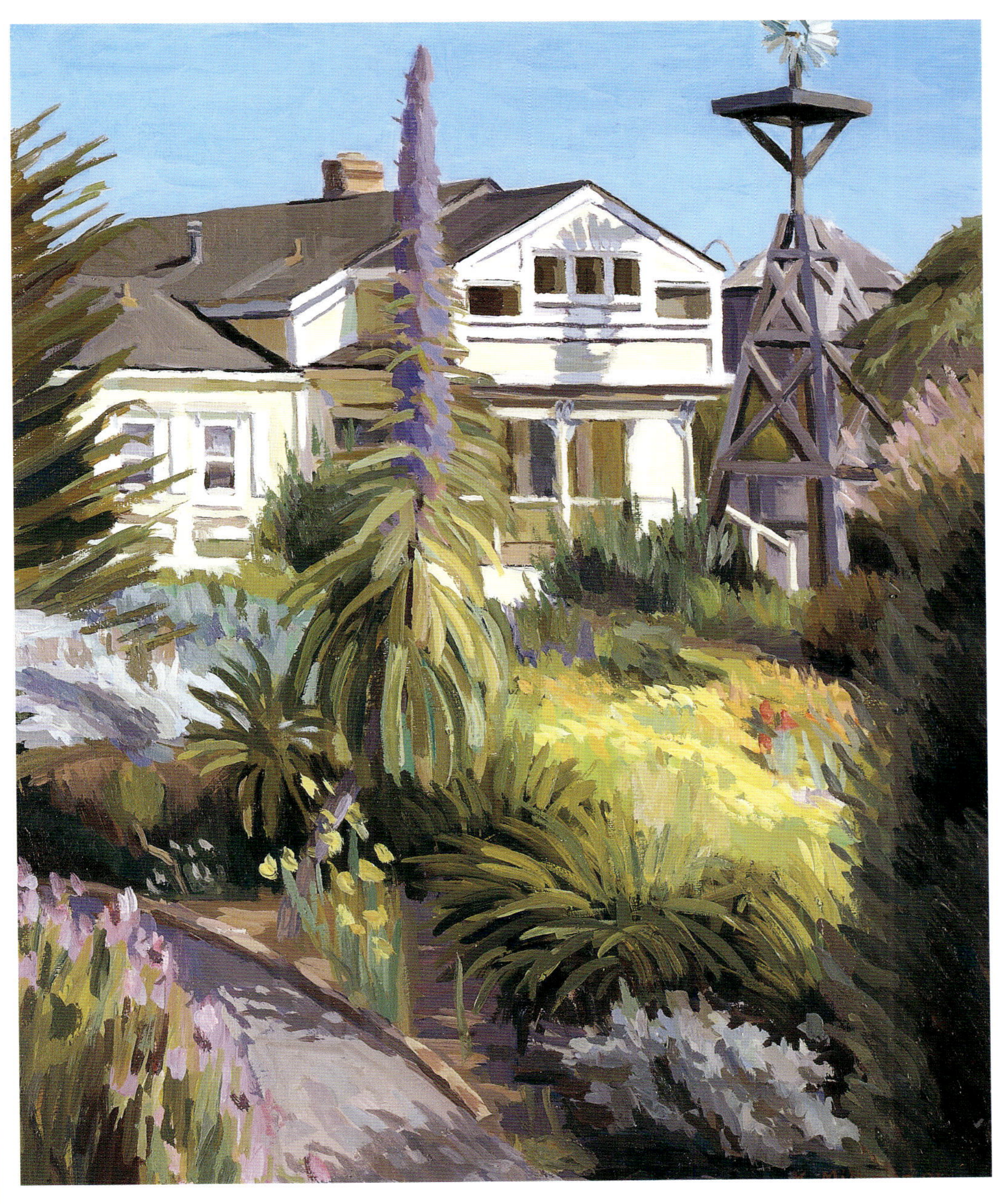

Kasten–Heeser House 2001, Oil, 18" x 14"
In the collection of Tim and Laura Zadel; San Jose, California

Jerome Ford's overland trek up to Big River turned out to be just as harrowing. Beginning on a boat from San Francisco to Benicia, he traveled to Napa, and then Sonoma by stage. At Sonoma he bought three horses and two pack mules and then rode to Bodega Corners where he bought an eight-yoke team of oxen and hired two men to help. They headed north into what was largely wilderness. Without roads or bridges, they followed narrow trails and had to swim across every creek and river, making for a slow, treacherous trip that only the hardiest might attempt.

When crossing what is believed today to be the Gualala River, one mule drowned and the other swam downstream and ran away. Losing the mules was critical because they carried the food supply and blankets. For another day and a half, they slept under saddle blankets and ate only berries. The three men were able to replenish their supplies and get a square meal when they reached the Portuguese Ranch near the Navarro River, where they rested for two days. Finally, after ten days of slow, difficult travel, they reached the mouth of Big River, which Ford alternately called the *Rio Grande* and the *Bull Don*. The Spanish used the first term while the latter was Ford's version of the Pomo Indian name *Booldam*, which means large stream.

But slow as they were, they still arrived a month before the *Ontario*. On later days, Ford noted in his diary that he would sit at the Point until sunset searching for sight of the ship. He made this entry about his own arrival at Big River:

> *Rio Grande, Thursday, 17, June 1852: Arrived last evening at six o'clock but owing to the tide being so high were unabled [sic] to cross the river with our animals so we crossed over leaving our Animals behind. This morning have got them across so we are at Journey's end. This is a rather pleasant Place. Am stopping in the House I bought of the Blacksmith.*

The shipwrecked Kasten occupied a crude log cabin on the southeastern headlands, probably the only such structure in the area. The next day Ford wrote:

> *Today have been looking about, defining Boundaries. Mr. Caston [Kasten] has a claim on the point, which with the claim I purchased takes up the whole of the Point. All living here now are six—"Warner," "Caston," myself and three Germans. The Harbor is a very large Bay and River entering from the Mountains some twenty miles up.*
>
> *Have taken up the next claim on the river. Have erected a Bough House. Land is quite well timbered and very well sheltered. Spent the night in the Bough House for the purpose of killing Elk in the morning. Early this morning we were woke up by the "Elk Whistle," and within the distance of 100 yards there were about 20 Elk, but they had got our location by scent and vamoosed before we could get our rifles. Have few stores and not*

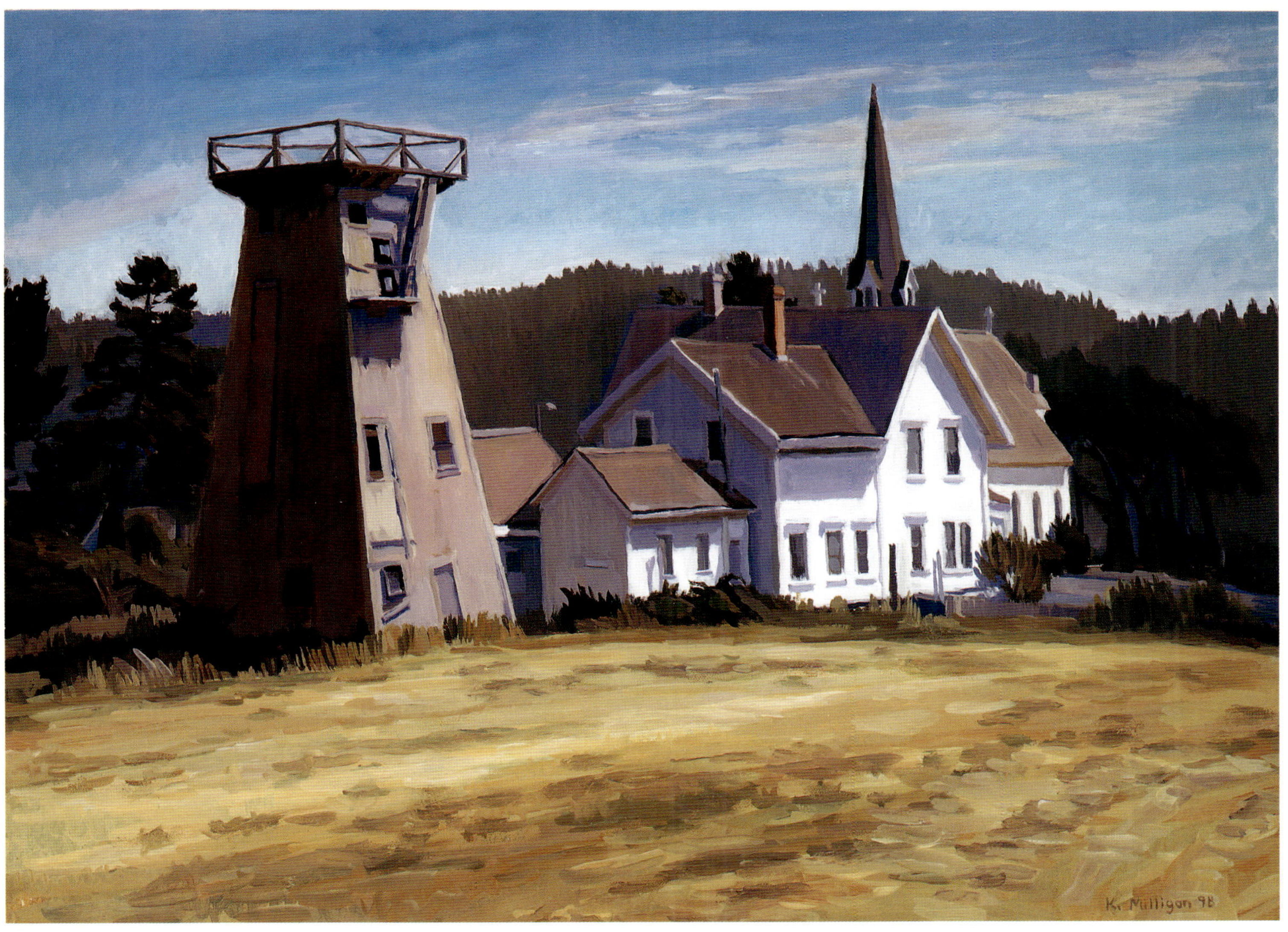

Captain Lansing House and Water Tower 1997–98, Oil, 18" x 24"

The David Frederick Lansing home is thought to be the third oldest in town. Lansing has a prominent place in Mendocino history, having captained the brig *Ontario*, which brought mill equipment and workers from San Francisco in June of 1852. Lansing served as harbor master and shipping superintendent for the Mendocino Lumber Company until 1874. During this time he mapped the underwater rocks and reefs of the Bay and rescued a number of people from ships wrecked there. He often said he had witnessed the drowning deaths of 50 people in Mendocino Bay, due not only to shipwrecks and capsized rowboats, but also falls from the cliffs and being washed off the rocks. He is credited, too, with building the county's first 180 feet of railway, making it possible to move lumber to the Point for shipping. Laid on Big River Flats, these tracks were later connected to more on the Headlands, where remnants can still be found.

Arriving in 1852, William Kelly became the township's largest individual landowner in 1854 when he bought out the departing Kasten. In 1861 William and Eliza moved into this home overlooking a large pond and the Bay. William Kelly was, apparently, a friend to the Chinese and once interceded to save the life of a Pomo Indian man, Busah, who devoted himself to Kelly and his family. When Daisy was a child, Busah carried her around town strapped to his back on a cradle-board, and he slept outside her bedroom door to keep a watchful eye. In 1975 new owner R. O. Peterson donated the Kelly home to Mendocino Historical Research, Inc. Now open to the public as the Kelley House Museum, it also houses the library and offices of MHR, a non-profit organization dedicated to researching, archiving and preserving the history of the region.

(Visit: www.mendocinohistory.org)

Note: Daisy, daughter of William and Eliza, changed the Kelly name to Kelley, adding the "e" later in life.

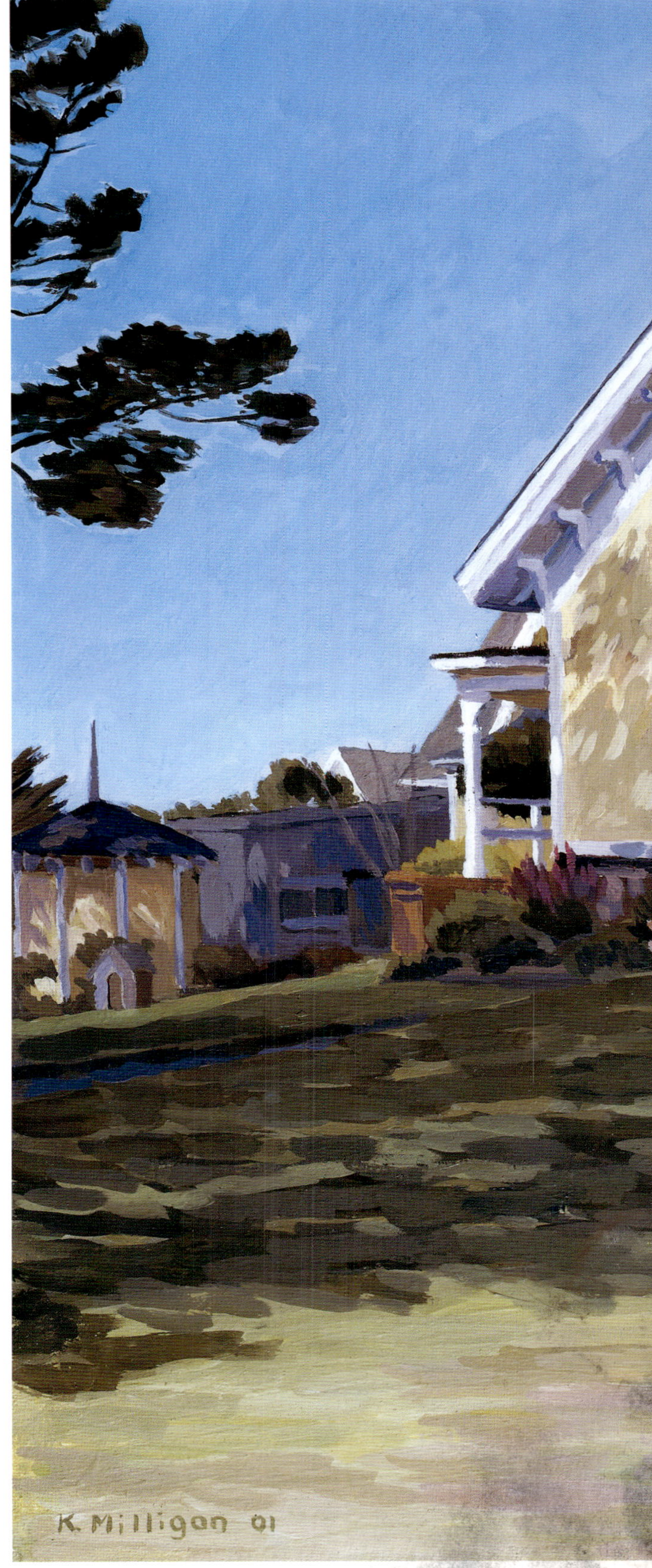

Kelley House 2001, Oil, 18" x 24"

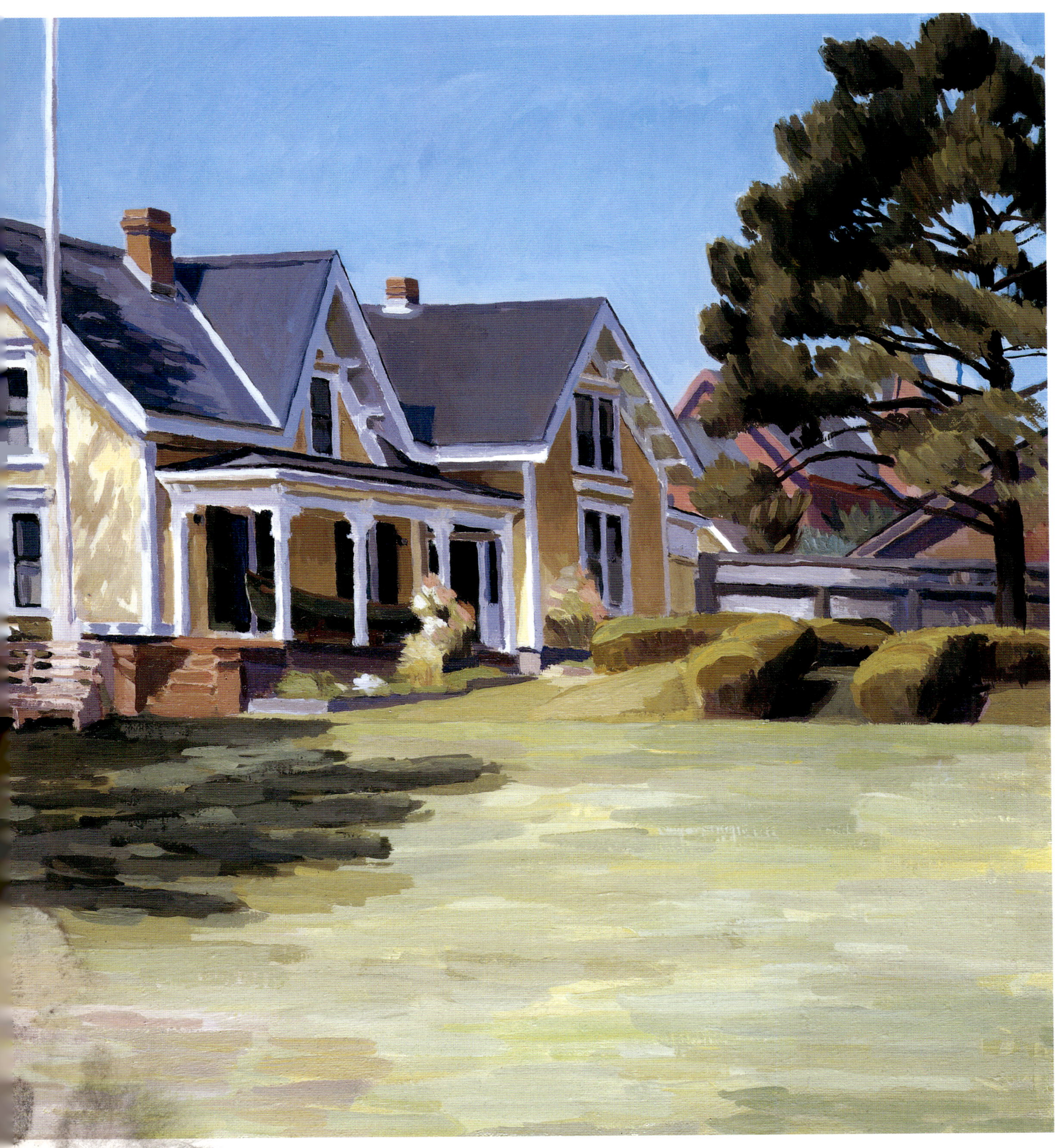

much to do with. Expect the ship every hour.

While waiting for the arrival of the *Ontario* he reported in his diary: *"Went up the river to visit the Germans at their camp."* He identified Gebhard Hegenmeyer, his brothers George, John, and/or Joseph, as part of this group. Other early white settlers were Russians who built a storage shed at the inlet now called Russian Gulch.

On July 19, 1852 the *Ontario* sailed into Mendocino Bay, and E. C. Williams recorded in his diary:

We found Mr. Ford, who had started out some days in advance of our sailing with horses and oxen, already on the ground, and as the summer winds had begun we hauled the ship inside the point with the stern close to the shore and landed her cargo.

The men and mill machinery were put to use as they immediately began construction of the mill on the Point, but workers were unable to complete the roof before the winter rains began. As a result, the mill did not begin operation until the spring of 1853. Years later in 1912, E. C. Williams recalled in a newspaper article for the *Mendocino Beacon:*

Difficulties connected with the building of the mill were many and great. Our millwright proved wholly incompetent; men became dissatisfied and left at a moment's warning and their places could only be filled by sending to San Francisco and bringing men overland up the coast. Before the mill had its roof on the storms began; for many years the memory of that winter came back to me as a horrible nightmare. But spring came at last and the mill was finished and we began shipping its output to market at the rate of 50,000 feet a day.

Getting the huge logs from Big River up the cliffs and out to the Point was so difficult that construction on a second mill, called the Page Mill, was begun down on Big River Flats in 1853. Fitted with new, larger circular saws that could handle the giant trees, its capacity was about 60,000 feet in twelve hours. But the logs milled into boards on the Flats had to be hauled to the Point for drying and shipping, which included getting them up to the top of the steep bluffs. Under the direction of Captain Lansing, some of the very first railroad tracks in California were laid to connect the new mill to the storage and shipping yard.

Boards went onto lumber cars pulled by oxen or horses to the bottom of the cliff. There, a stationary steam engine winched the cars up the steep incline while the teams were walked up the hill. Hitched again to the cars at the top, they pulled them along the headlands to the shipping yard at the Point. After drying somewhat, boards were loaded one at a time onto wooden *apron chutes* and slid down to the decks of schooners anchored below. In later years *wire chutes*, long lines fastened to buoys, allowed ships to moor beneath them while loads of boards and passengers on "trapezes" were slid down

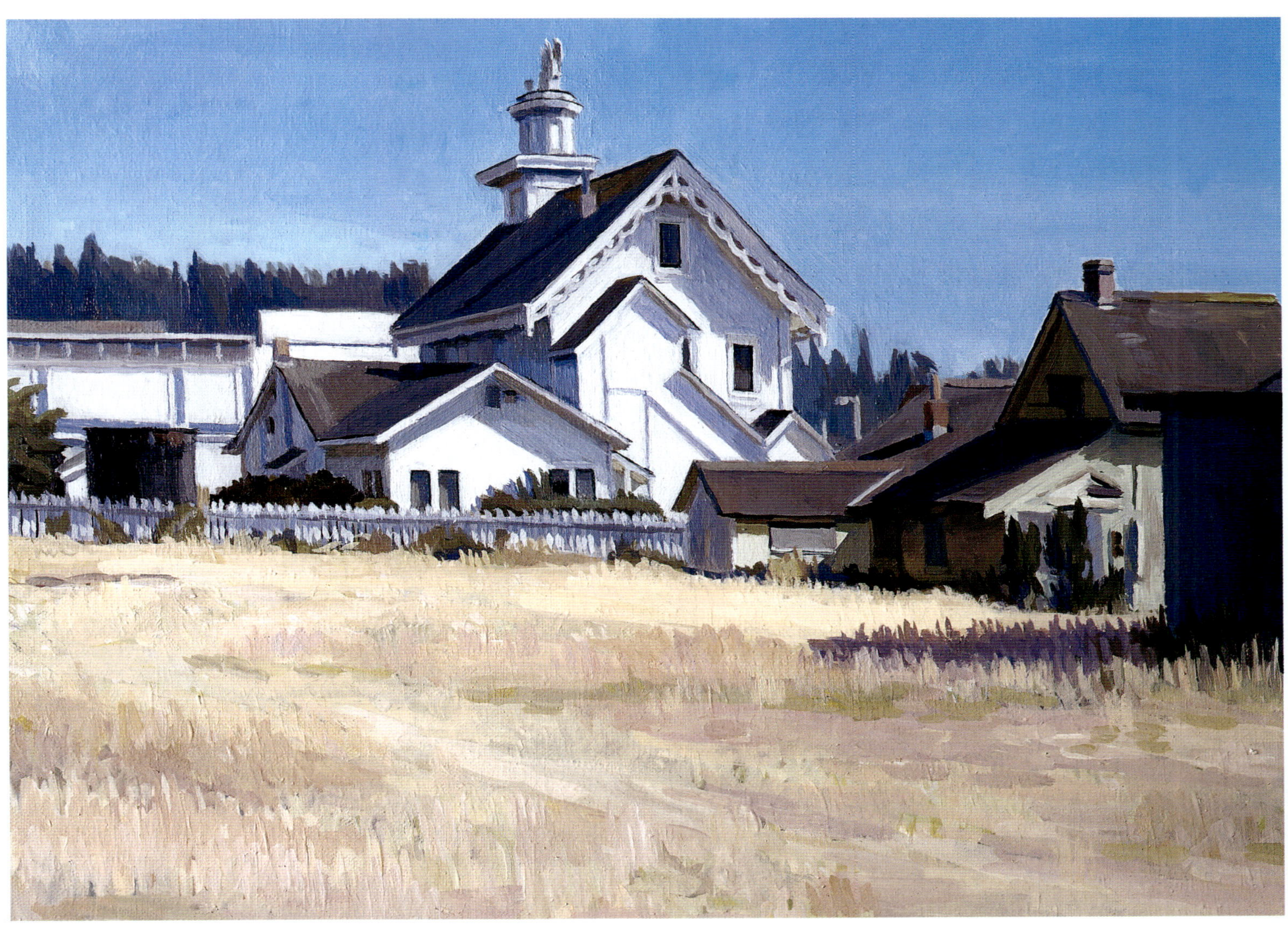

Masonic Hall with Hegenmeyer House 2000-01, Oil, 14" x 18"
In the collection of Jack and Jeanette MacCormick; Mendocino, California

Gebhard Hegenmeyer resided in the house at right, behind the Masonic Hall. He was one of the order's charter members as of 1866. The Hegenmeyer brothers were among the first settlers Jerome Ford noted in his diary after his arrival at Big River on June 17, 1852. Gebhard's brothers left the area, but he remained to become the blacksmith for the mill, and he crafted the ironwork of the Masonic Hall, including some decorative chapiters atop columns inside the building.

Until late in the century, there was no actual post office building. The Postmaster simply fulfilled the duties at his place of business, often a general store, as was the case with Woodward. Despite how the postal service identified it, the town was generally referred to as Mendocino City, distinguishing it from the region or county. (Similarly, to the south, the town of Greenwood had its post office designated as "Elk," but the town is usually still called Greenwood by anyone who's been a resident for more than 25-30 years. "Newcomers" call it Elk.)

In 1858 William Heeser, who came to Mendocino the previous year, paid $6,000 for most of William Kelly's land holdings. This included everything west of Lansing and north of Ukiah Street to the ocean—about 200 acres. Kelly held on to a good portion of property between Main and Ukiah Streets and on Lansing Street, where he opened numerous businesses and helped others start their own, leasing his properties. He also operated stores on western Main Street in partnership with early businessmen Rundle and Woodward. Eventually he opened his own store on the corner of Lansing and Main.

Heeser surveyed and divided the land north of Main with the two spacious east-west streets: Ukiah and Little Lake, as well as three narrow carriage roads: Albion, Calpella and Covelo. Then he split the property into smaller lots affordable for the working-man, to purchase. It is said he never foreclosed on any of them. But he retained the two-block area in the center of town, unbroken by Calpella Street, for his own business interests. This was across Ukiah Street from his home which was originally Kasten's. In 1865 Heeser married Laura Nelson, daughter of Alfred Nelson, Sr., one-time friend of Henry Meiggs.

Heeser was also a major force, with J. B. Ford, in getting a road constructed eastward toward the central valley and Ukiah. They donated $30,000, and Heeser contributed the surveying skills. Having to traverse both valley grasslands and many miles of heavily forested mountains, the first leg followed the south side of Big River to the inland community of Comptche. From there, one route went to Boonville, where a road had already been built to Cloverdale. From Boonville, High Gap Road went northward to Ukiah. Low Gap Road, another route from Comptche to Ukiah, was originally called Heeser Road. Soon stagecoaches could reach Mendocino over inland routes, bringing mail, freight and passengers, though all were vulnerable to bandits.

Meanwhile, the lumber business flourished. The first mill on The Point was closed in 1858 to concentrate efforts on the Page Mill down on Big River Flats. It burned in 1863, but was rebuilt immediately with a larger and better facility with the saws on an upper floor and the planing mill below. Nearby, some houses were built and rows of small cabins for the bachelors who worked at the mill. (Later, in the 1890s, a man living in a company cabin and eating in the cookhouse got $35 cash for a month of six twelve-hour days per week. If he saved $10 a month for a year, he could buy a lot in town. As soon as he could get a house built, he could marry.)

Mendocino's population had grown from 28 in January 1855 to 700 in 1865. The homes of most of the founders were east of Kasten Street, while the town grew mainly to the west, focusing on the lumber company. There were hotels, boarding houses, saloons, livery stables, laundries, specialty shops and several general merchandise stores. At the end of Main street just west of the City Hotel, one of these was operated by William Heeser. He opened the upstairs as the first meeting place for an order of Masons that was forming. In 1868 he donated land for a Masonic Hall at the corner of Ukiah and Lansing. He was a charter member of the Mendocino Lodge and held the position of Senior Warden and then Secretary.

The town was thriving and forward-looking by the fall of 1870 when disaster struck. A fire started in the St. Nicholas Hotel located on the northeast corner of Kasten and Main where Gallery Books is now. This was formerly the California Hotel, one of the oldest in town. Because of the winds, it burned westward toward the lumber company, destroying everything in between—about 25 buildings. William Heeser allowed his store to be burned as a backfire to halt the blaze at Hotel Street (later Heeser Street), which saved the Company's cookhouse and lumber storage yard.

The loss of those homes and businesses, including J. E. Carlson's City Hotel, was a terrible blow to the town, but the spirit of Mendocino has always been strong. Rebuilding began immediately, and many of those structures are still standing and in use today.

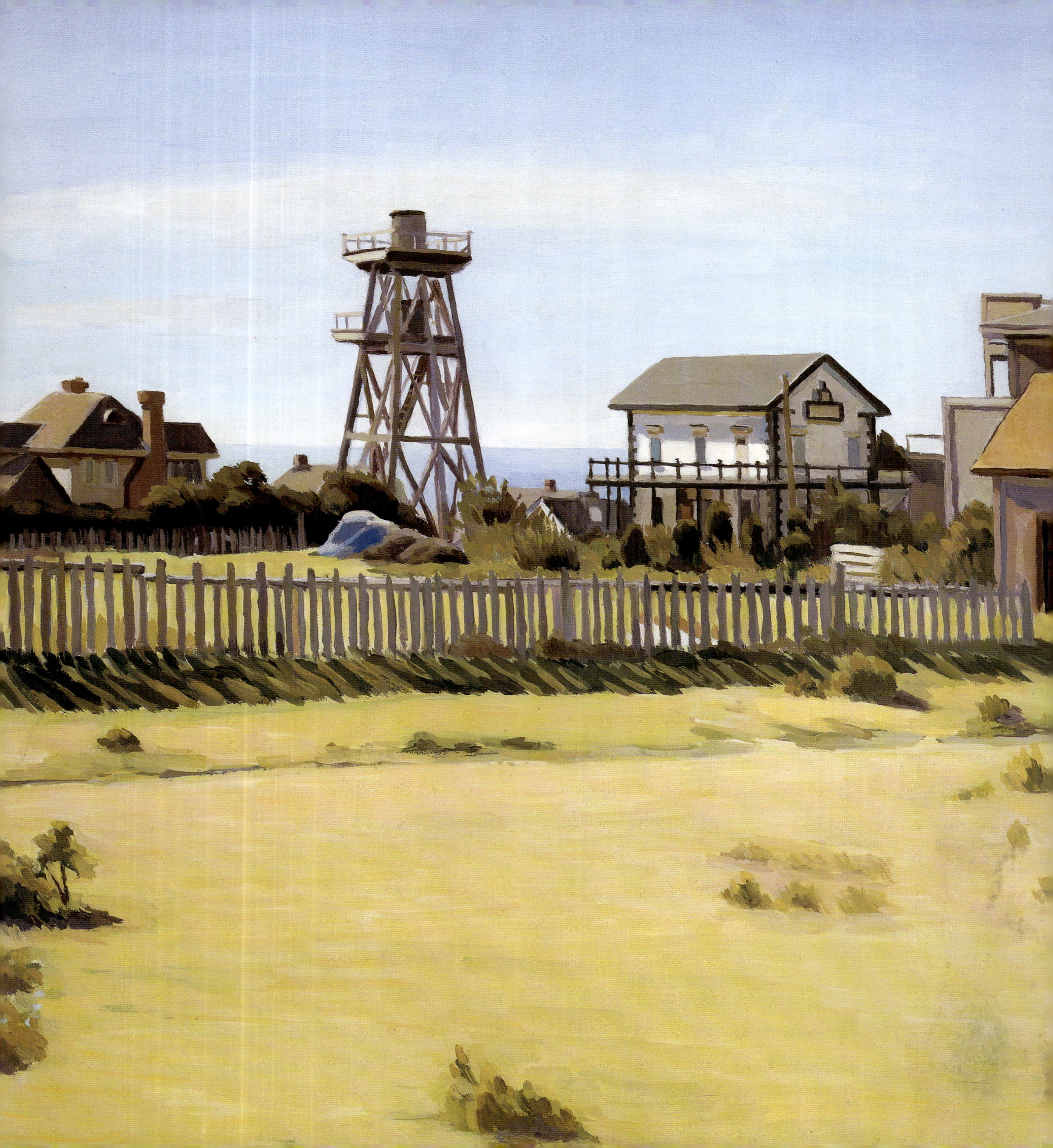

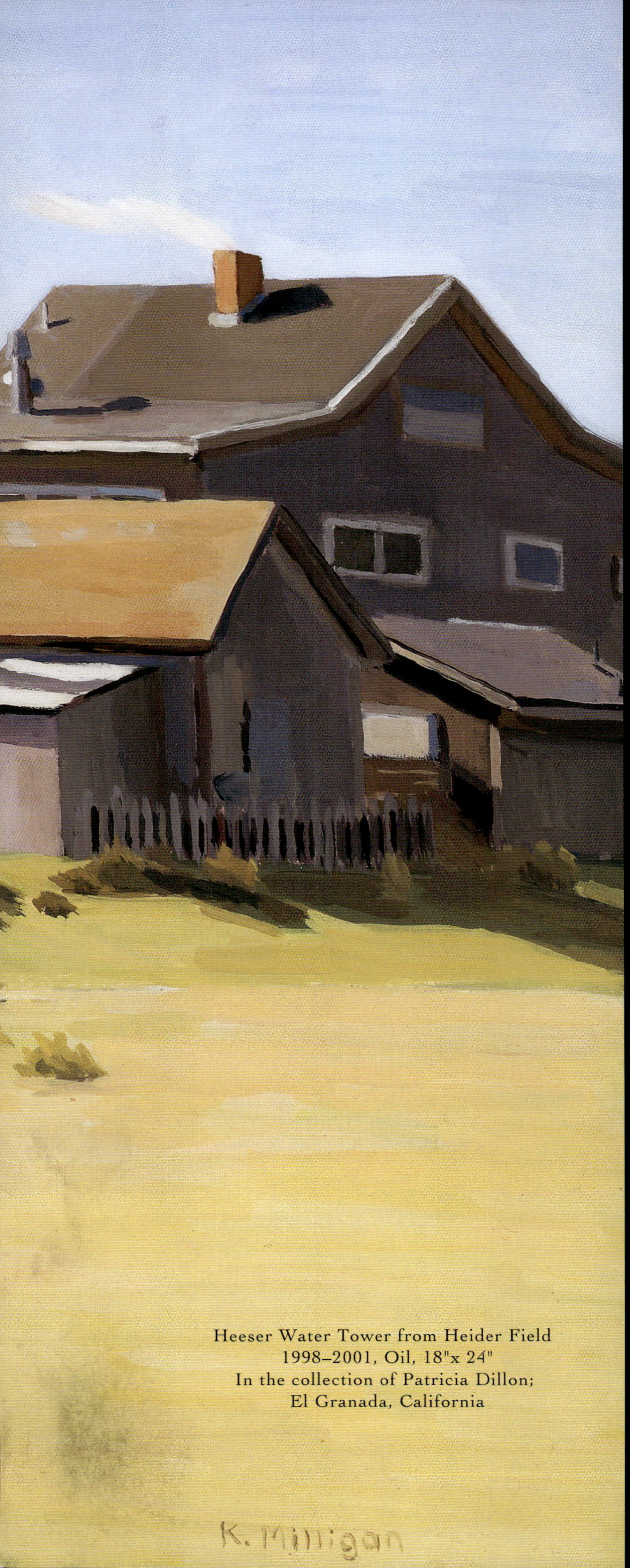

Heeser Water Tower from Heider Field
1998–2001, Oil, 18"x 24"
In the collection of Patricia Dillon;
El Granada, California

Lumber Mill Days

From the beginning, those who settled in Mendocino wrote home to relatives about the pleasant climate and financial opportunities they had found. Many New Englanders, especially those with experience in the lumber business, flocked to the town. The homes they built reflected the architecture they left behind.

Many European ethnic groups came looking for a more comfortable life. A large number of Finns settled on the Mendocino Coast, but mostly to the north around Noyo and to the east near Comptche, where the untimbered valleys were put to use raising food and grain crops to feed the workers and the animal teams essential for the lumber and milling industries. In Mendocino, the largest ethnic group proved to be the Portuguese, most of whom came from the Archipelago of the Azores, also called the Western Islands. The next chapter focuses on their influence on Mendocino, but it should be noted that these people had their pioneer women as well.

When 15-year-old Maria Julia Silvia came alone on a ship around the Horn in 1869 to marry Manuel Thomas Ramus, whom she'd never met, she was the first Portuguese woman in Mendocino. In the flurry of rebuilding after the great fire of

1870, Manuel Ramus opened a saloon on west Main Street, about midway between Kasten and Osborn Streets. Next door was the Ramus home and a boarding house run by Mary Julia, who was also greatly respected as a healer. She learned to speak not only English, but also enough Pomo and Chinese to study the herbal medicines of Indians who lived down on the Flats and of her Chinese neighbors on Albion Street. (It was probably the strength of this friendship that led to her sale in 1903 of the Ramus holdings to the Hee family, despite the prejudices of the time.)

In 1871 she gave birth to their first child, who died in infancy, as did their fourth. However, they were fortunate to rear seven others, born between 1872–92. Though by 1878 she had three small children and was running a successful business, Mary was still lonely for the community of Portuguese women. It was probably she who convinced her husband to send for his nieces from the island of Flores. The five Thomas sisters came to Mendocino between 1878–86, married and reared families in homes along or very near western Calpella Street, sometimes called the "Street of the Sisters."

Little is known about the early Chinese women who settled in Mendocino. Following tradition they were largely sequestered in the sanctuary of their families, but they, too, must be considered pioneers who kept the houses, reared the children and provided the refuge of traditional home life for their hard-working husbands, who dealt daily with the prevailing culture.

As elsewhere, there was a class system in Mendocino with racial and cultural prejudices. A handful of woodsmen and mill workers rose to wealth and power, but most of those were of Anglo ancestry.

With the influx of new residents from all walks of life and the rebuilding after the 1870 fire, the era of growth continued through the 1880s–90s. Western Main Street was soon built up again on the north side of the street, including the impressive new Carlson's City Hotel. On the south side, the lumber-drying yard stretched eastward nearly to the Ramus holdings. The property for some distance beyond was owned by the lumber company and largely inhabited by Chinese, including a two-story rooming house and store, originally the Joel Fisher Hills store, run by Eli Tia Key. There was at least one other Chinese store, as well as various small dwellings with their truck gardens. Where Kasten meets Main, the southern row of Main Street businesses began. These included William Kent's meat market, Stone's jewelry store, a photographic parlor, and several other buildings including the Good Templars' Hall and the Ford house. The latter is the only structure still standing on the south side of the street as a lone reminder of how different Main Street appeared in the 1800s.

By 1884 the school-age population had not only out-

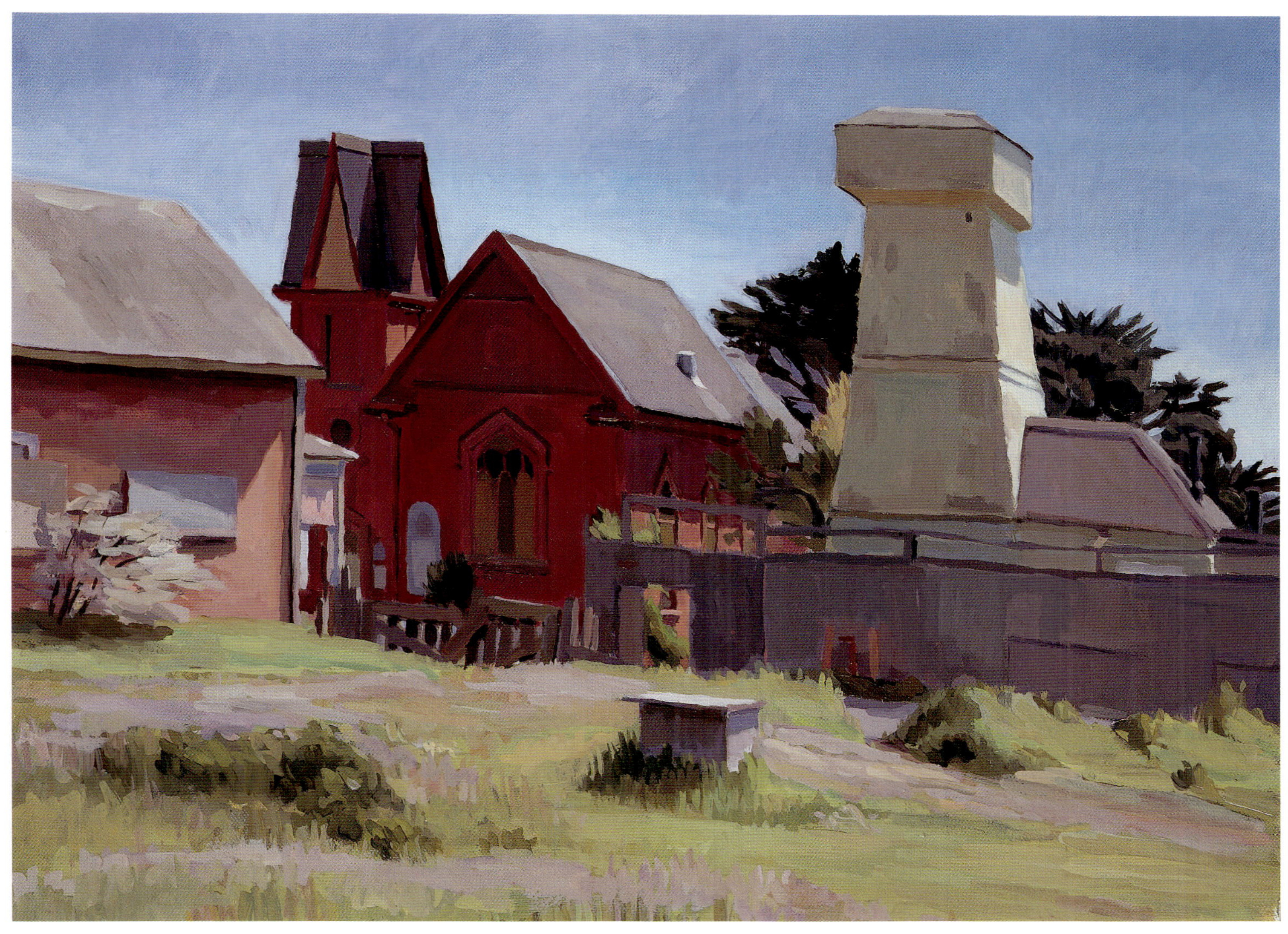

Old Baptist Church 1999–2000, Oil, 14" x 18" Private collection

The Eliza Owen Kelly Memorial Baptist Church was built especially for her in the fall of 1893. It was dedicated in June 1894, with the Reverend John Simpson Ross of Caspar presiding. Though she'd been attending the Presbyterian Church where her father-in-law Peter Kelly was one of the founders, she grew up a Baptist. As Mendocino's population increased, William Kelly built this church for her and fellow worshippers. Reverend Ross frequently officiated there, while Eliza sometimes preached. She often played the organ at services and kept the church in use until her death in 1914. The beautiful red building with bell tower and stained glass windows has remained an architectural icon for parts of three centuries. Since 1975 it has housed the community's health food store.

grown its first school and space in the old church, it now had classes spilling over into the Masonic Hall across the street. A successful school bond election bought property at the northeast corner of town between Little Lake and Pine Streets. By July 1885 a substantial school building opened and served the community until it was destroyed by fire in December 1929. It was rebuilt in a different shape and directly on the corner where it housed the Grammar School until 1976, then the Middle School, later an alternative school. It is currently the town's recreation center. In 1894 a high school opened on the hill behind the four houses called Banker's Row on land donated by William Heeser. The new school graduated its first class of five boys and two girls in 1896.

Inland, up and down the Coast, men harvesting the timber lived in numerous woods camps all along the watercourses. Likewise, mills and towns sprang up at the mouth of virtually every creek and river, but Mendocino remained the most important port and the center for the Coast's commercial interests, the place where people went for business, banking, cultural events and relaxation.

In 1870 William Heeser organized the Bank of Mendocino and in 1871, the Mendocino Discount Bank. By that time he had already served as a Justice of the Peace, a Notary Public and one of his two 3-year terms as a County Supervisor. In 1877 he began publishing a weekly newspaper called the *Mendocino Beacon.* In a Salutatory he wrote for the first edition, he explained its name:

> *The Beacon by its friendly light warns the mariner of the dangers of the coast, and serves to guide him safely into a harbor; and so it is, or should be the function of the newspaper to shed abroad the beams of intelligence and to honestly and fearlessly point out the evils of social and political life, which are the shoals and reefs which endanger and often wreck the bright prospects of individuals as well as communities.*

Under his direction as editor and publisher for some thirty years, and then for another sixty under his son August's control, the paper never missed an issue. The *Beacon* continues today, though its offices are now in Fort Bragg. From October 1877 through December 2000, the *Beacon* office resided in the same building on Ukiah Street. (This was the southern edge of the lot Heeser set aside in the center of town.) It remained the only structure on the two to three acre parcel until 1894. Because the *Beacon* building also housed Heeser's banks, where the vaults still exist, this area became known as Bank Square. Late into the 20th century it provided a center for community celebrations such as July 4th, entertaiment including dog and pony shows, and other gatherings like tent revivals. Today there are structures on three of its four corners, including a church and the post

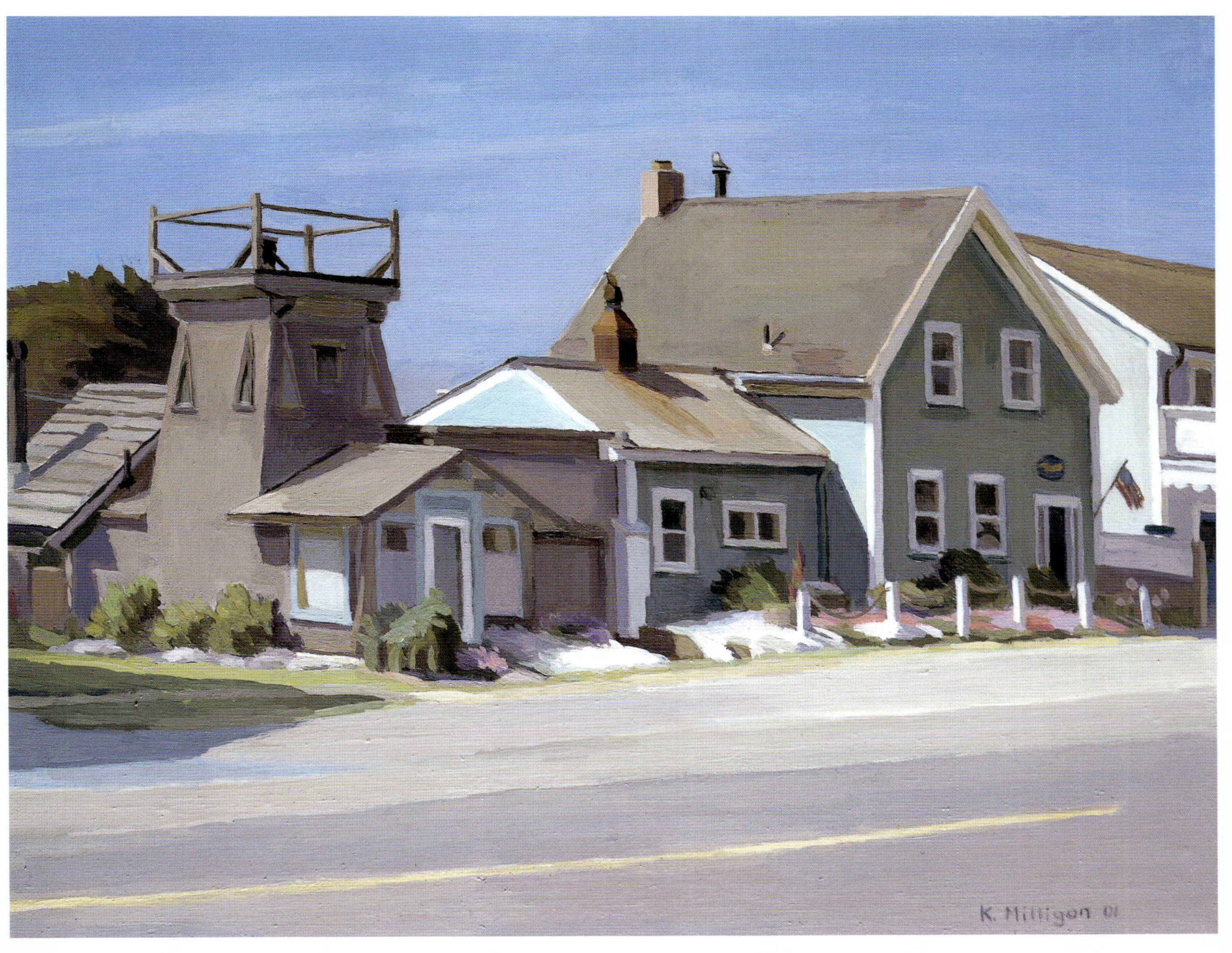

John Dougherty House 2001, Oil, 14" x 18"
In the collection of David Bellis and Margaret Wrightson; Alameda, California

The John Dougherty family was one of the first eight that J. Chester Ford (son of J. B. Ford) remembered attending the earliest Protestant Church. An 1868 survey of the town shows Dougherty owned a 71' x 160' lot stretching between Ukiah Street and Albion Street, which at the time ended at the western boundary of his property. This is the second lot west of Kasten Street. The back of the building, facing the ocean, has been greatly modified to enhance its current role as a Bed-and-Breakfast Inn.

office. For a while it was called Heeser Field, but is now designated Heider Field in honor of John Heider, the man whose foresight led to its preservation as open space.

In the productive days of the Mendocino Lumber Mill, the Bay was often filled with ships waiting to receive lumber; in 1878, eleven were counted in the harbor at one time. Mendocino Bay was one of only four harbors along the Redwood Coast (comprised of Sonoma, Mendocino and Humboldt Counties) able to accommodate deepwater ships. Since these vessels could not get close enough to the loading chutes, flat-bottomed barges called *lighters* took loads out to them.

However, most lumber went onto the smaller craft commonly called *doghole schooners*. Less than two hundred tons and usually two-masted, these more maneuverable ships could enter the shallow waters of tiny coastal inlets—likened to a hole barely big enough for a dog to turn around in—and position themselves beneath the apron chutes. Though wire chutes were in common use in the 1870s, Mendocino didn't install its first until 1902. Vessels were also built in several harbors on the Coast, but only a few at Big River.

Schooners named *Golden Rule* and *Corinthian, Barbara, Ocean Pearl* and *Electra* traveled between Mendocino Bay and San Francisco, bringing supplies in and taking redwood lumber out. But some met their fate in the Bay's treacherous waters including the *Storm Cloud, Bobolink, Alfred, Ella Florence* and *Harriet, Golden State, La Paz* and numerous others. As steamers became more prevalent, ships like the *Yaquina* and the *Mary D. Hume*, the *Los Angeles* and the *Sea Foam* carried passengers and freight as well as lumber. James Piersol wrote about his experience traveling on one of these steamers around 1916:

> *On Voyages south, the Sea Foam's hold would be filled with lumber, and lumber would be lashed securely on the ship's deck as high as the Captain's bridge. With all that weight and buoyancy, the run down the coast was usually very pleasant, but on the return trip, with only a small amount of freight in the hold, and no ballast, the little vessel bounced around like an unruly cork even in the calmest weather.*
>
> *In addition to carrying lumber and freight, the Sea Foam also provided two or three staterooms available for paying passengers. Residents of Mendocino who had business in San Francisco would usually buy a one-way ticket south, preferring to return by train to Willits. There, they would take a stagecoach over the mountain to Alpine, where they would catch a ride on the logging train to Fort Bragg. From Fort Bragg it was only a two-hour stagecoach ride to Mendocino. It was the long way around but much better than experiencing the almost certain seasickness the rolling voyage north*

on the Sea Foam would bring.

As time passed, the children of the first citizens grew to adulthood and made lives of their own. The Fords left Mendocino for Oakland in 1872, in order to give their children broader educational opportunities. J. B. Ford took over the San Francisco office of the lumber company but visited often to keep an eye on operations. His son Jerome Chester Ford, the first white male born in Mendocino, returned in 1874 to run the lumber company. He courted Alice Hills, but lost her to Joshua Grindle. Chester did not marry until 1900 when he wed the widow Almeda Brayton. Upon her death, he married another widow, Minnie Belle Brainard, who had two children. Chester Ford had no children of his own, but his surviving siblings, who did not return to live in the town, married and had offspring.

David Lansing passed away in 1877, ten years after his wife died. Their surviving daughters married and some moved away. The youngest, Helen (Ella), was a dressmaker and milliner in town until her marriage in 1885. She and sister Julia Morrow sold much of the family property at the eastern end of town, including the site for the second elementary school.

Three of J. E. Carlson's children grew to adulthood with son John Jr. assuming management of the City Hotel. Bessie wed Captain Henry Nelson, and her twin sister Kate married James Albert Nichols, brother of Joseph H. Nichols, who was partner in the Jarvis-Nichols Store with Henry Jarvis. Their daughter Edith Nichols married Auggie Heeser, son of William and Laura Heeser, whose first son Willie died very young. Auggie, like his father, was a powerful influence in the town, especially as the editor of the *Beacon* and in his own donation of property.

William and Eliza Kelly had four children. Russell Blair, the second child, died in his early twenties of a long-endured heart ailment. Elise Abigail and Otis William both married, but it was undoubtedly the first child Daisy who is of the most interest and the one who added the 'e' to Kelly, making it "Kelley" in later years. Born in the town in 1859, she is said to have run into the Carlson Hotel during the fire of 1870 to alert and help guests escape. At age twenty, Daisy married Alexander MacCallum, the bookkeeper in her father's store. This young Canadian was soon a businessman in his own right, serving as a partner in the store and becoming Postmaster there in 1885.

As a wedding gift, her parents had a lovely home built for them in a lot to the north, with the house on Ukiah Street but facing south toward Albion Street. The Kelly House on Albion Street also faces south toward Main. Years later, Daisy had the house moved to its present location on Albion Street, only a few steps from the back door of her widowed mother's home, now the

Kelley House Museum. Alexander and Daisy reared two children, David and Jean, neither of whom married. MacCallum had business interests that took the family away from the Coast at times. They had to move to San Francisco in 1896 when a business partner died. After Alexander's death in 1908, Daisy came back to stay, remodeling and adding on to the original structure; probably at the same time she had it moved. Daughter Jean stayed in San Francisco but visited often. David was a bank teller and remained close to his mother, who was well respected in town. Daisy's ninety-four years of life were marked with courage, care, generosity and selflessness toward friends, family and those in need. Serving with Red Cross emergency aid workers in the Bay Area after the 1906 earthquake, she was in charge of the distribution of food, clothing and housing in tent cities. In addition, she organized the relocation of victims with relatives who lived out of the ravaged area. Photographs show her at work in Oakland and San Francisco helping others during the crisis. Even into the early 1950s it was common to see Daisy entertaining guests on her porch. She died in 1953, but her house remained in the family until it was sold in 1966. The new owners turned it into a charming Bed-and-Breakfast Inn with a renowned bar and restaurant.

Fire has always plagued Mendocino, a community almost entirely comprised of wooden structures. It was not until 1887 that a fire company was formed and acquired its first hand-pumper, kept in a new engine house opposite the Central House Hotel. In October 1923 a new chemical fire truck was first used to save the Manuel Lawrence house. Mendocino is still served by an excellent volunteer fire company. Over the years, several fine homes have been lost; fires have taken stables, a church, a school and a bank. But most often it was hotels and saloons that burned and had to be rebuilt or abandoned to a new owner.

From the earliest days, saloons were a part of Mendocino. By 1868 there were two hotels with bars and three separate saloons, all for some 400 to 500 men. Not surprisingly, it was one of the most lucrative kinds of businesses. The majority of workers lived in rough woods camps up the rivers, where they were generally well fed, but they craved the recreations of town, where they could find alcohol, card games and female company. Early Portuguese saloons also served as social clubs where patrons could speak their native language and, perhaps, ease some homesickness.

Despite the Victorian mores of this frontier town, prostitution was readily available. James Peirsol recounts an incident around 1910 in *My Boyhood in Mendocino*:

> *The day of the big fire at Big Lil's house of prostitution, the volunteer fireman turned out in full force to check the blaze. Inspired to Herculean efforts by Big*

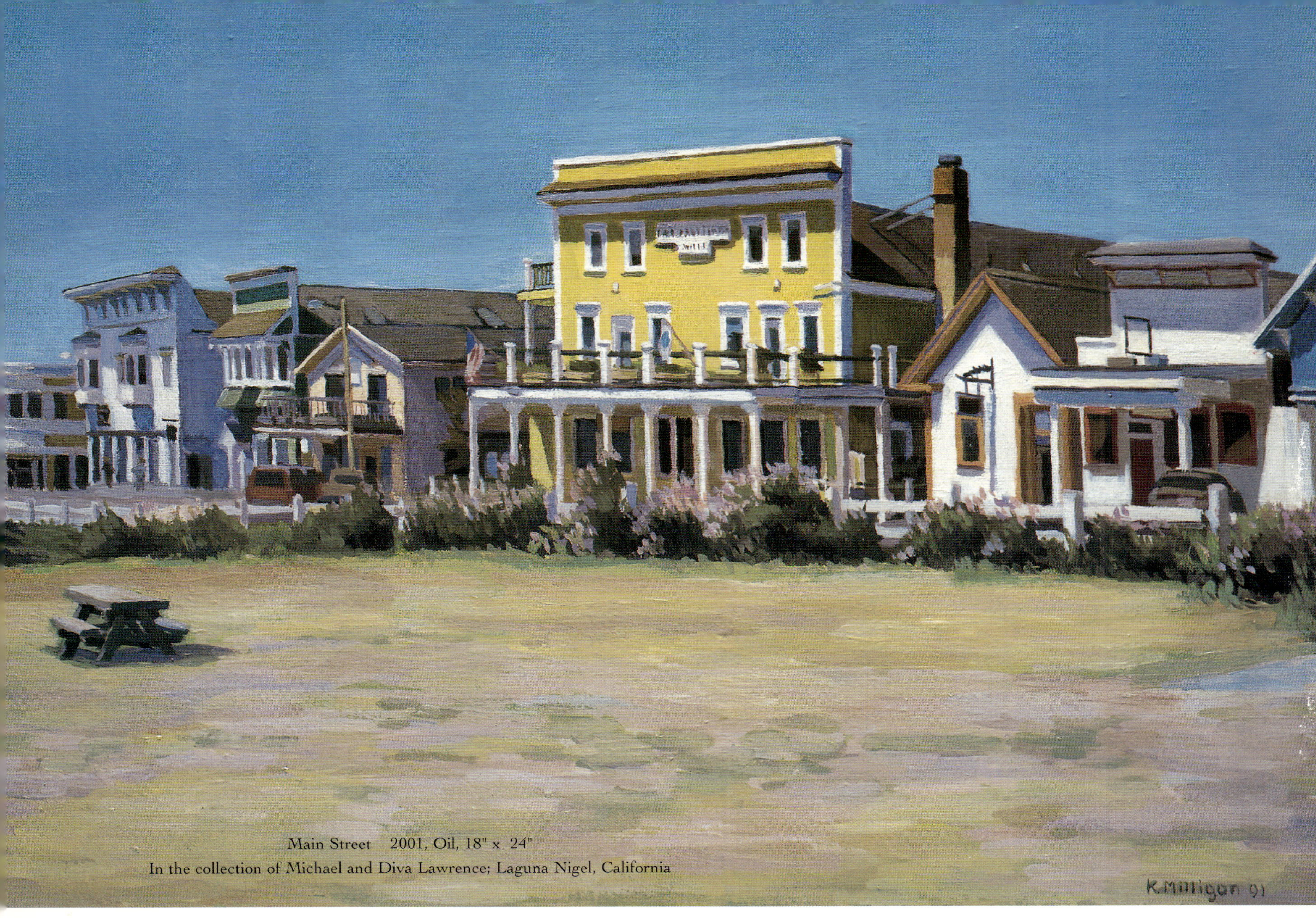

Main Street 2001, Oil, 18" x 24"
In the collection of Michael and Diva Lawrence; Laguna Nigel, California

On pleasant summer evenings in the late 1800s, the Native Sons of the Golden West played on Main Street in front of the Hotel. Jeweler Bert Stone was the only band member who wasn't Portuguese. The Bever Brothers opened a boarding house in 1878, first calling it Temperance House, then the Central House. Business was so good, they expanded, adding a false front. Between 1901–27 it was known as Central Hotel, then Hotel Mendocino. In 1928 new owners Albert and Georgiana Brown changed the name to Mendocino Hotel. They leased it to numerous people over the years, including Joe King, John Silvia, and the Hee family. It changed hands at least six times between 1944–74. In 1975, under the ownership of Robert O. Peterson, it was thoroughly remodeled and refurbished. Though it is again a jewel of central Main Street, its front facade is probably the only remaining part of the original building.

Lil's kimono clad girls, who bravely stood by shouting ribald encouragement and advice, the fire laddies were able to hold the loss to less than $500. This was a great disappointment to the Ladies of the Presbyterian Guild who, having won the battle against Demon Rum, hopefully anticipated another victory. "It would have only been righteous retribution if THAT PLACE had burned to the ground," my mother muttered when informed of the fire department's success.

Many men as well as the town's Ladies were concerned about the negative influence of alcohol. The children of numerous families went hungry when the breadwinner spent his already-meager paycheck in a bar. Change was often given in tokens for free drinks to keep customers coming back, a practice that also kept the patron's cash pay in the bar's account. Public drunkenness and the resultant brawls were an eyesore and hazard to passersby. Inebriation undoubtedly aggravated domestic violence and led to other crimes.

As early as 1865 the International Order of Good Templars (I.O.G.T.) organized in town, and over the years its members attempted to bring temperance to Mendocino. In 1909 when the precinct, which included the town, was voted "dry" by local option, there were some seventeen saloons. All of these businesses had to find a new way to survive. Several saloons became general merchandise or grocery stores, one a pool hall, one a garage, one a sausage factory. But this didn't stop the consumption of alcohol. It was available in Fort Bragg and several other communities that voted to stay "wet." And some saloonkeepers in Mendocino still sold liquor on a private basis, avoiding the overhead costs of a legitimate business. It's no surprise such a spirited frontier town, tamed as it was becoming in the new century, would have these "blind pig" operations, bootleggers and customers willing to take a few chances with the law to "wet their whistles."

Mendocino City has been blessed with a unique mix of qualities characteristic of early western towns. It had its cow town false-front saloons and hitch racks, but also a pristine Gothic church and a brightly painted Chinese Temple. It had ships and sawmills, a railway without a locomotive and daily stagecoaches that were often robbed at gunpoint. It had its tragic losses, devastating fires, shipwrecks and mill disasters, though it fared better than many others in the 1906 earthquake.

Nearly every home had a tall water tower topped with a windmill, all spinning in the near-constant breezes, and townsfolk competed to raise the tallest flagpole. Miles of picket fence (no shortage of wood, after all) encircled yards to keep wandering livestock out of carefully tended personal gardens.

Mountain lions were sometimes sighted in the middle of town, and there was a pond on Main Street large

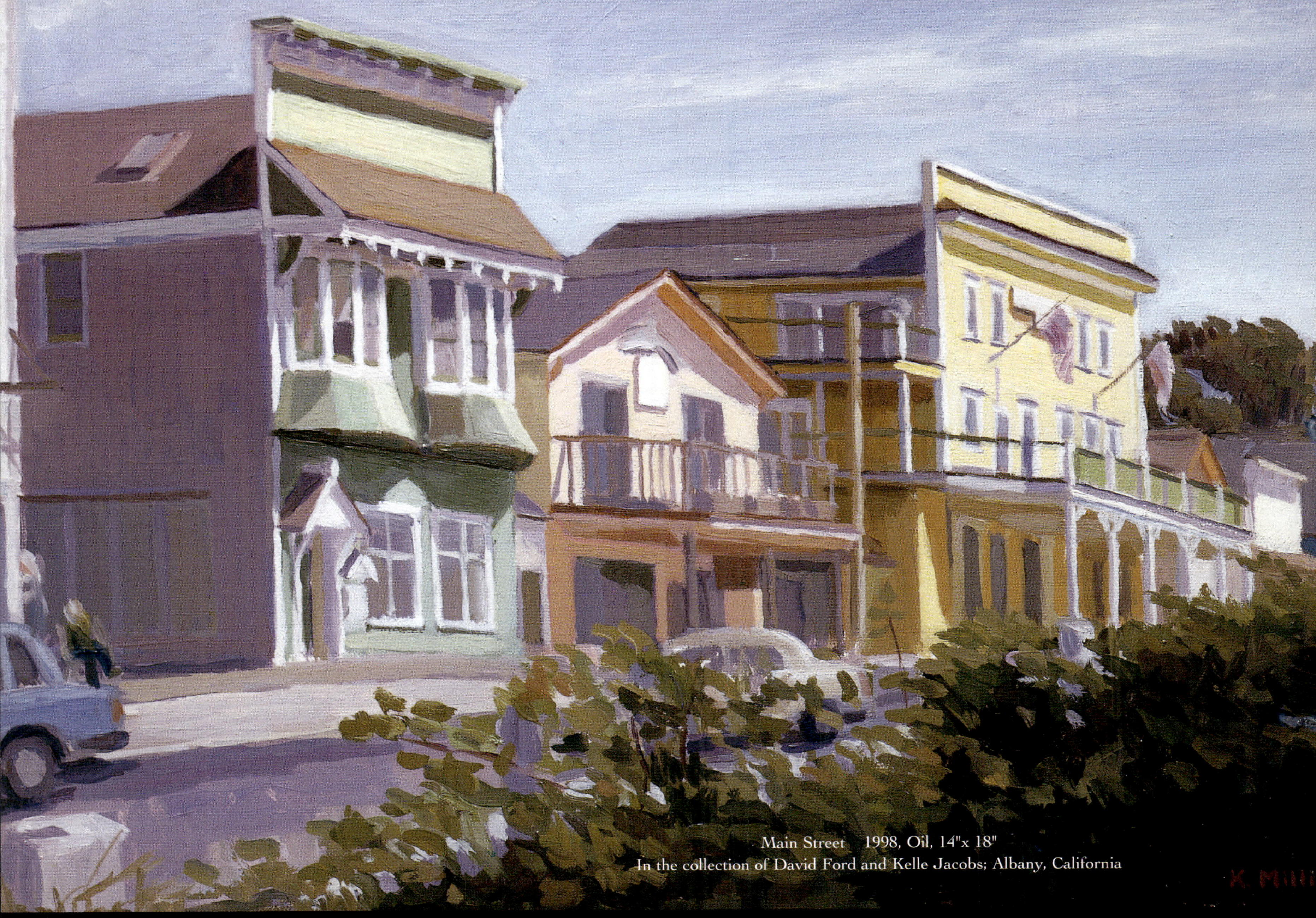

Main Street 1998, Oil, 14"x 18"
In the collection of David Ford and Kelle Jacobs; Albany, California

Mendocino Temperance Parade

With coat tails flying and a battered coronet pointed skyward, the Reverend Fisher resolutely played chorus after chorus of "Hold the Fort For I Am Coming" as he led a group of loudly singing Presbyterian Sunday school children down the four blocks that constituted Mendocino's Main Street. The children's voices did little to enhance the Reverend's coronet playing, but it was all in good cause. The coronet was symbolic of Gabriel's trumpet heralding the good news that on the morrow the town's electorate would go to the polls to decide whether or not, by local option, Mendocino would become a "dry" town.

—James K. Peirsol's *My Boyhood in Mendocino, 1905 -1917*

enough for the Kelly children to have their own boat. Parades were common celebrations for Pentecost, Decoration Day (Memorial Day), the Glorious Fourth (of July), the Apple Fair and any other good excuse. The July Fourth parade continues to this day. The residents also gathered for plays and operettas, political and religious assemblies, fancy-dress balls and community parties, fireworks displays, sports competitions and other varied entertainments such as magic shows, circuses, horse races and later, bicycle and auto races.

Some Pomo Indians lived on Big River Flats while others followed their old migration patterns and came once a year to the Coast to fish and stock up on dried abalone. They traded their exquisite baskets for food and old clothing. Traveling the Coast Road, cattle were sometimes driven through town, as were other animals, such as a flock of turkeys, conveniently just prior to Thanksgiving in 1885. The town had Chinese laundries with drying clothes stretched across Main Street, pool halls and bowling lanes, a soda bottling works and roller skating rinks.

It was for some eighty years a vibrant, picturesque, industrious community, a lusty yet cultivated seat of life and commerce on the rugged Redwood Coast.

The End of an Era

It took little more than those eighty years of logging to exhaust much of the lumber supply along the Mendocino Coast. As the timber in the Mendocino City area was depleted, the huge mill became obsolete. With most of the large trees already harvested in the coastal region, the search for new timber moved inland. Better roads, vehicles and railways made it possible to log without depending on ships for transportation. Smaller mills were constructed near sites where trees were felled. Thus, with on-site milling taking place inland, the need for a large-scale coastal mill was greatly diminished. To its benefit, Fort Bragg's operation had the advantage of a diesel railway connection to Willits.

Other factors, including the Depression, maritime strikes and shifts in the kind of lumber preferred by consumers, resulted in sporadic operation between 1931 and 1934, when the mill closed. Between 1852 and that closing, Mendocino processed and sold some 7.15 billion feet of redwood. Then in the summer of 1938, a fir log raft belonging to the Benson Lumber Company broke up outside Mendocino Bay while it was being towed from the Columbia River to San Diego. About half the logs were salvaged and towed into the Bay. The old inactive Mendocino Mill reopened for one last job: cutting 3,500,000 board feet from the salvaged fir logs, while the Mill produced its last hurrah. It was closed for good

November 30, 1938.

Merna Brown, granddaughter of pioneer John Q. Brown, niece of Antone Braga Lemos and first cousin of Jack and Rich Lemos, shared her personal recollections in a 1945 *Mendocino Beacon* article:

> *With the dismantling of the Mill on Big River, come memories of my childhood. The Mill was a dominant feature in the lives of all that lived in the town of Mendocino. It lay south of the town about a quarter of a mile from the bay and ocean.*
>
> *Perhaps my earliest memory of the mill was the sound of the whistle. As I snuggled in my bed, the 6:30 A.M. whistle would blow and I would hear my father's departure. In a half an hour the day's work began with another blast from the whistle. All of our lives were set to the mill whistle. At noon (the whistle blew) we knew that it was time for our midday meal. At 6:00 P.M. the day's work ended with another blast from the whistle and that meant that father would return to the warmth of his home.*
>
> *However, the mill had other sounds besides the whistle. If there was a good stiff land breeze, in the mornings we could hear the engines, the hum of the saws, the trimmer, the re-saw and the rhythmical flap of boards on the sorting table. All these sounds blended into a composition almost melodic accentuated by the whine of the crane. I can plainly see and hear it now—the red mill set against a background of dark evergreens and azure sky—at our feet the green salty water and clean white sand covered with beached driftwood.*
>
> *Sad were the days when the mill closed. The depression came to the redwood industry and our lives were affected in various ways. As long as the mill stood, even though idle, there was always hope that someday the big wheels would turn again.*

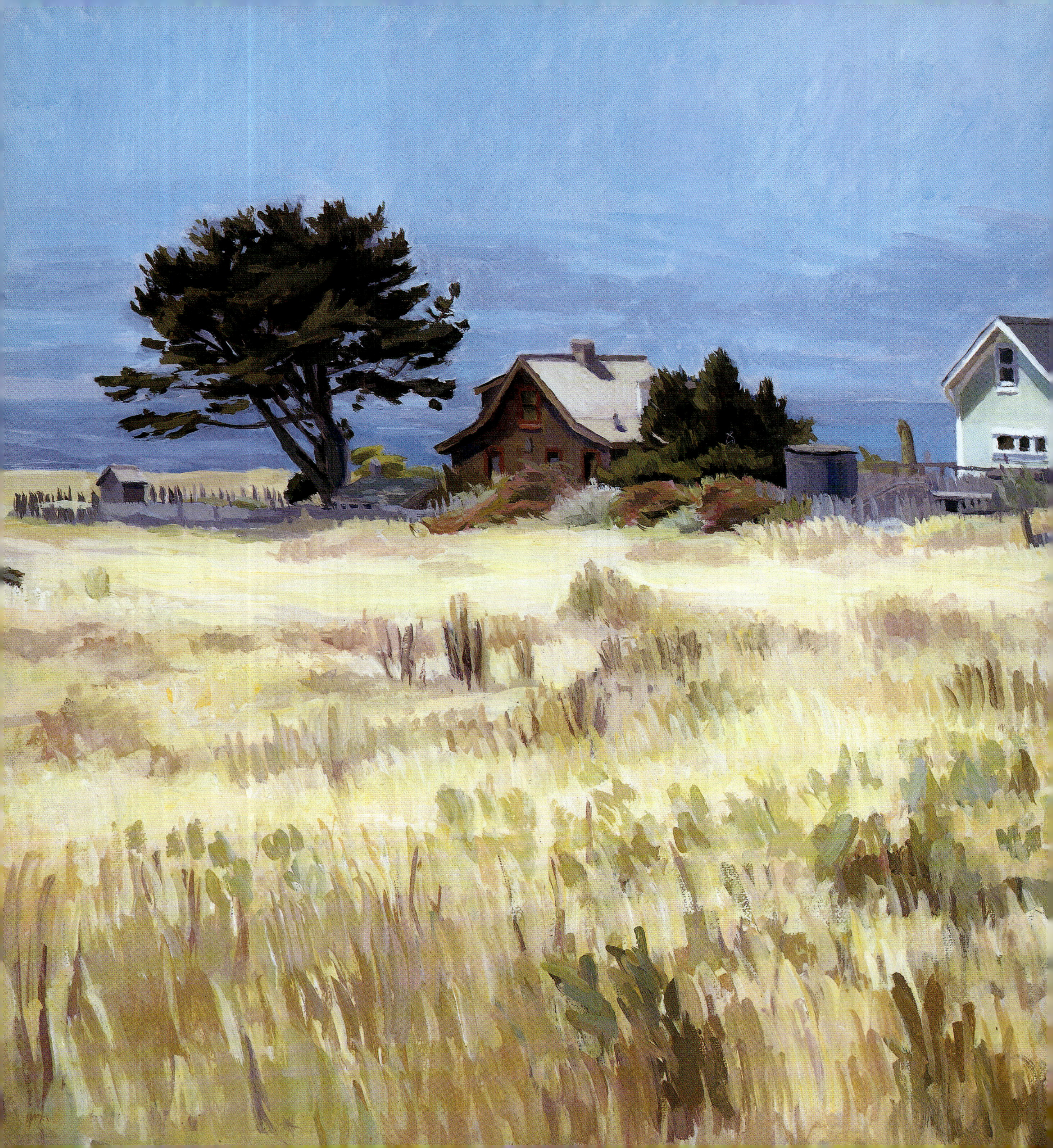

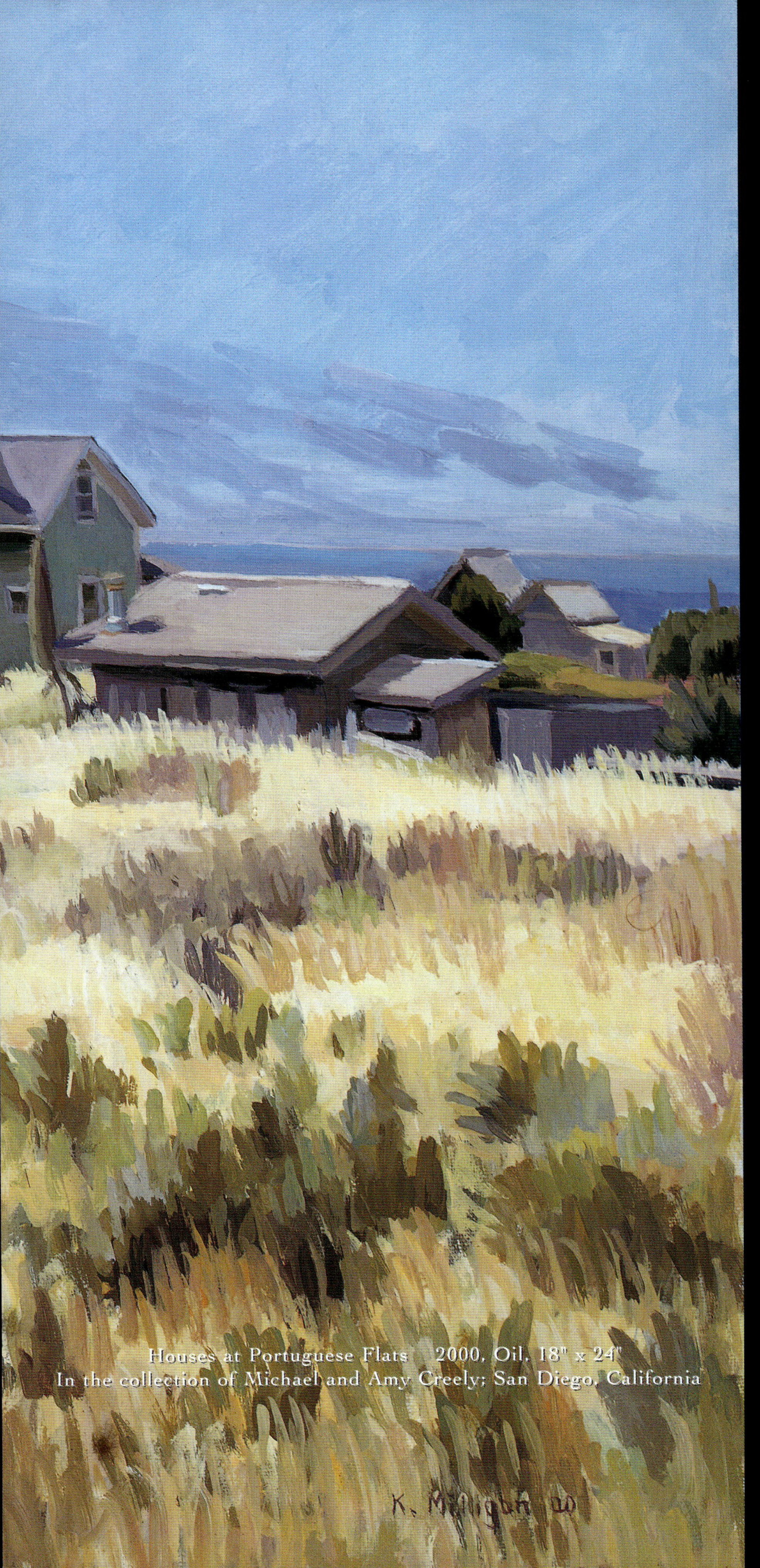
Houses at Portuguese Flats 2000, Oil, 18" x 24"
In the collection of Michael and Amy Creely; San Diego, California

Portuguese Settlers

Mendocino's rich Portuguese history dates from the 1860s, when its original pioneers began to arrive from the Azores, a group of islands located 900 miles west of Portugal. The men were known for their seamanship, sailing small wooden boats to hunt whales. Some, like Frank Mendosa and Domingo Valador, were whalers as young men in the late 1800s, but traded the high seas for jobs in the Mendocino lumber industry. Several earlier arrivals, including the Ramus, Neto, Luis, Lazarus and Lemos families, opened hotels, boarding houses and saloons, most west of Kasten with the majority on Main Street. The men sent back to their homeland for brides, who often traveled alone on sailing ships around the Horn, to marry men they'd never met. Most settlers also convinced family members to come join them for opportunities California offered but were lacking in the

Azores. Portuguese also came from mainland Portugal from eastern U.S. states where they first landed, and some from the Hawaiian Islands.

The 1860 census includes 8 Portuguese men among 477 total residents. Of 1870's total 474 residents, 14 were Portuguese. Two of the men were married, but one wife was Scottish, the other from Massachusetts. The 1880 census lists 87, including some 30 families. By June 1900, the census taker registered 233 Portuguese as part of the total of 927 residents.

In addition to the names mentioned prominently in these chapters, there are numerous others, with various spellings, that echo through the town: Alameida, Andre, Caetano, Coelho, Dias, Faria, Fayal, Fraga, Freitis, Gomes, Jermias, Lenhares, Luiz, Madera, Pereira, Salvador, Silva, Valladao and Vieira. Others chose new names or spellings—or had them changed by their employers—and some were quite Anglicized: Allen, Bettencourt, Brown, Lawrence, Lewis, Mathews, Osborne, Perry, Quaill, Rodgers.

Besides work in the woods and the mill, many Portuguese found success in the hotel and saloon business. Their patrons could enjoy a sense of community and speak in their native language. One of these hotels, the three-story Lisbon House, was built in 1861 and is located next to the Dougherty House west of Kasten Street. The ornate balustrades on the second-story porch railing were carved by J. D. Johnson and feature hearts and diamonds. In 1906 the Lisbon House passed into the hands of Italian families, becoming first Joseph Borgna's Sempione Hotel and then the Paoli Hotel. Today it houses several offices and shops.

Pioneer Portuguese resided in primarily three areas. Most settled first in town, centering around western Calpella Street. Later arrivals built on the more level southwestern section (Heeser, Rundle and Kelly Streets), which became known as Portuguese Flats. Others moved up Little Lake Road to Fury Town east of present Highway One. The Portuguese community constructed some fifty-seven houses, and forty-six are still standing.

These new Californians—almost entirely Catholic—worshipped at St. Vincent's and later, St. Anthony's, Catholic Church. They brought with them their Old World customs, like the Celebration of the Pentecost, a tradition observed in Portugal for more than 600 years and commonly maintained in New World communities. In 1901, they built Crown Hall as a center of Portuguese events. It also served as a church where many could attend services closer to home than at the Catholic Church across town and up the hill.

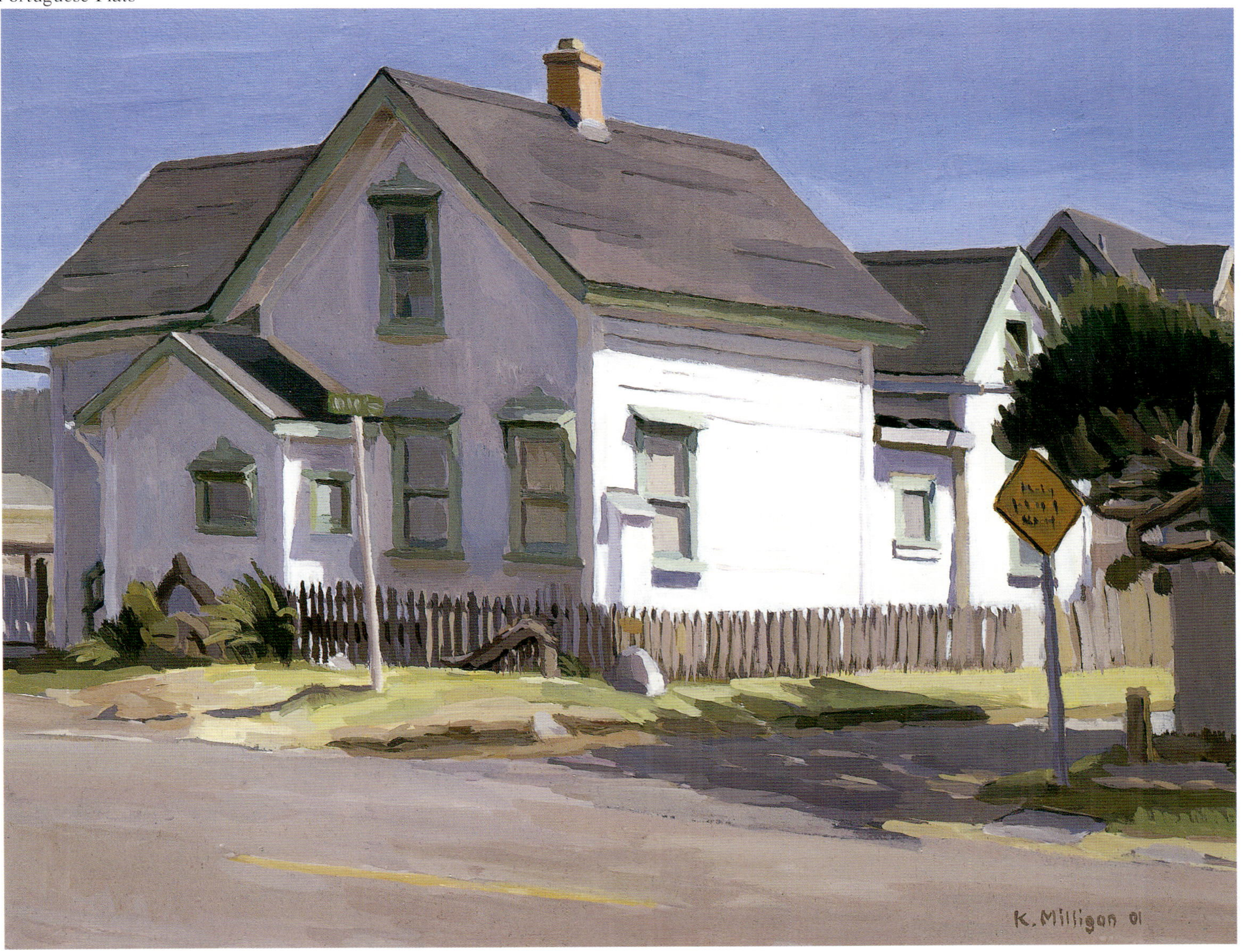

Valador House from Across Ukiah Street 2001, Oil, 14" x 18"
In the collection of Ken and Carol Lawlor; Las Vegas, Nevada

Like several other Portuguese immigrants, Domingo Valador left the Azore Islands as a whaler and worked in the lumber business when he arrived in Mendocino. In 1881, Domingo and his wife Marian bought this house for $700. It was the first house built on Portuguese Flats (1871). Marian was the daughter of Rosa Thomas Jerome, one of five Thomas sisters who lived in the western section of town.

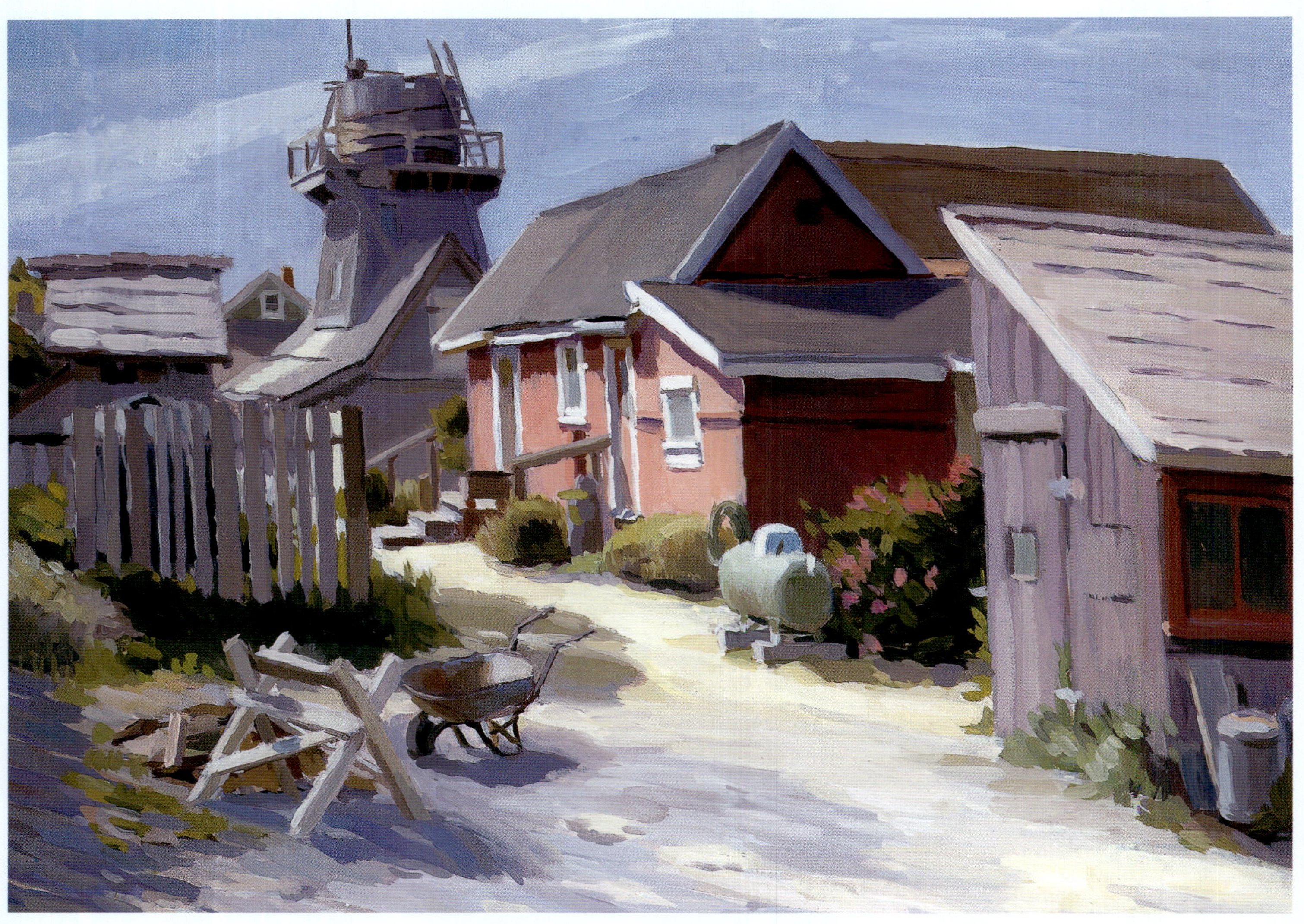

King House with Wheelbarrow 1999, Oil, 14" x 18"
In the collection of Dr. Laxman Kamath; River Hills, Wisconsin

Joseph King, Sr. left the Azores Island of São Jorge at the age of 12 as a cabin boy. By 1874 he made his way to Mendocino, where he worked in the sawmill. After he courted and married Joaquina Thomas, one of the Five Sisters, they moved into one of the homes on Big River Flats near the mill. Some time later—apparently before 1905—they moved to a small house on the corner of Calpella and Heeser Streets. Across the street was the home of her sister Maria, who arrived in 1886 and soon after married Antone M. Bettencourt. In 1916 Joseph King bought two cabins located on the Point from the Mendocino Lumber Company and had them moved and joined to the original structure.

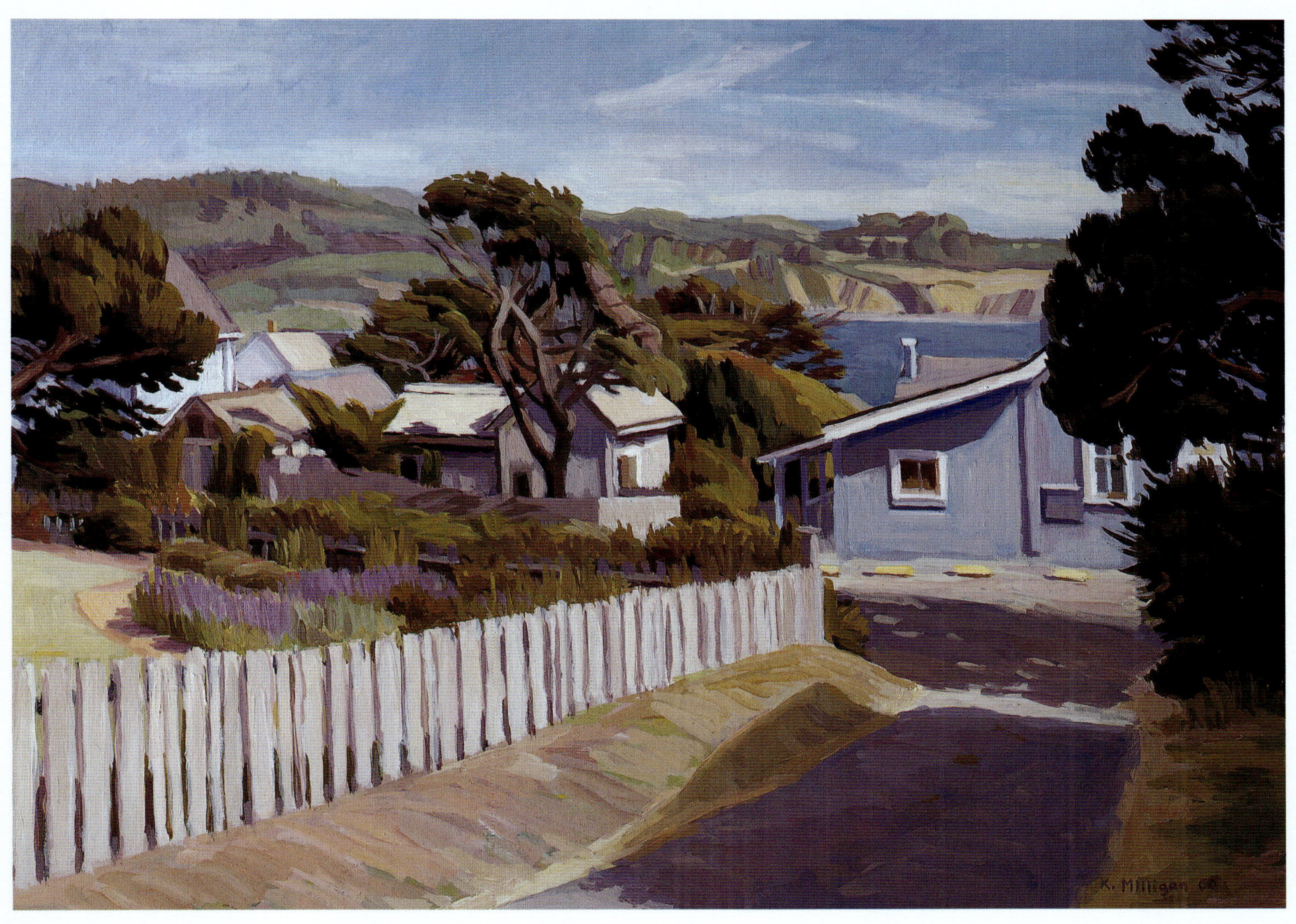

Crown Hall from Woodward Street 2000, Oil, 18" x 24"
In the collection of Shannon Kluever; Long Beach, California

During the 1890s, Portuguese citizens raised funds to build Crown Hall. It was completed in 1901, and a party was held there in October. The first Pentecost was celebrated in it May 1902. For some years, church services were held at the Hall, with many Portuguese attending here instead of the Catholic Church. The community marked the building's centennial anniversary with a New Year's Eve party on December 31, 2001. During the last 100 years, the building has been the site for wedding receptions, concerts, theater performances and numerous other events, not only for the entire Mendocino region, but also for people residing outside the area (for information call 707-937-0672).

The Legend and Celebration of the Pentecost

During the 13th and 14th centuries, earthquakes and volcanic eruptions ravaged the Islands of the Azores, leading to drought and famine. It's believed a ship sailed into the port of Fayal on the Island of Flores, bringing food and necessities to the starving people. Portugal's Queen Isabella was so moved by this act of charity, she donated her crown, which was brought in a procession to the Cathedral of Lisbon, as an offering of thanksgiving. Known as the *Angel of Peace*, she dedicated her life to helping the suffering poor in her country. Thus developed the dual purpose of the celebration to honor the religious holiday of Pentecost and provide charity to the neady. Pentecost is the Seventh Sunday after Easter that commemorates the descent of the Holy Ghost upon the disciples.

The Mendocino observance of the Pentecost not only embraced the aspect of good will toward mankind but also demonstrated it by feeding everyone in town. During the late 19th century, men and boys would cover the entire town, going from house to house taking beef and bread to everyone while playing music, singing, and carrying banners and flags.

The most revered symbol associated with the Pentecost celebration has always been Queen Isabella's crown. Each year a new young woman is selected to wear the symbolic crown.

Frank and Joe Pacheco ordered the original crown for Mendocino, formed of gold bands, from the Azores Island of Terceira around 1885-86, and their family cared for it between celebrations. The new crown was first worn by Mary Ramus. Over time this crown became so fragile it could no longer be worn by the chosen queen, and finally had to be carried on a satin pillow during the parade.

During the seven weeks between Easter and Pentecost, the crown was displayed on altars decorated with flowers and candles in seven different homes, rotated weekly. The honored, chosen families would welcome neighbors to come and pray at their home during the week. A rosary service often concluded the evening meal, followed by singing songs of praise accompanied by cymbals, drums, triangles and tambourines.

The Pentecost weekend included a blessing of the bread, a large and lively party and a parade led by the Queen who wore or carried the crown. Her royal attendants joined in the procession that moved through town between the Church and one of several locations. Before the building of Crown Hall, festivities were held in private homes, in halls like the Odd Fellows or Foresters, and sometimes at the Lisbon House. The Native Sons of the Golden West Band would play as they marched in the parade.

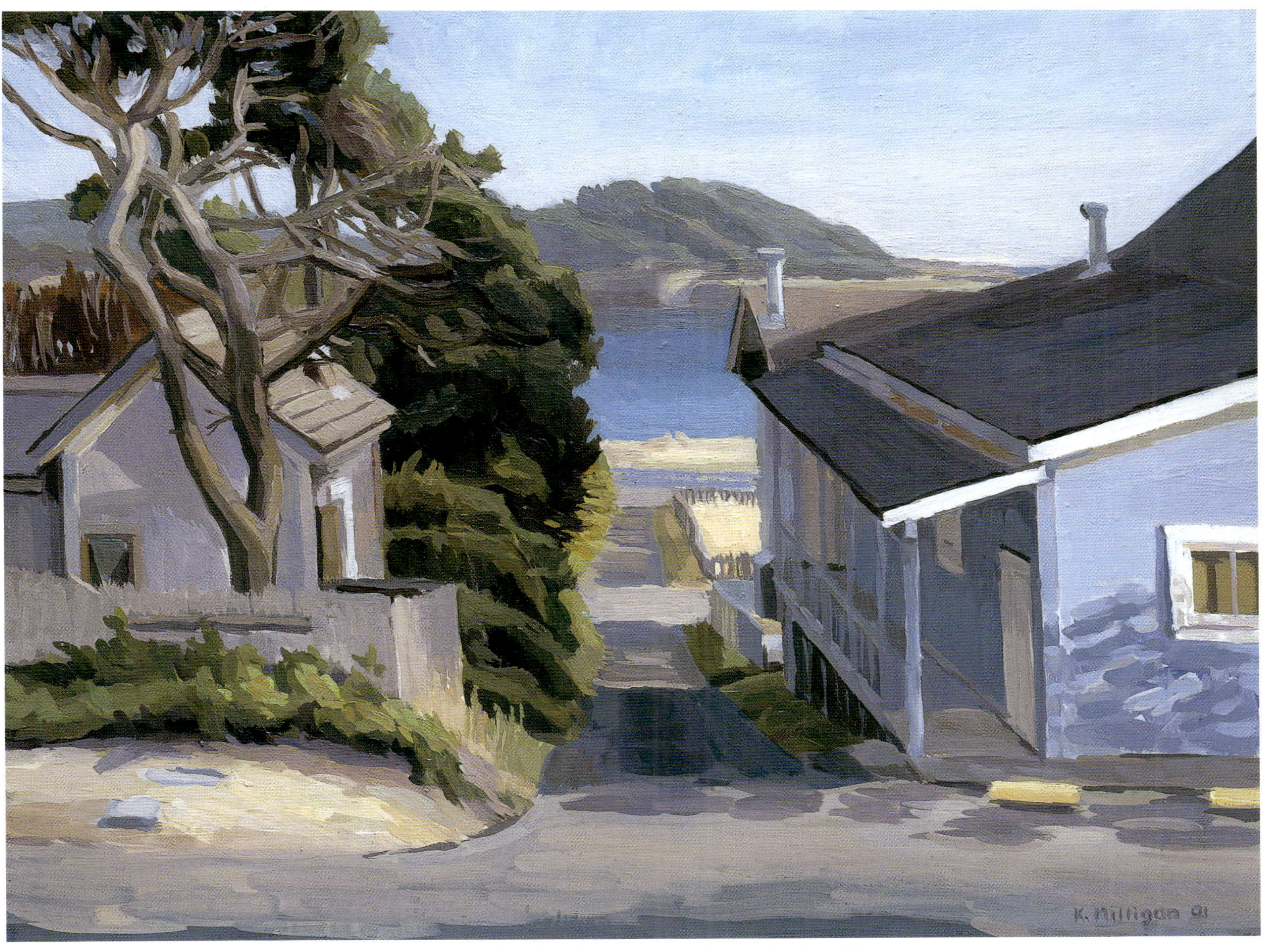

Crown Hall with Osborn Street 2001, Oil, 14" x 18"
In the collection of Tim and Laura Zadel; San Jose, California

For its first 62 years, Crown Hall was the Mendocino site for the Celebration of the Pentecost. In 2001, 78-year-old Richard Lemos, youngest of 10 children, recalled fond memories of the Pentecost Celebration at Crown Hall, *"It was a chance to see my older brothers Art and Jeff and sister Priscilla . . . They would all make the trip up to Mendocino for the event. . . . When I was a kid, I would run around Crown Hall (during the Pentecost Party), with my friends . . . We would end up falling asleep on the wooden benches, as our parents would stay late into the evening visiting with long-time friends."*

Later, the local community raised 60 silver dollars to replace the worn-out original gold crown from 1885 with a new silver crown. They sent the coins to the Azores where they were melted down and made into the new crown, which is still used today. The first to wear it was Mamie Bettencourt, who was the chosen Queen for the first Pentecost celebrated at the newly built Crown Hall in 1902.

The new Crown Hall provided a party site where participants could dine and dance and socialize late into the evening. Favorite traditions include performing the *Chamarita* folk dance and feasting on *Sopa*, a savory beef dish cooked in huge kettles and served over bread seasoned with mint and cinnamon.

In 1964 the Portuguese communities of Mendocino and Fort Bragg consolidated their celebrations in the larger town to the north. Lifetime resident Foggy Gomes commented, *"It was a sad day when the celebration was moved to Fort Bragg. It was so enjoyable at Crown Hall that us 'old timers' have many fond memories."*

At this writing, efforts are under way to return some form of Pentecost observance to the historic hall in Mendocino, perhaps alternating years with Fort Bragg. For years Rosamond Rodrigues has been the Keeper of the Silver Crown, tending to it with great care and reverence between celebrations. The gold crown was donated to the Kelley House Museum and is on display there in the Lemos Library.

Alvin Mendosa has lived for 50 years in this house on Little Lake Street. Built around 1910 and located just west of the Art Center, it is sometimes called the Henry Gordon House after its early owner, Alvin's great-uncle. (This should not be confused with the Henry T. Gorden House on School Street.)

Many of the Mendosas lived in Fury Town. Alvin's uncle William recalled, *"I planted the palm trees here when nephew Morris was born, fifty-one years ago (December 1924). I remember my neighbor, Emil Seman, Sr. when he lived next door. When I planted those he just laughed. He said, 'They will never grow.'"— William Mendosa, c.1950.* Seventy-seven years later, the palm trees have grown to 30 feet high beside the house on Little Lake Road, just east of Highway One.

—Quoted excerpt from *Mendocino County Remembered, An Oral History* by Bruce Levene.

Alvin's uncle Gus Mendosa was known as a straight-faced practical joker who loved to spin yarns for tourists. Gus's wife Alma, a teacher at various schools in the county, became a beloved principal of the Mendocino Grammar School. Alvin's son Mitch is currently a teacher elsewhere in Mendocino County.

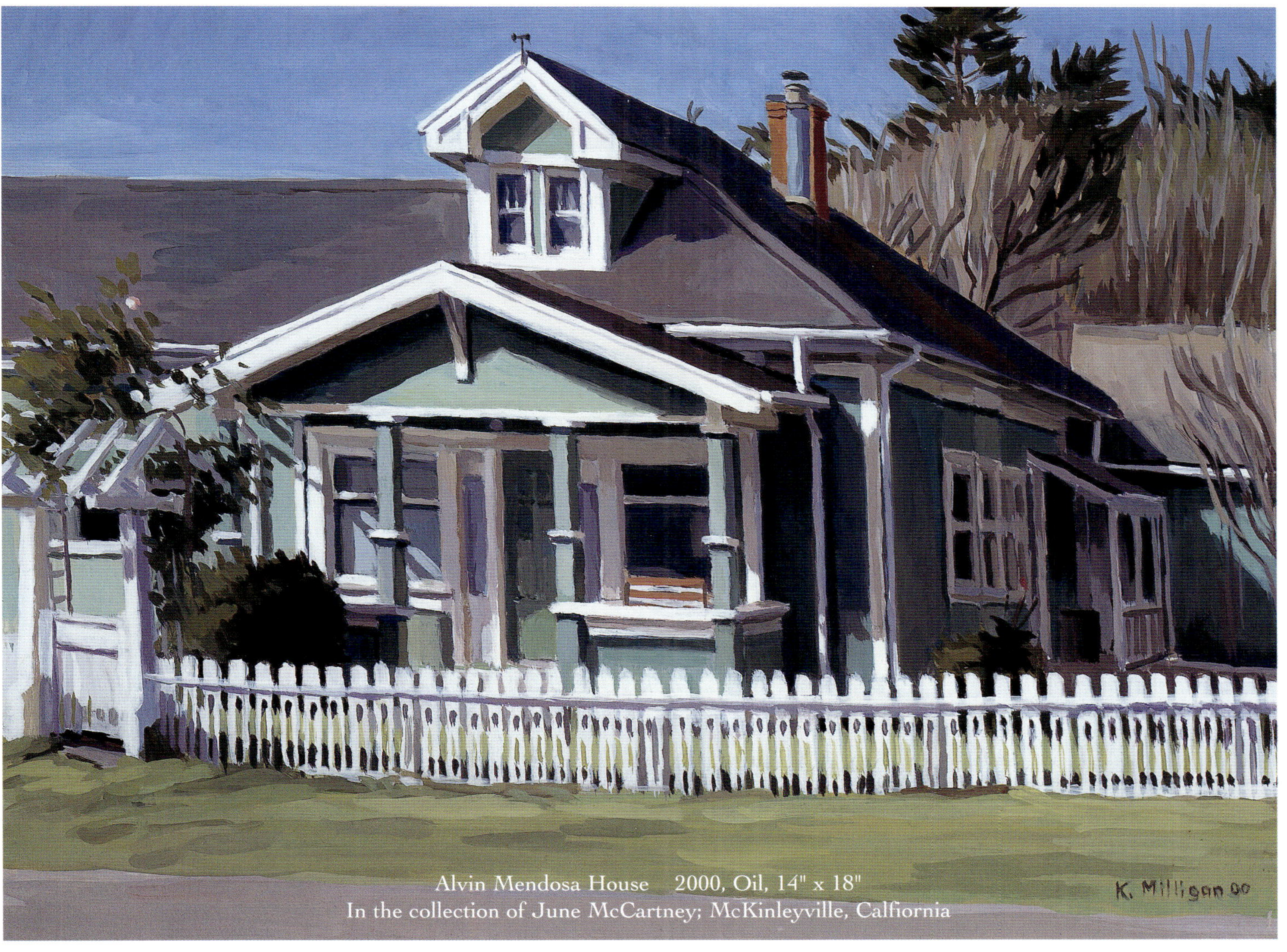

Alvin Mendosa House 2000, Oil, 14" x 18"
In the collection of June McCartney; McKinleyville, Calfiornia

One Portuguese Family: the Mendosas

Frank J. Mendosa, originally Francisco Jose Mendonca, left the whaling trade in the Azores and came to Mendocino c.1869. He worked in the woods for a time and later at the mill. He became friends with Antone Lopes who arrived from the island of São Jorge in 1873. Lopes is pronounced and sometimes spelled Lopps. In 1882 Frank and Antone bought land together in Fury Town and built neighboring homes on Little Lake Road. Later, Antone's sister Isabel Jacinto Lopes came to join him and met her brother's good friend. Isabel and Frank married in 1887. They were known all their lives as a hard-working team who seldom argued, even while they reared eight children separated in age over 11 years. Their work ethic and strong love for each other saw them through many difficult situations, which accounted for the ten-member family's ability to survive and thrive in an isolated country town.

Frank, who had sailed around Cape Horn twice in his late teens, shared these experiences with his children, telling vivid stories about his adventures at sea. Working on a small boat, Frank was part of a crew that harpooned whales, which were allowed to pull the boat around until they tired and then could be hauled onto the mother ship. He spellbound the children with stories of how the whales would often smash the boat with their huge tails.

According to his grandson Alvin, Frank was glad to get away from that kind of work. The young immigrant gained experience as a *water slinger* and a *whistle punk* before working his way to *bull puncher* in the woods. As a result, he was an experienced woodsman when he took a job at the Mendocino Lumber Company mill on Big River Flats, a position he held for years until he was severely injured in 1902. While operating the muley saw, his right arm got caught in the rope. As it tightened, he was thrown from his feet with his arm nearly severed. The foreman finished amputating the arm at the mill, after which he was brought home on a buckboard and treated by Dr. James W. Milliken.

Grandson Alvin Mendosa says that according to the family,

> *He was only paid a half day's wage (the day of the accident) and had to pay for the doctor visit himself.*

After recovering from the accident, Frank and Isabel opened a saloon in a small building they owned on Lansing Street, site of the current store. Later, they added a small restaurant referred to as a *chophouse.* Beer and wine were served out of large wooden kegs. The only sale on their opening day was one nickel beer! However, the business developed and ran successfully until the town was voted "dry" in 1909. The restaurant business was unable to succeed without the revenue generated from the sale of alcohol. The windows and doors were boarded up when the saloon-restaurant closed, and the resiliency of the family was tested again.

That year, they decided to convert the chophouse into a grocery and hardware store. Later, in 1919, without losing a day of business, more space was created by building over the existing structure, creating the main part of the store, which was the hardware-building supply department. Since it was common for people to construct their own homes in the early years, building supplies were always in demand. The grocery sold many bulk items out of bins including rice, beans, flour and coffee. They also carried fresh vegetables grown in the family garden in Fury Town.

The two parents and eight children composed a formidable work force. The only girl, Mary, worked as a cook in the chophouse and as a bookkeeper for the business. Since neither parent could read nor write in English, customers would put their mark on a piece of paper with a list of the items purchased, and Mary would later record

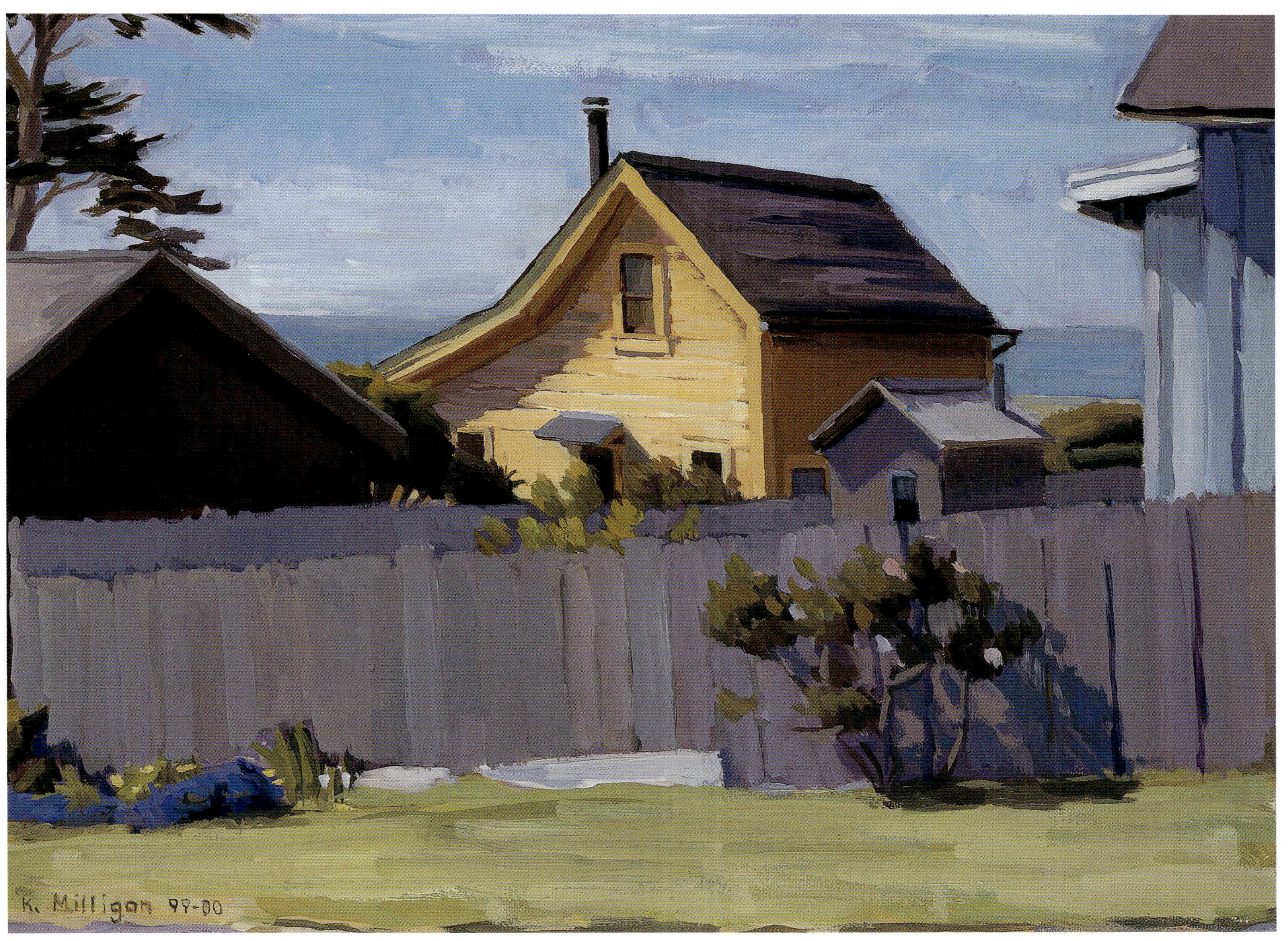

Yellow House with the Pacific Ocean 1999–2000, Oil, 14" x 18"
In the collection of Shara Stamler; Bodega Bay, California

the transactions into the books. As they grew up, the seven brothers tended the family garden and delivered groceries using bicycles and hand-pulled wagons. The older brothers worked in the woods and the mill and turned their paychecks over to their parents, who paid the children an allowance. William Mendosa (1896-1980) once commented:

My father in turn gave us five dollars a month. That does not seem like a lot now, but in those days five dollars was quite a bit of money.

William recounted how he was drafted into the family business:

I had to leave school my second year in high school. My sister was working in the store, and she wanted to get

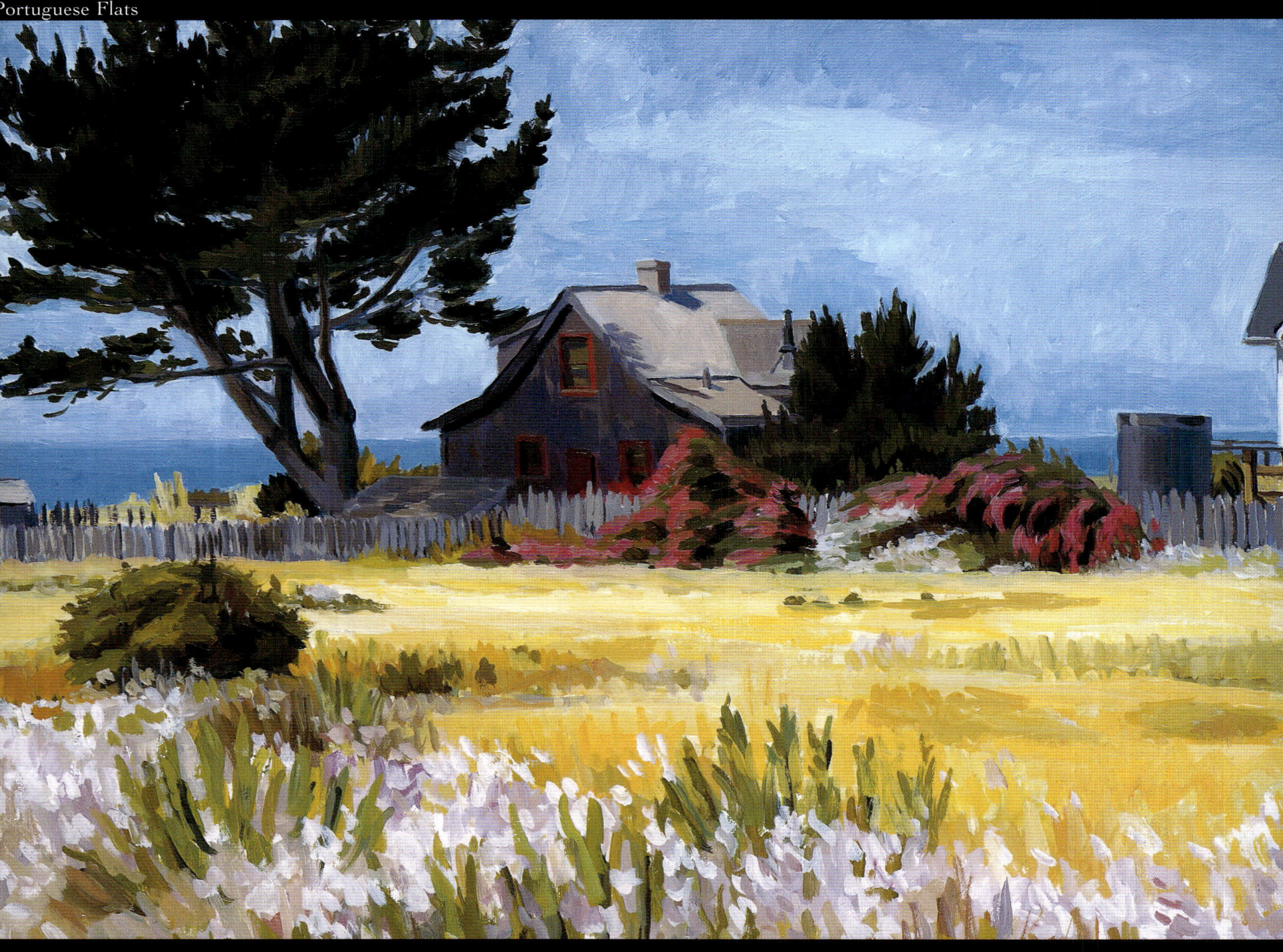

Shake House with Field and Rosebushes 1999, Oil, 14" x 18"
In the collection of Reed and Kathleen Pugh; Winchester, Massachusetts

Golden Field at Portuguese Flats

For years, I observed the town from an easel while painting in fields, back streets, balconies and looking down from hills. Details of the town's sights and sounds imbedded themselves in my memory. In time, I became so familiar with my surroundings, I could recognize the sound of a particular gate closing behind me, or how the ravens made their click-clock call as they flew out of the cypress trees beside Crown Hall, over the west end fields, and circled the leaning Carlson water tower. In the summer months, this field is a favorite location to paint. From my easel, I can look across yellow, dried grass and paint views of the rosebushes and pine trees next to west end houses set against

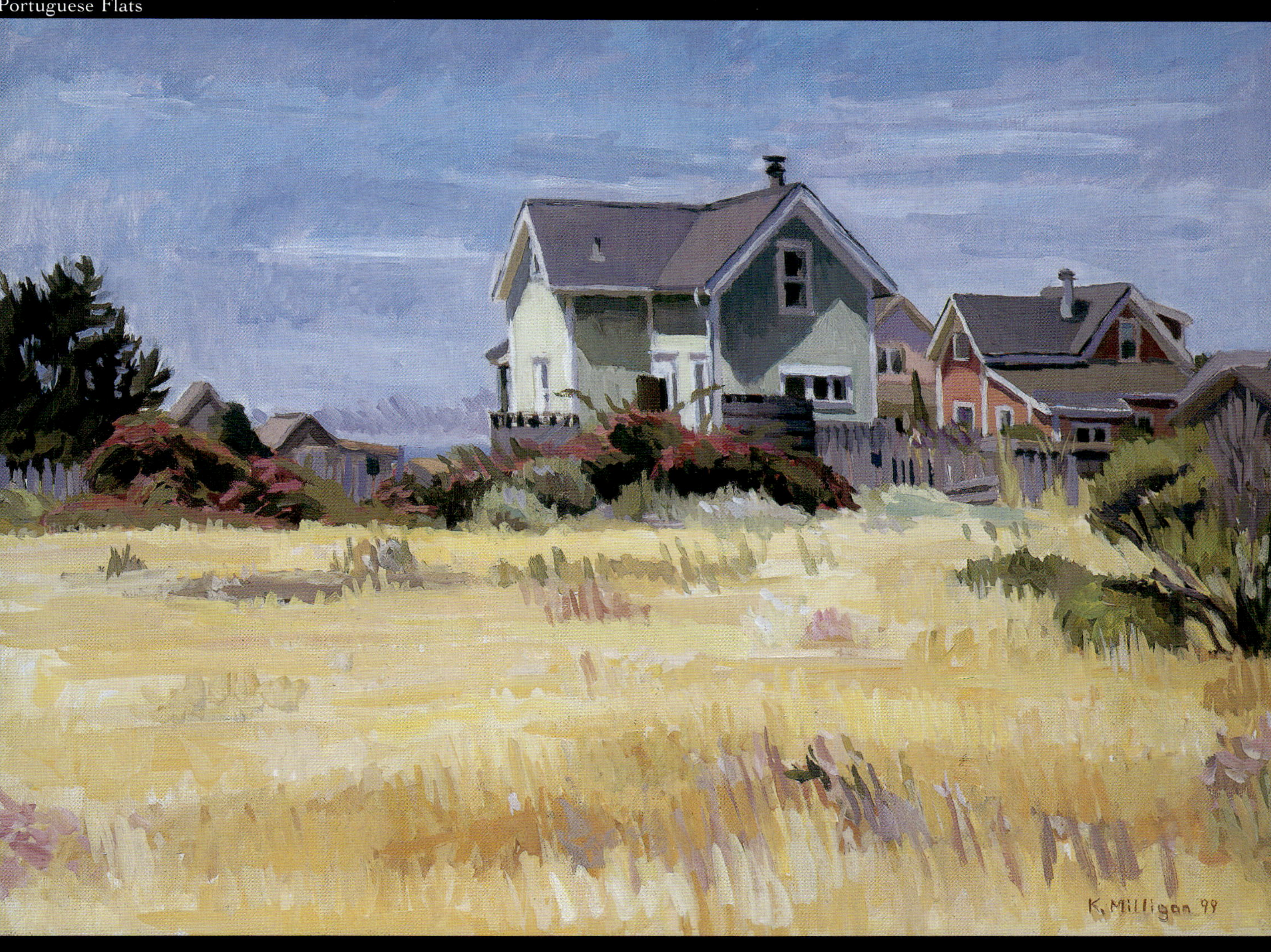

Green House with Red House 1999, Oil, 14" x 18"
In the collection of Mario Duarte; San Francisco, California

the ocean and sky—all forming a perfect harmony. On many afternoons, a fog bank will sit just offshore and slowly make its way onto land, overtaking the houses on Kelly and Rundle Streets, then moving toward my easel in the open field. As the mist approaches, I brace the canvas from the fog line gusts. This pattern is often repeated as the fog bank moves back and forth, creating a breezy condition at the leading edge. On rare hot days, the marine layer remains offshore, and it stays calm over Portuguese Flats. A wispy ribbon of fog may curl around the Point into Mendocino Bay (forming a transparent curtain between headlands and Bay) and is drawn up Big River as the heat rises, shimmering, off the golden field.

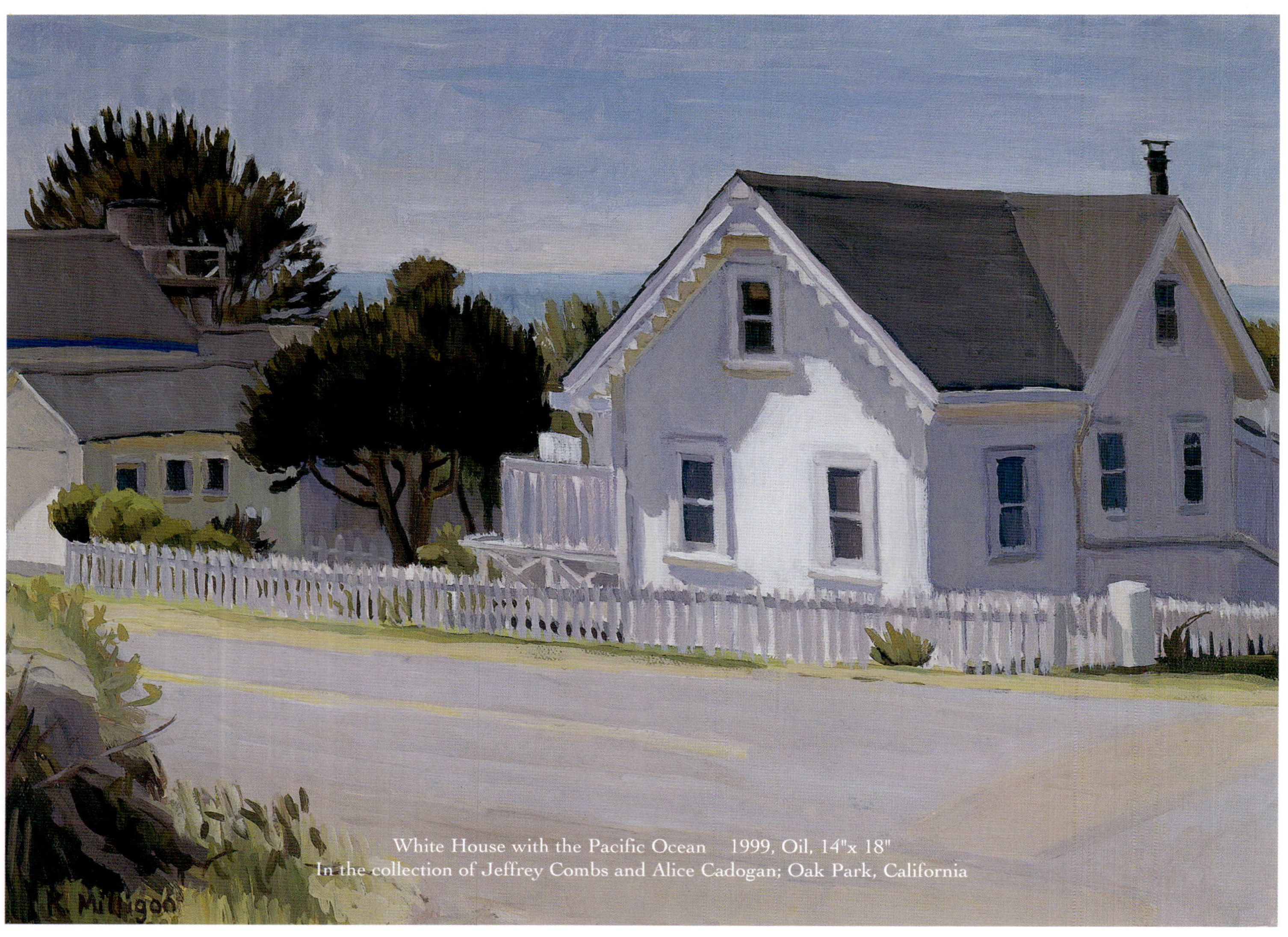

White House with the Pacific Ocean 1999, Oil, 14"x 18"
In the collection of Jeffrey Combs and Alice Cadogan; Oak Park, California

married, so what happened was that I had to go there. I took private lessons. I wanted to continue on with high school but what are you going to do? The options weren't there when I was young. We just did not have the money. We had to struggle for a living at the start. I worked there and enjoyed my work very much. I had charge of the store for well over fifty years. It was a long time, but it did not seem like it.

The family business survived the closing of the mill. According to William:

We had a lot of tough going here. When they dismantled the mill here, we thought we were goners.

There were other hurdles such as the Depression and the war. Five of the boys left to serve in the armed forces during World War I. John (the third oldest boy) was gassed overseas, which led to tuberculosis. Fortunately, he recovered at Mare Island Hospital after the war.

It seems that nothing stopped the Mendosas. The store continues to be an integral part of the community.

The Lemos Family

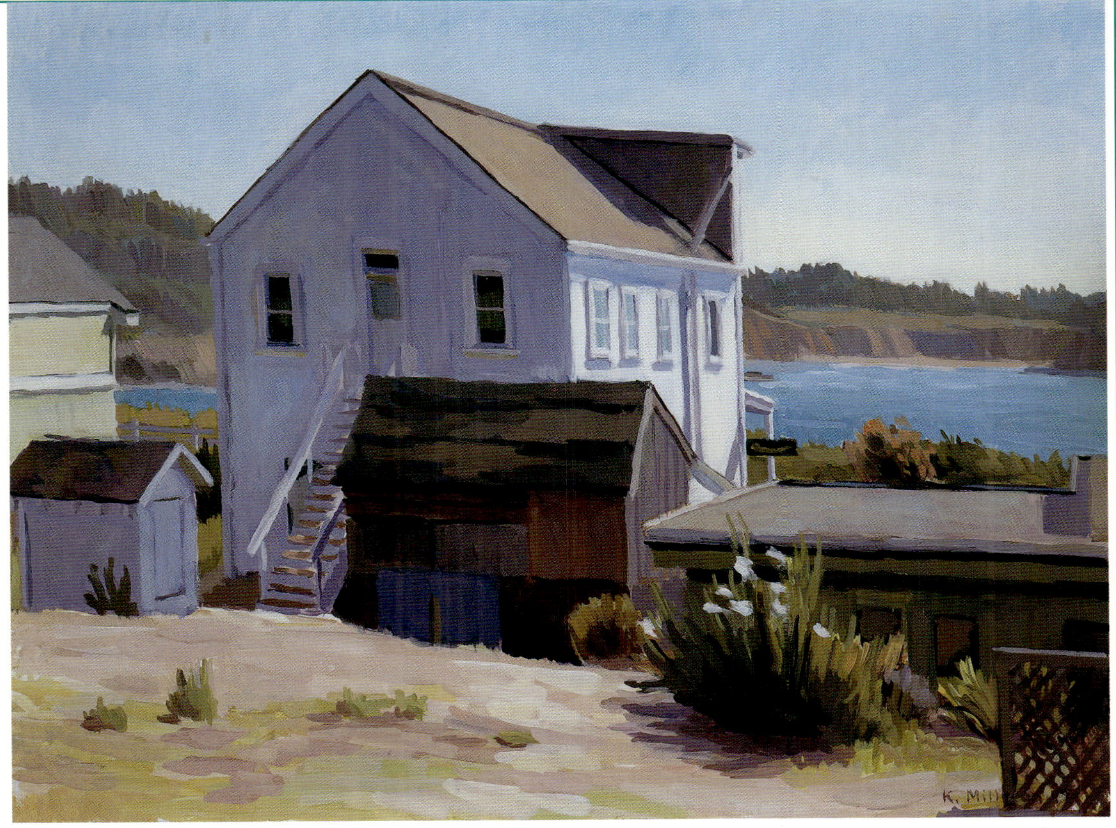

Lemos Saloon 1999, Oil, 14" x 18"
In the collection of Andrèe Bryan; St. Helena, California

Fernandez Lemos came from the Island of Flores, opening the Lemos Saloon and Boarding House on west Main in 1886. When the town was voted "dry" in 1909, he converted the saloon into a grocery store with a pool table in back. On the last day, friends were invited to come to the bar and drink the remaining 50 gallons of wine. Herman Fayal (1893–1988) reported, *"I was sick for a week."* Antone Braga Lemos, youngest brother of Fernandez, arrived in 1903. Locally known as Mr. "B," he spoke four languages and for 38 years ran a shop cutting and dressing hair. He and wife Amelia, daughter of John Quaill Brown, reared nine children in a two-story house on Lansing Street, with Antone's barbershop on the first floor. It is currently the Mendocino Café. His sons John (Jack), and Richard, still live in Mendocino. Many members of the Lemos Family continue to play an important role in Mendocino's educational community, especially at the high school level.

Alvin and his cousin Jeanette Mendosa Hansen are the last Mendosas living in Mendocino City, but other members of the family still live and work in the county. Alvin's uncle William once described the strong family bond:

Sometimes you hear of brothers and sisters not speaking to each other . . . but that was all the bunk as far as we were concerned. We were a very close-knit and loyal family.

Portuguese Flats

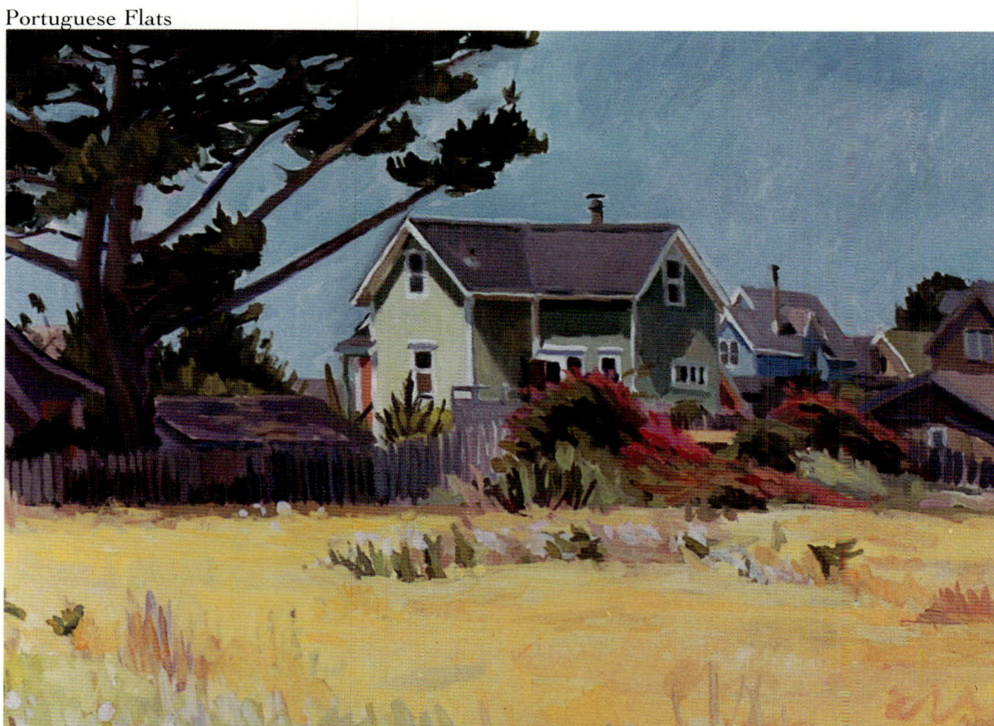

Green House with
Pines and Rosebushes
1999, Oil, 14" x 18"
In the collection of
George O'Toole; San
Francisco, California

Portuguese Flats

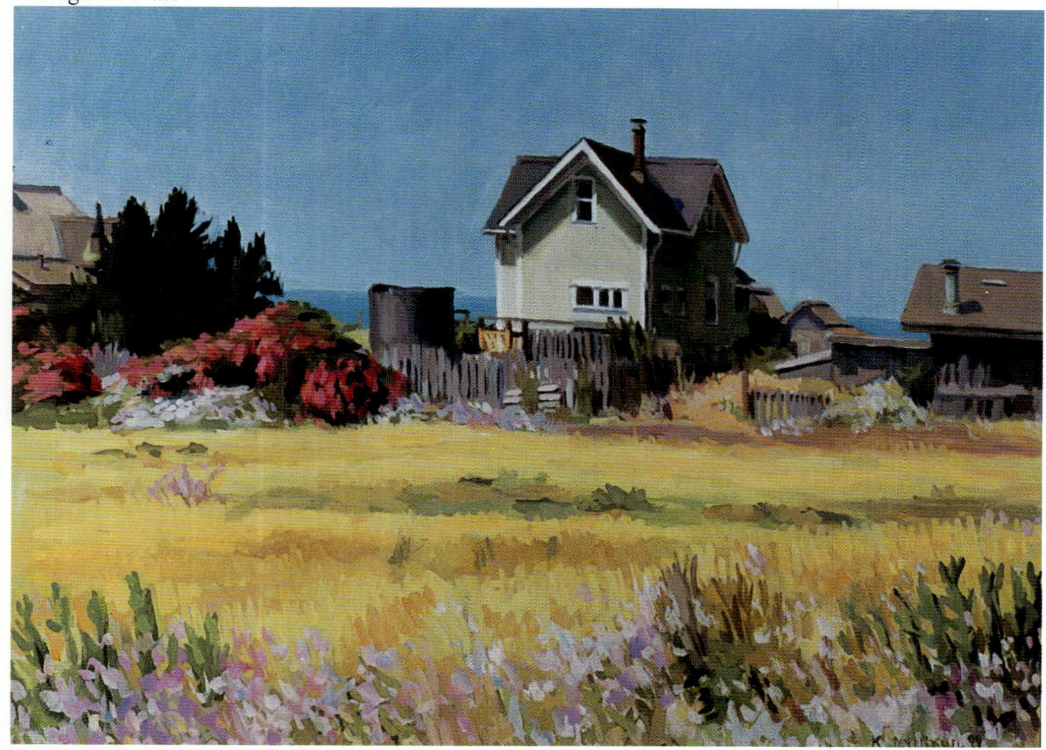

Green House with Rosebushes
1999, Oil, 14" x 18"
In the collection of Donald
and Maureen Gazzaniga;
Auburn, California

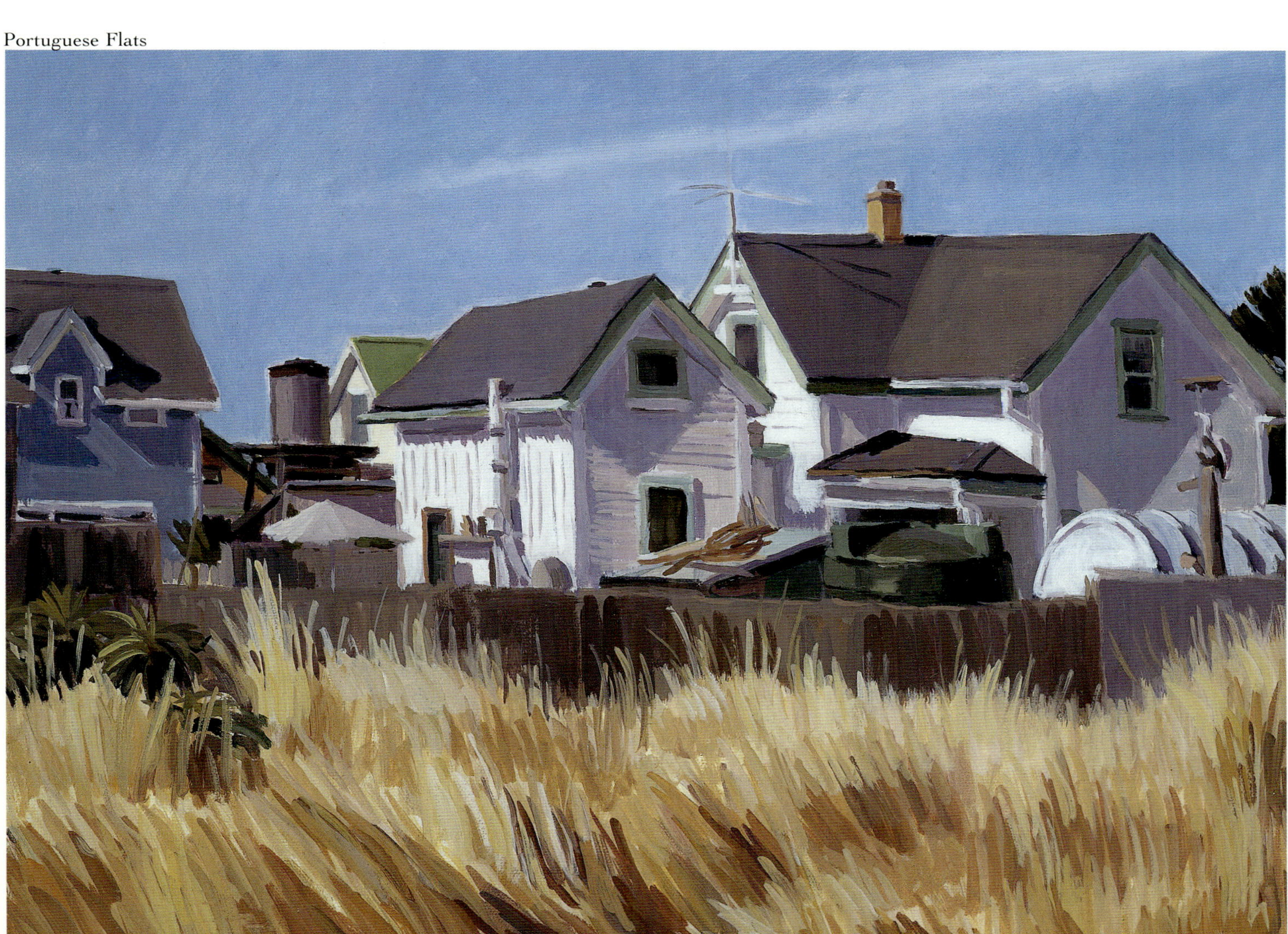

Valador House with Field 1998, Oil, 14" x 18"
In the collection of Paul and Sandy Dietrich; El Sobrante, California

Domingo Valador, Jr. and his wife Dolores first lived across the street in the Joseph Diaz house, where they reared five children. Then they moved to this home where they stayed until the late 1990s. Domingo followed in his father's footsteps, trying various jobs in different lumber mills in the area. Domingo, Sr.'s first job at the Page Mill was making shingles. The old record book shows that in 1932 he earned $2.12 a 12-hour day, which came to $55 per month for 26 days of work. Granddaughter of Domingo and Marian, Nancy Valador, was chosen to be the Queen of the 1961 Celebration of the Pentecost on the 60th anniversary of Crown Hall.

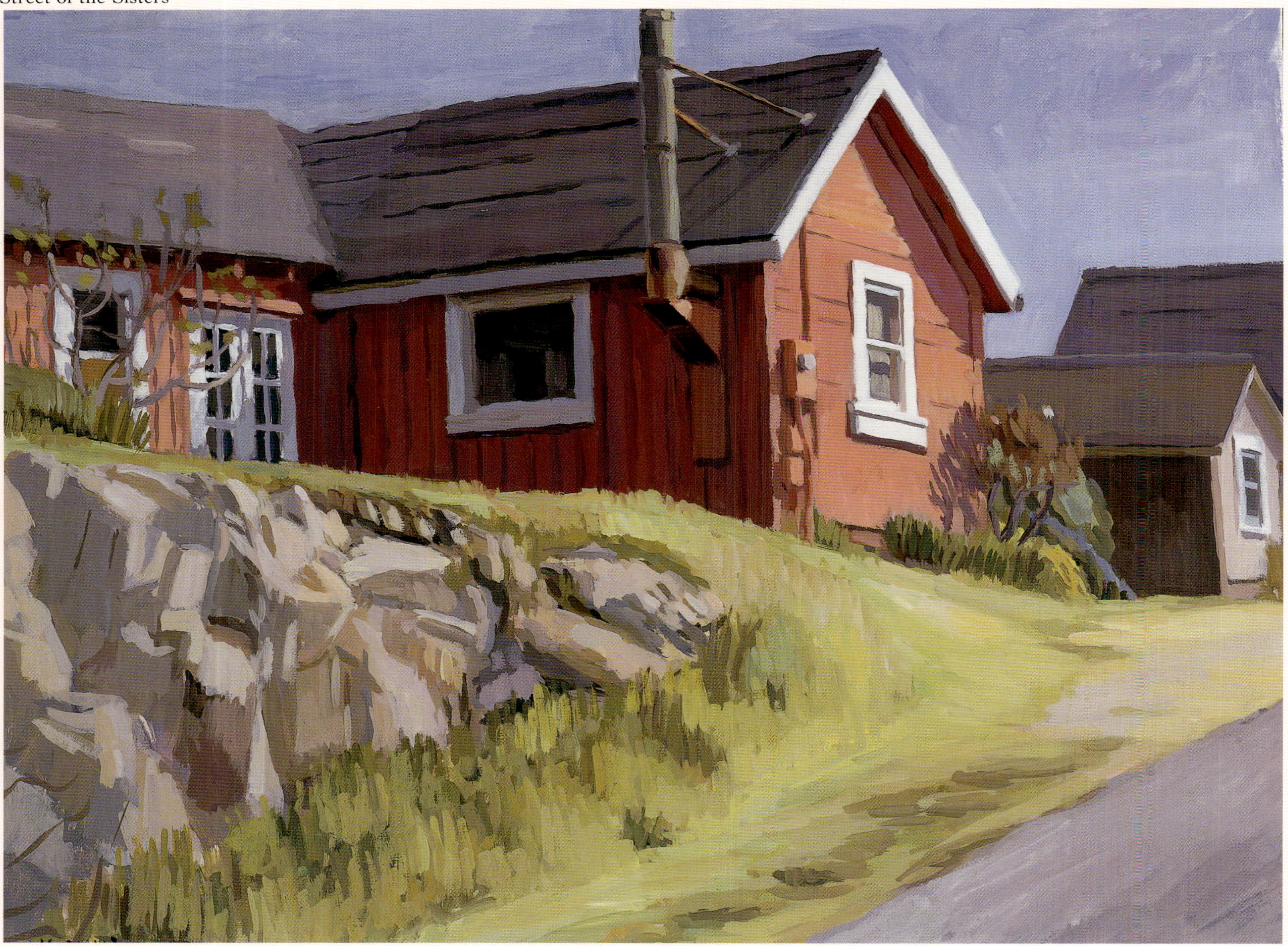

Joseph King House 1999–2000, Oil, 14" x 18"
In the collection of Bruce and Nancy Nelson; Fresno, California

The Street of the Sisters

The five Thomas Sisters came from the Azores island of Flores between 1878–1886 and created a small community of their own, settling in homes all along western Calpella Street with one sister around the corner of Williams Street on Little Lake Street. Farthest west at Heeser Street were the homes of Maria and Antone Bettencourt and, across Calpella, that of Joaquina and Joseph King.

Annie, born in 1853, arrived in 1878, the first. Rosa, born in 1847, arrived in 1879. Marianna, born in 1851, came with her in 1879. Joaquina, born in 1858, arrived in 1882-83. Maria, born in 1866, arrived in 1886, the last.

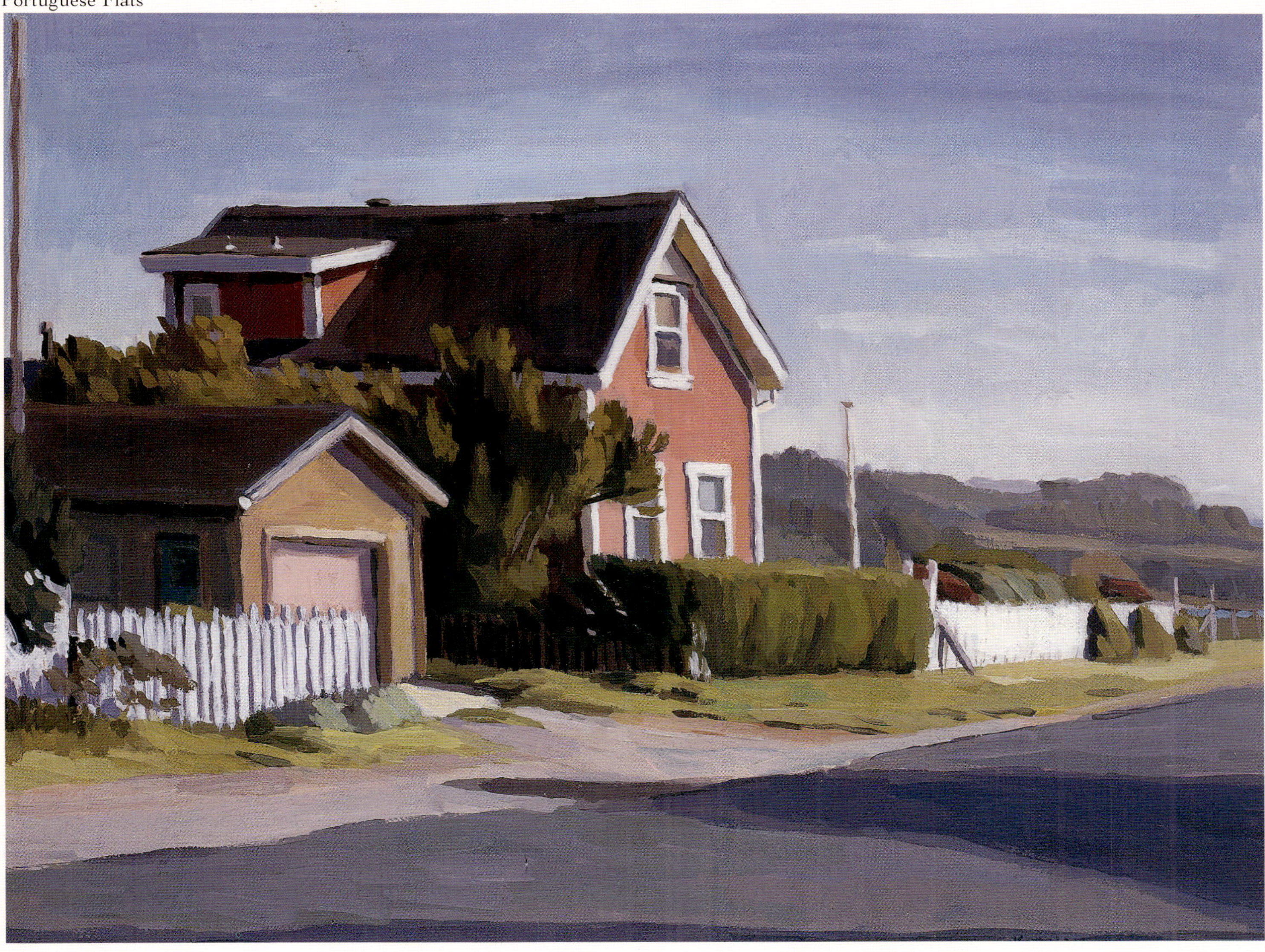

Manuel Lawrence House 1999–2000, Oil, 14" x 18"
In the collection of Kris and Lisa Anne Milligan; San Ramon, California

Echoes of the Past

On New Year's Eve, the men would gather and go from house to house, serenading their neighbors on Portuguese Flats. The singers might be accompanied by a concertina and would perform late into the evening. The spirited group was known to perform even in the rain, which was often the case in December and January, with the hosting family providing encouragement, food and drink.

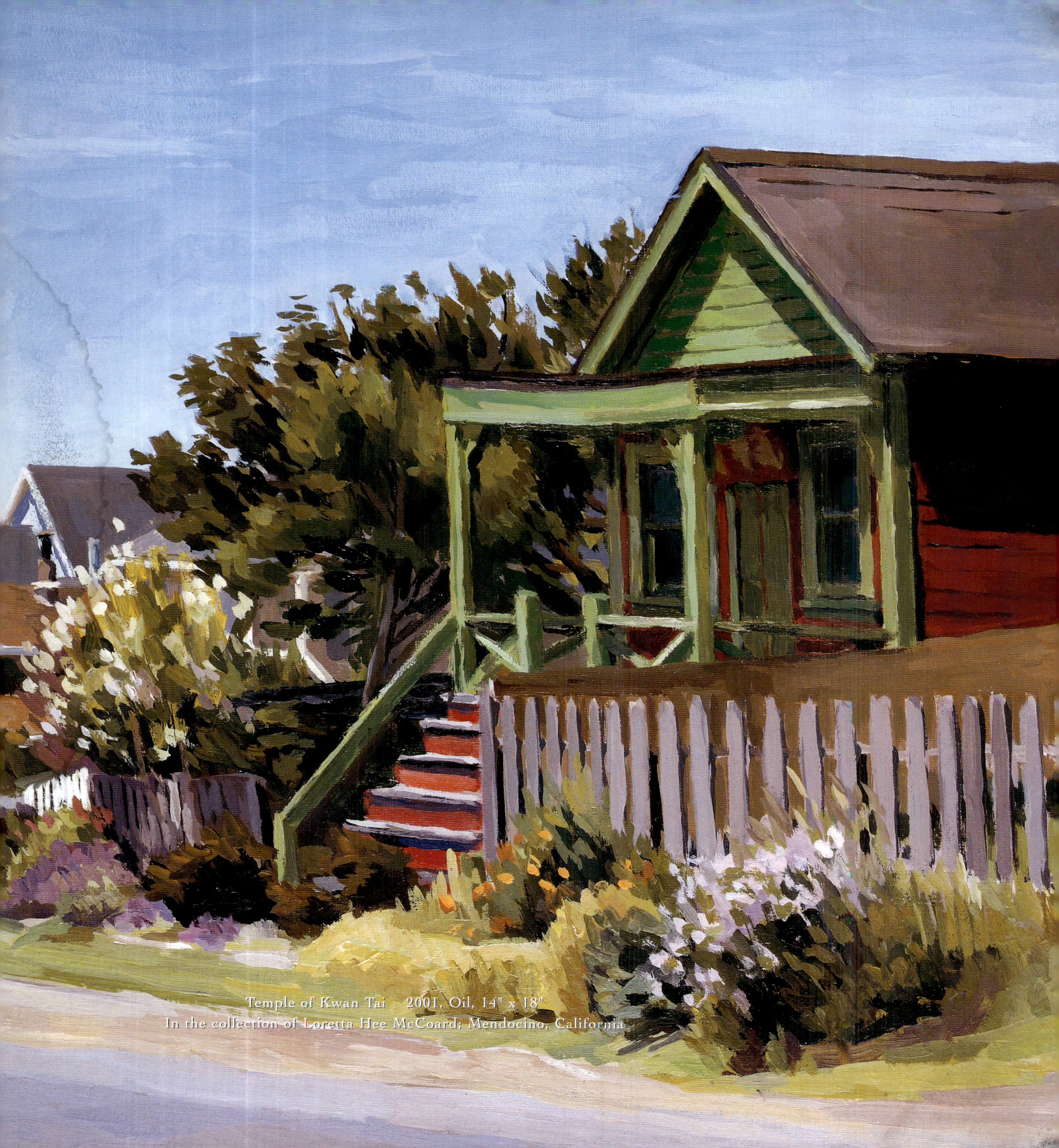

Temple of Kwan Tai 2001, Oil, 14" x 18"
In the collection of Loretta Hee McCoard, Mendocino, California

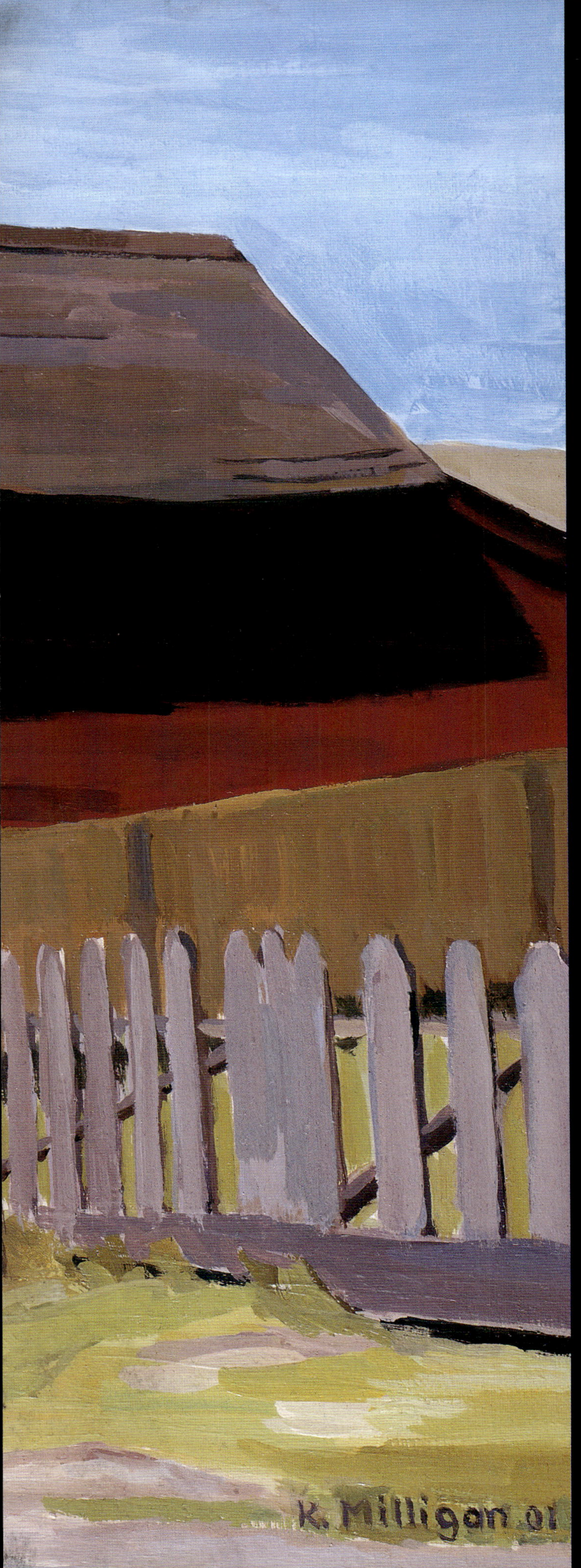

Chinese Settlers

Oral history traces Mendocino's first known Chinese settlers to a wooden junk that landed at Caspar Beach around 1854. It's believed this was one of five boats manned by farming families that, using the Black Tide Current, wind power and rowing, sailed up along the coast of China, across to the North American continent and down to California, headed for San Francisco. Each thirty-foot boat was loaded with blankets, clothing and a food supply necessary to survive the year-and-a-half-long trip. Three boats were lost at sea; one ended up on Carmel River Beach; and one landed at Caspar. According to Mendocino resident George Hee (1897–1977), his grandfather Lee Sing John (also called John Sing Lee, Joe Lee or John Song) was one of the men who then walked from Caspar four miles south to the early community of Mendocino, where he was able to find work.

Before long other Chinese arrived, but most came in on boats from Monterey or San Francisco. Many of the early settlers like Lee Sing John and Eli Tia Key (also known as Eli Tai Kee and other variations) took their first jobs as cooks in the lumber mills and woods camps.

There was also one logging job for which many were well suited: *water-slinger*. Redwood trees felled on the ridges and steep slopes needed to be moved down to the rivers where currents could transport them to the mill. Bull teams dragged huge, linked sections of logs down through rough terrain over a "corduroy road"

Not only do English spellings of Chinese personal and place names vary, but also, one finds much variation in the written names of individuals. Generally, a person had three names. The first was the family name (surname). Next was commonly a "generational" name (often given to each child in the family, even first cousins: the entire generation)—a character chosen from a poetic scroll in that particular family's ancestral temple. The final name was what we might call a "given" or first name. So when a man said his name was Lee Sing, non-Chinese thought of him as Mr. Sing rather than Mr. Lee. Also, the word *Ah* (a courtesy title like *Mr.* or *Mrs.*) was often mistakenly recorded as the person's first name. When looking over lists of Chinese residents, it's amazing to see how many seemed to have the first name Ah!

It's also notable that almost every one who emigrated to California was listed as coming from the Canton district, capital of Guangdong Province (though that may only have been their embarkation point and not their original home).

---

of nearly buried smaller trees laid across the route. This lifted the logs off the earth and eased much of the drag, but friction built up as wood scraped over wood. Lithe young men, often Chinese, served as water-slingers. Running beside the skid road with buckets carried on a long pole across their shoulders, they sluiced water by the dipperful onto the skids in front of the first log. It was strenuous and dangerous work.

The Chinese were most often relegated to the jobs others didn't want, including those considered "women's work," such as laundry, housework and cooking. Chinese cooks were prized in the woods camp cookhouses, as well as in private homes. An 1874 memoir by Charles Wordhoff evokes life in a woods camp:

> *A logging camp is an assemblage of rude redwood shanties, gathered about one larger shanty, which is the cook-house and dining hall, and where usually two or three Chinamen are at work over the stove, and setting the table. The loggers live well; they have excellent bread, meat, beans, butter, dried apples, cakes, pies, and pickles; in short I have dined in worse places.*

Lee Sing John and Eli Tia Key both moved into the village of Mendocino as soon as they could. Employed at the Caspar Mill cookhouse and later by the William Kelly family in Mendocino, Lee Sing John was fortunate to have his wife Fong Sun Choy come from China before the Exclusion Act of 1882 prevented most Chinese immigration. Additionally, most Chinese men residing here before the Act were no longer allowed to send for brides or wives waiting in Canton. Since, in California and most other states, it was illegal for them to marry Caucasians, the vast majority of Chinese men lived and died a bachelor's life. The Lees had two sons and three daughters, the youngest of whom died in infancy. The second child, first daughter Lee Gum Yip (Annie), later married Chow Ah Hee. In the confusion about surnames, Chow Ah Hee yielded and became Mr. Hee instead of Mr. Chow. It is through the Hees that the family maintained its Mendocino residency.

During the 1860s, while cooking at Daniel Milliken's Camp and home, Eli Tia Key saved enough money to open a store and lodging house in adjacent buildings owned by the Lumber Company on the south side of

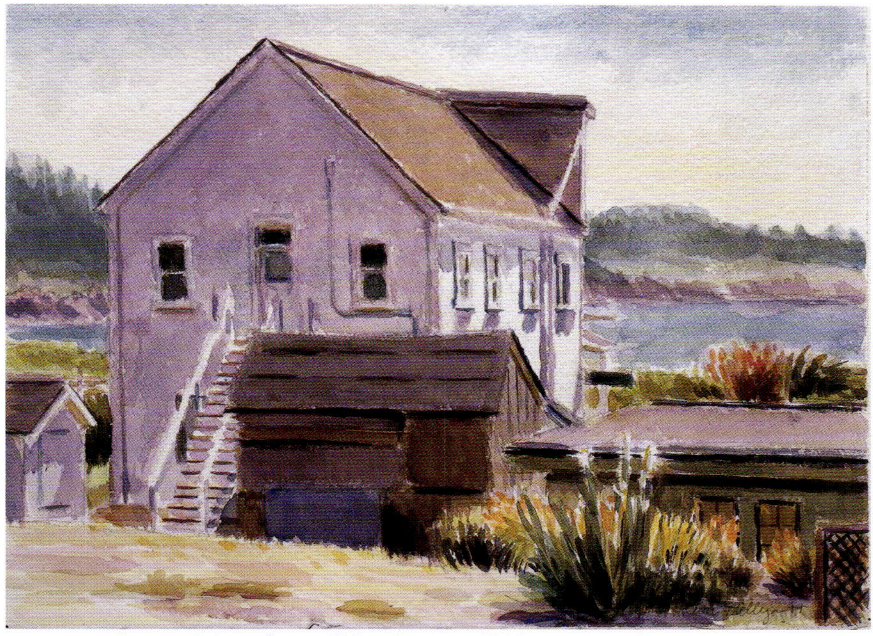

Lemos Saloon from Albion Street 1999, Water color, 11" x 15"

The majority of Chinese dwellings not located on the southwest end of Main Street were found on Albion Street, mostly west of Kasten, near the Temple of Kwan Tai. This view is from directly below the porch of the Temple, facing southwest toward Main Street. Just to the left of the frame is the lot once belonging to Manuel and Mary Julia Ramus, sold to the Hee family in 1903.

western Main Street. The store mainly served the needs of the local Chinese population and advertised as early as 1874 in the *West Coast Star* that it offered tea, rice, tobacco, spices, silk and fireworks, as well as clothing and matting.

Eli Tia Key's wife, Su Wang, was a Pomo Indian adopted by a Chinese family. She bore him three sons and a daughter. The eldest son Look Tin Eli and the youngest Look Poong-shan also called Lee Eli, were educated in Mendocino and went on to become respected and influential businessmen in San Francisco. As confidential advisor to the Russo-Chinese Bank of San Francisco, Tin Eli handled the business dealings of Chinese clients both at home and abroad, with Lee Eli serving as an assistant. Tin Eli was also a manager of the Sing Chong Company, the largest importer of Chinese and Japanese goods in the United States. He was a prominent organizer of the China Mail Steamship Company, and the president of the Canton Bank of San Francisco.

Apparently some Chinese children attended public school in Mendocino in the 1800s, including those from the Hee and Eli families. Unfortunately, later laws prohibited this. In 1890 Laura Nelson Heeser started classes for Chinese students in the building that once housed the town's original school near the northwest corner of Ukiah and Lansing Streets.

Despite being excluded from public school and often having their homes and businesses burned to the ground, the Chinese found Mendocino less dangerous than some other Coastal communities. Violent acts were committed north in Westport and Fort Bragg. In 1892 at what has become known as The Incident at Pudding Creek, a mob attacked a Chinese camp working on a railroad tunnel east of Fort Bragg. More than one hundred white men forced 40 workers from their camp at gunpoint in the middle of the night during a driving storm, all the way to the Noyo River. Told to leave town and not return, they walked through the storm, south to Mendocino, where they were offered temporary shelter.

Prejudice was based on numerous cultural and religious differences and on the largely mistaken idea that the immigrants took employment away from other workers. Though Chinese continued to labor at jobs other men shunned, when times were hard, they became a convenient scapegoat.

When August Heeser reported the Incident at Pudding Creek in the *Mendocino Beacon*, he suggested the mob did not reflect the feelings of the local community. He wrote:

> *The rank and file of the men who drove the Chinese out was composed of men who have no interest here.*

His statement would lead one to believe the white mob was comprised of transient workers who would be "here today, gone tomorrow." In fact, among the 23 suspects arrested and indicted by a Grand Jury, three were prominent business leaders of Fort Bragg—the postmaster, the leading physician, and the president of the Knights of Labor for Mendocino County. It is not clear if Heeser was in denial about the depth of the public prejudice or was not aware of the facts.

In Mendocino City most of the Chinese lived in cabins at the western end of town on lumber company property, on the ocean side of Main Street. Many cultivated truck gardens and sold their produce in the community. However, an 1890 map shows Chinese dwellings elsewhere. They lived on Kelly property close to where Eliza's Baptist Church was later built, and also next to the Temple Kwan Tai on Albion Street, as well as Albion Street west of Kasten.

It also shows two Chinese laundries, one across Lansing from the Kelly-MacCallum Store and the other on the northwest corner of Main and Kasten, opposite the Jarvis-Nichols Store.

Many Chinese retained traditional clothing, and the men kept their hair braided in the characteristic queue: a long single pigtail. Until the Chinese law was abolished in 1911 with the fall of the Manchu Dynasty, a man would not be allowed to return to his homeland without his queue. Throughout California, these important personal and cultural symbols were often the target for harassment, as seen in these memories of James Peirsol from the *Mendocino Historical Review*: *My Boyhood in Mendocino, 1905–1917*:

> *There was also a China Town near the point. It consisted of eight or ten closely grouped redwood shacks which, from time to time, would burn down and immediately be rebuilt by the industrious Chinese who asked neither aid nor pity from the rest of the townspeople. This area, with its Joss House and Oriental smells and furnishings, was a place of special interest to the white youngsters of the community. At first we would gather on the outskirts of the compound and shout in unison: "Ching Chong Chinaman sitting on a rail. Along came a whiteman and chopped off his tail." But when we found that this type of harassment brought little retaliatory action—and more specifically, when we got better acquainted with several of our Chinese classmates at school and learned that they were no different from the rest of us—China Town became one of our favorite haunts.*

Temple of Kwan Tai

California Historical Landmark #927

In a tiny back room a wooden bench served as a bed, providing a resident priest with living quarters right inside the Temple. The building has always been painted in the same colors. Traditionally, red has represented *joy* and green, *harmony* and *prosperity*. In present-day Chinese custom, red also stands for *good luck*.

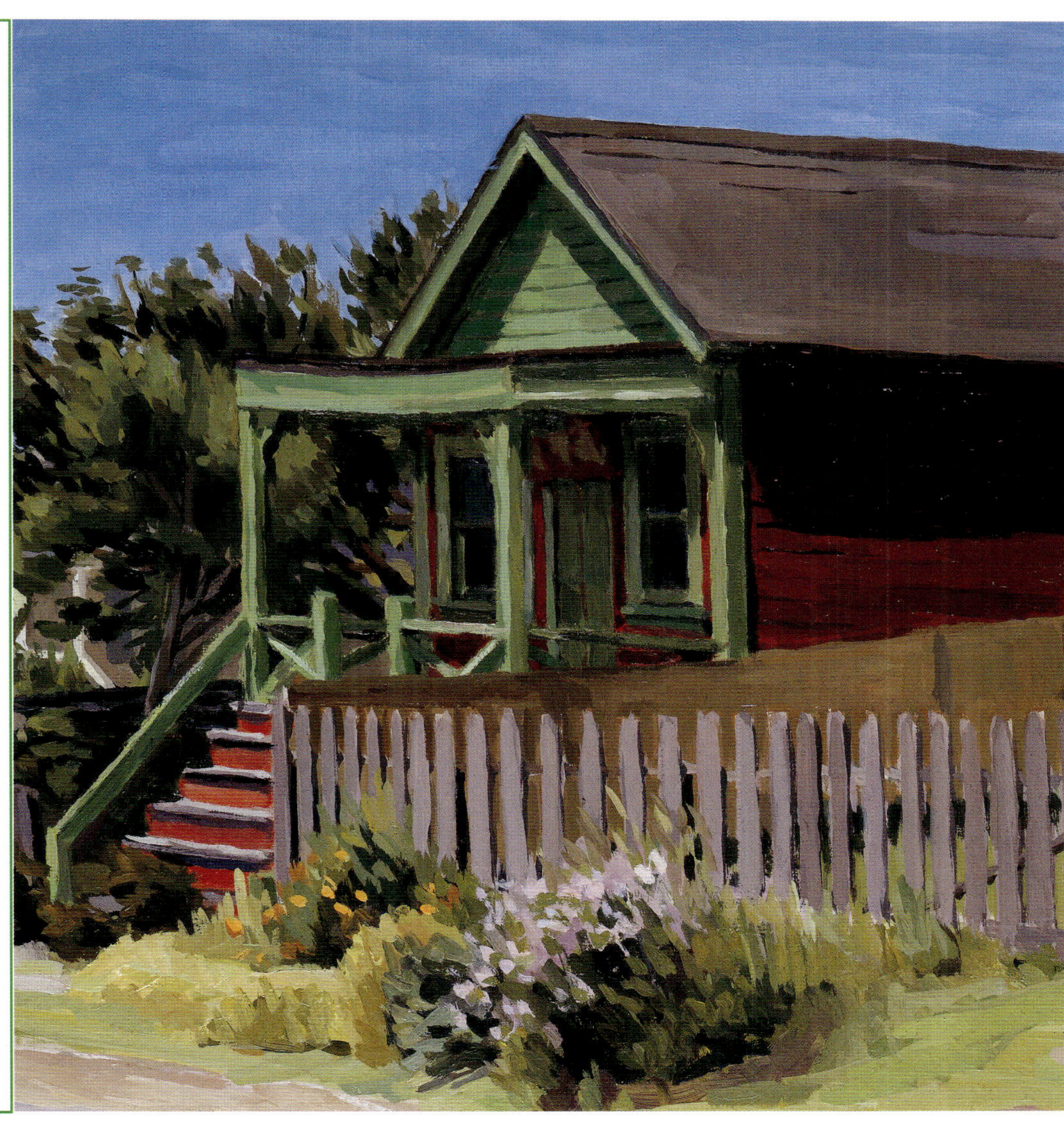

The Temple of Kwan Tai

What Peirsol refers to as a Joss House should more correctly be called a temple, and, fortunately, the one-story wooden building serving as a shrine to legendary folk hero Kwan Tai (also spelled Gwan Di) was not among the buildings burned. It stands today as the most visible reminder of the early Chinese pioneers. In 1867 W. H. Kelly sold the 33' x 80' lot on Albion Street for around $170 in gold to Ah Sy. It is believed he represented the collective Chinese population in the purchase of the property. Deeded to Lee Sing John in 1871, it has been in that family's keeping ever since. Oral history from George Hee (Lee's grandson), dates the beginning of the Temple to the 1850s before the time the land was deeded by Kelly, and notes it was enlarged in 1875.

According to a typically patronizing account in the November 4, 1882 *Mendocino Beacon:*

> *A Chinese temple or Joss House has been built in this place and was formally opened on Monday last. . . . We were informed that the meats and drinks with which the table was covered are the refreshment offered to the Joss.*

After remaining some time on the table, which seems to be an altar, they are eaten by any worshipper who pleases. Firecrackers and bombs were exploded, and the ceremonies closed amid the noise essential to all conservative Chinese ideas.

This notice no doubt incorrectly identifies the occasion as the opening. Instead, it could have been a dedication, re-dedication or other celebration, as the Temple would already have been in use for years.

Over the front door hangs a sign with gilt characters naming the Temple and the god honored within. This is believed to be the original sign made of old-growth redwood, which explains how it has survived over the years including being blown down in a storm. The Temple honors Kwan Yu, a general during the Han dynasty who fought valiantly in many battles before he was captured in the year A.D. 219 along with his son Kwan Ping. He was executed for his unshakable loyalty to Liu Pei of the House of Han. For more than a century he remained the model of military virtues and ability and was officially recognized as a deity in 1594, entering the Chinese Pantheon as Kwan Tai, the god of war, representing integrity and loyalty. Even today many pray to this god for assistance, especially with business enterprises.

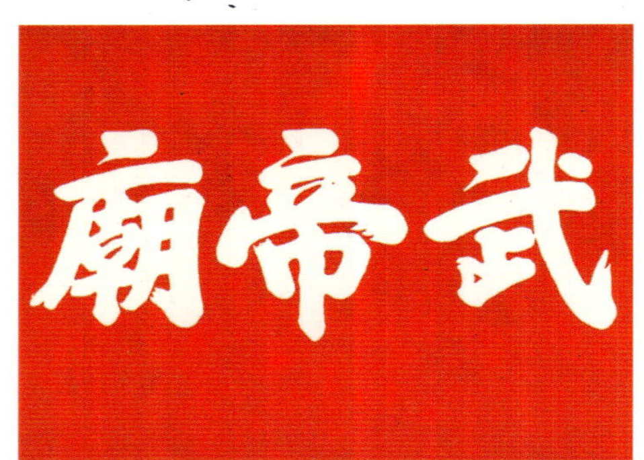

The Temple itself is one large room opening into a smaller back room that served as living quarters for a priest. The interior is furnished with simple wooden benches along the side walls and two altars for offerings of food, wine, candles and incense. Behind the altars on the Temple's rear wall, hung an ancient painting that depicted Kwan Tai, Kwan Ping and sword-bearer Ju Chang. On the side walls are gilt characters on green boards offering praise for Kwan Tai:

His spirit ranges throughout heaven and earth—his accomplishments fill heaven and earth.

Another instructs visitors:

Burn incense (in worship) and enjoy good fortune (as a result).

In 1979, thanks to the efforts of Lee Sing John's great-granddaughters Lorraine and Loretta, the unique red-and-green building was designated California Historic Landmark #927. In her application to the State, Lorraine Hee Chorley explained its significance:

The Mendocino Joss House is the only remaining Chinese Joss House in use along the Pacific north coast of California, north of San Francisco and south of the Oregon border. The Mendocino Joss House also remains as the only surviving reminder of a once substantial Chinese community with its own history and its own customs.

Lorraine and her sister Loretta Hee McCoard obtained a grant and organized fundraising projects that resulted in a major structural renovation in 2000–2001. Prior to restoration, the building was showing its age from some 150 winters exposed to Pacific storms. Its walls leaned, its beams were severely bowed, and parts of the floor were unsafe. With a new foundation and support beams, the Temple appears ready to handle the next 100 years.

On October 13, 2001, the sisters hosted a celebration to thank county officials and local volunteers and to rededicate the Temple. The event began with a parade through town led by lion dancers from Santa Rosa. On a clear October afternoon, from the Temple porch, Lorraine Hee Chorley, as well as a representative of the National Trust for Historic Preservation and local politicians addressed members of the community. Those gathered were treated to festive noisemakers, fortune cookies and cups of a newly created Temple of Kwan Tai Tea while they enjoyed demonstrations of lion dancing and martial arts.

Though the Temple has always been Taoist rather than Buddhist, on this day Buddhist nuns came from The City of Ten Thousand Buddhas in Ukiah to bless its dedication. They chanted the authentic Kwan Tai blessing, during which some of the nuns moved inside to perform the rest of the ceremony in private. Afterward, many locals and tourists made their way up the nine steep Temple steps to view the interior and, if they wished, make offerings by lighting candles and incense.

In the past the Temple was only opened to the public on rare occasions. Before 1950 only Chinese were allowed to step inside, but now it can be viewed by appointment and later will have regular hours and docents. For more information about visiting the Temple, assisting its preservation or obtaining Kwan Tai Tea, go to the www.kwantaitemple.org website.

In 1976 George Hee said,

> *When my mother was alive, I told her I'd keep (the Joss House) as long as I'm alive and it's up to the children to do it now.*

Even though most of the Chinese have left the area, third-generation Californians Lorraine and Loretta, George Hee's daughters, have carried on the family tradition and have lovingly maintained the Temple for the enrichment and enjoyment of others.

A visitor to the Kelley House Museum once wrote in Chinese in the guest directory:

> *There is no such place too far for the Chinese to reach. Where there are sunbeams, there will be Chinese: for that is the lustrous splendor of the Chinese race.*

Historian-author Sandy Lydon has interviewed descendants of the Quock family, who landed at Carmel River Beach on a junk, known to be part of a group of five boats that sailed from Manila and traveled around the Pacific to California. The Cantonese farmers, all from the same village, first went to Manila in order to learn to sail and navigate. After the farmers received their training, the five boats embarked from Manila but were separated on the long voyage. Quock family members mentioned the "Mendocino Junk" during the Lydon interviews as possibly being one of the other four boats that were part of their contingent. The Quock Family's stories and their fishing village at Point Lobos are featured in the book, *Creating California: The Point Lobos Story* by Sandy Lydon.

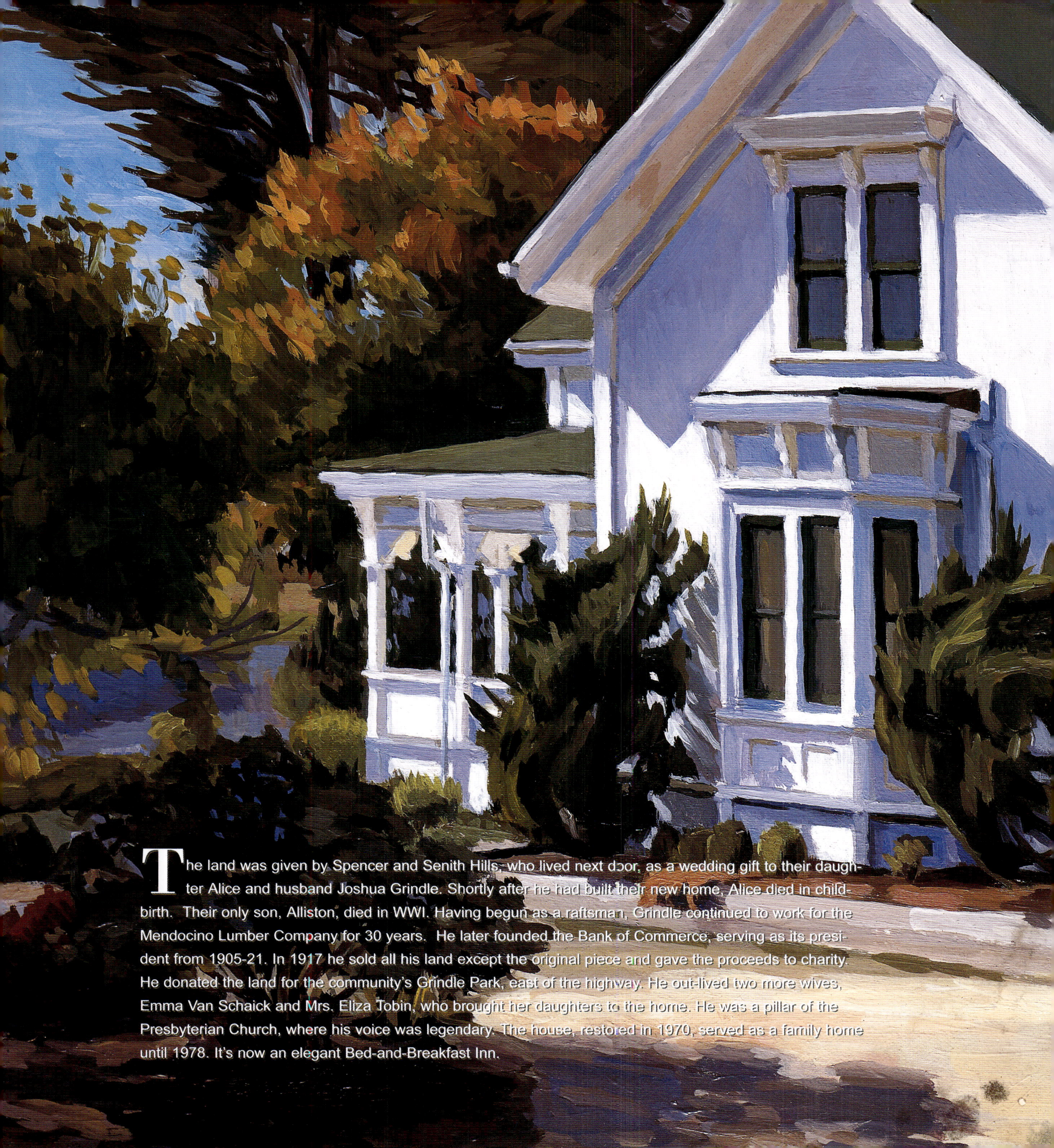

The land was given by Spencer and Senith Hills, who lived next door, as a wedding gift to their daughter Alice and husband Joshua Grindle. Shortly after he had built their new home, Alice died in childbirth. Their only son, Alliston, died in WWI. Having begun as a raftsman, Grindle continued to work for the Mendocino Lumber Company for 30 years. He later founded the Bank of Commerce, serving as its president from 1905-21. In 1917 he sold all his land except the original piece and gave the proceeds to charity. He donated the land for the community's Grindle Park, east of the highway. He out-lived two more wives, Emma Van Schaick and Mrs. Eliza Tobin, who brought her daughters to the home. He was a pillar of the Presbyterian Church, where his voice was legendary. The house, restored in 1970, served as a family home until 1978. It's now an elegant Bed-and-Breakfast Inn.

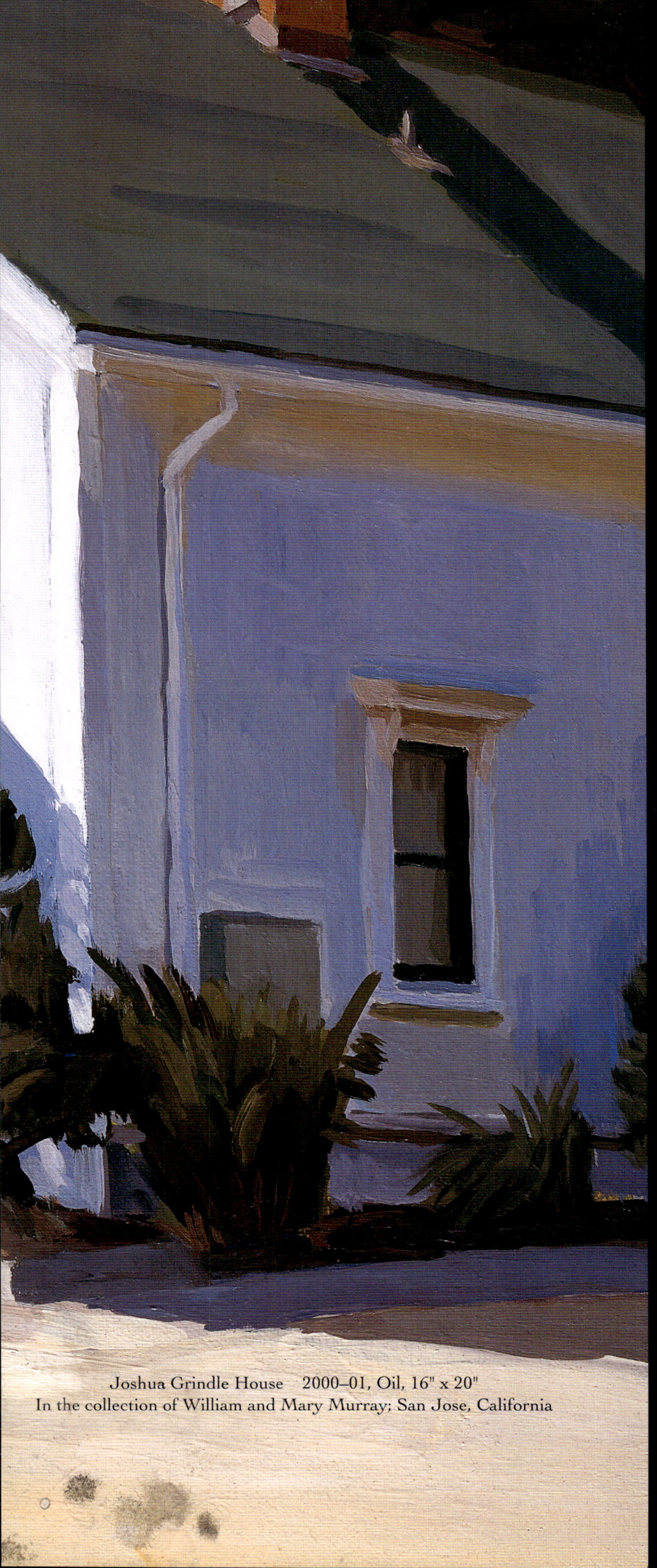

Joshua Grindle House 2000–01, Oil, 16" x 20"
In the collection of William and Mary Murray; San Jose, California

Houses & Churches

Every town is a collection of buildings—hotels, stores, offices, school, community halls, specialty shops—but the places where people reside and worship often reflect the most care and personality. The homes and churches of Mendocino were constructed by skilled woodworkers, many from New England, who imported that region's architectural look; others were willing to recreate it for clients who missed the style of their old homes on the East Coast.

Houses

Lumber company buildings were painted dark red while many unpainted homes, barns and outbuildings weathered to the rustic shades of ageing redwood. However, most homes and businesses were painted in either white or ochre. Nowadays, with an array of paint colors available, one sees more variety, but still within keeping for homes at the time.

Most houses were two-story, of simple design, often sheathed with horizontal channel siding. Shingles were also used as siding, sometimes arranged in ornate motifs, or with the corners of the shingles rounded to create a "fish scale" pattern. Other typical embellishments to the simple designs include bay windows, enclosed storm entrances, steep gables, gingerbread trim, corbels under the eaves, porticos over windows and brackets on porch posts.

A handful of men were the main builders and contractors of the structures that still stand or are most remembered. Edwards C. Williams, Albert Maxwell, Lauriston Avery Morgan, William Riley Hamilton and John D. Johnson are names that stand out. Charles Wellington Denslow was responsible for at least four fine homes, but the work was actually done by J. D. Johnson, who seems to be one of the most colorful, as well as the most notable, of the craftsmen.

Born in England, Johnson came to Mendocino in the early 1870s when his talents were most needed and bought a large parcel of property from David Lansing. It was located at the eastern edge of town, from Main Street up to Pine, bordering Evergreen Cemetery. Over the years he remodeled or added onto numerous structures and built many houses, some on contract. He built others to later rent or sell. One of these, the Justin E. Packard house, still stands as the last building on the northeast end of Main Street. It may be seen on the corner of Evergreen Street, once called Packard Ave., next to the Cemetery. Similarly, J. D. Johnson's own house still stands on Evergreen north of Ukiah Street, but its twin next door is now gone. At this location he housed funeral carriages and horses, as he also served as an undertaker. His place of business for both undertaking and carpentry was on Lansing next to the Masonic Hall. He never married, living alone instead on those premises for many years. There's a story that he left scaffolding up around this building for some 17 years. It became a real eyesore, even though he would say he was in the process of remodeling, thereby avoiding the payment of certain taxes.

Just a few of the other existing structures Johnson built or substantially altered are the Lisbon House Hotel, Lemos Saloon, Albert Brown House, Elisha Blair House, W. A. McCornack House, the first part of the MacCallum House, and homes for C. W. Denslow and relatives, including the Denslow–Morgan–Preston, Denslow–Borgna–Pesula, Denslow—

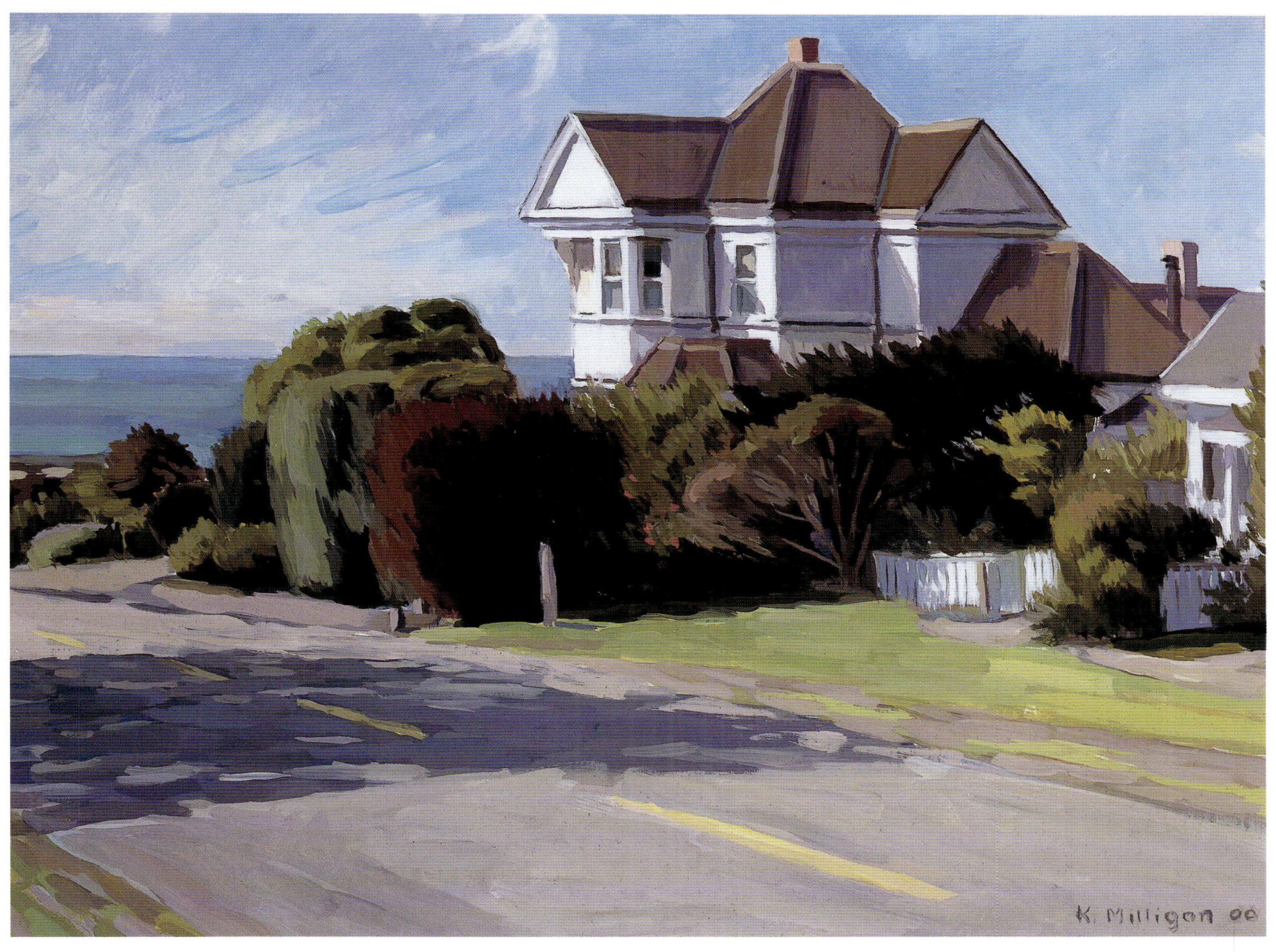

Morgan–Mullen House   2000, Oil, 14" x 18"
In the collection of David and Estra Devore; Nyack, New York

Lauriston A. Morgan, who married Cathrin Denslow, built this house around 1887 at the corner of Little Lake and Woodward Streets. Instead, they lived in the mansion her father Charles W. Denslow built for them a block east, where the Art Center is now. In 1892 J. William Mullen and his wife Charlotte bought it. Mullen became Postmaster in 1889 and filled that position until his death in 1928, though officially Auggie Heeser was Postmaster during the Democratic years between 1915–22.

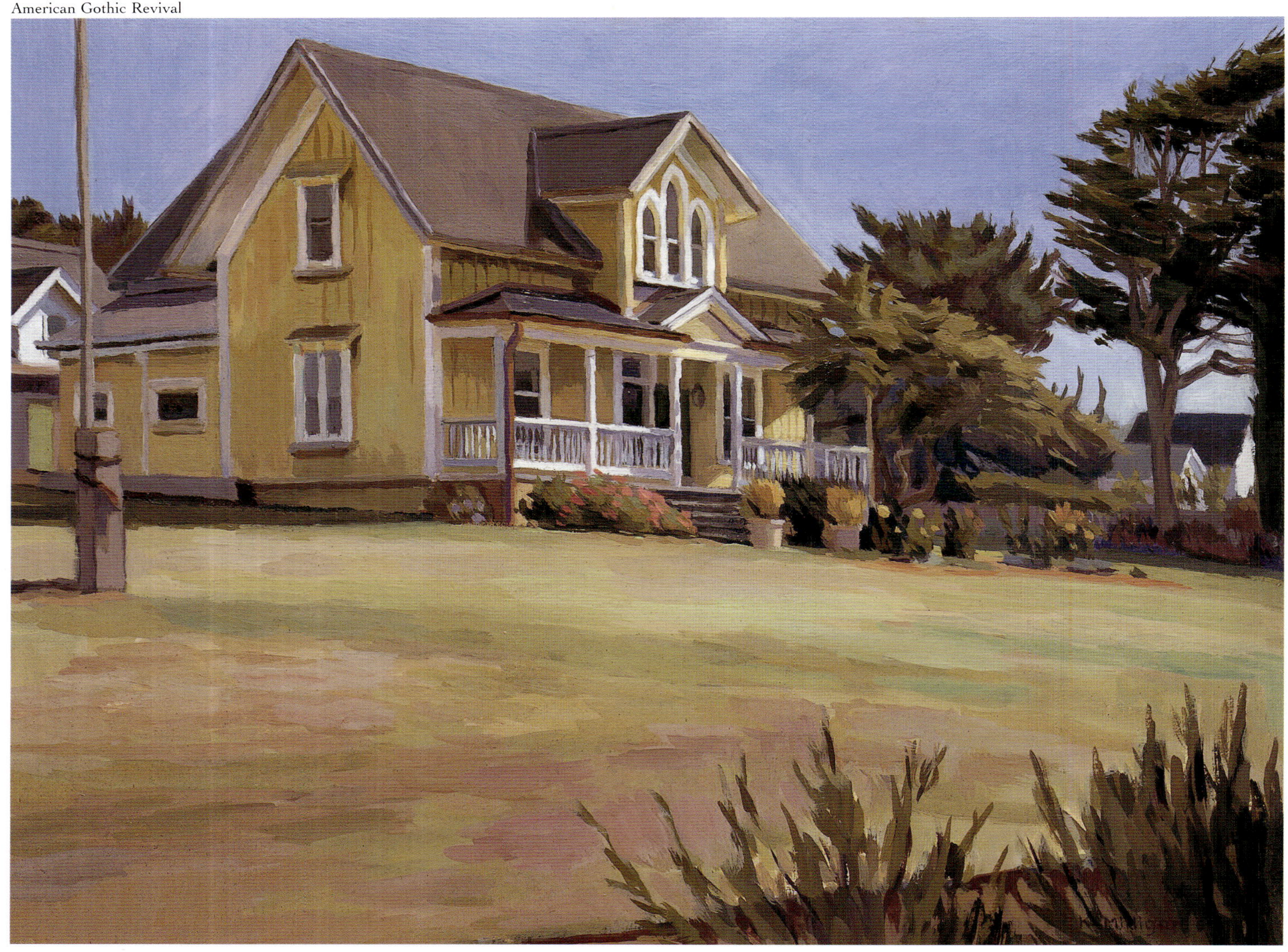

Denslow–Hayden House 2001, Oil, 14" x 18"
In the collection of Elaine Matthews; Mendocino, California

Charles W. Denslow, drawing on his own study of architecture, designed both this house (on Ukiah between Williams and Woodward Streets c.1877) and the Denslow-Maxwell House (at the northwest corner of Kasten and Calpella c.1880), but they were constructed by J. D. Johnson. C. W. Denslow, brother-in-law of Martha Ford, was the father of Cathrin, who married builder Lauriston A. Morgan. The Hayden name probably refers to Denslow's cousin Louise Hayden. The *Mendocino Beacon* reported a fire on Calpella Street in 1879: "*The wind was blowing a gale . . . it was by the most strenuous efforts and untiring labor of the citizens that the dwelling belonging to Charles W. Denslow was saved.*"

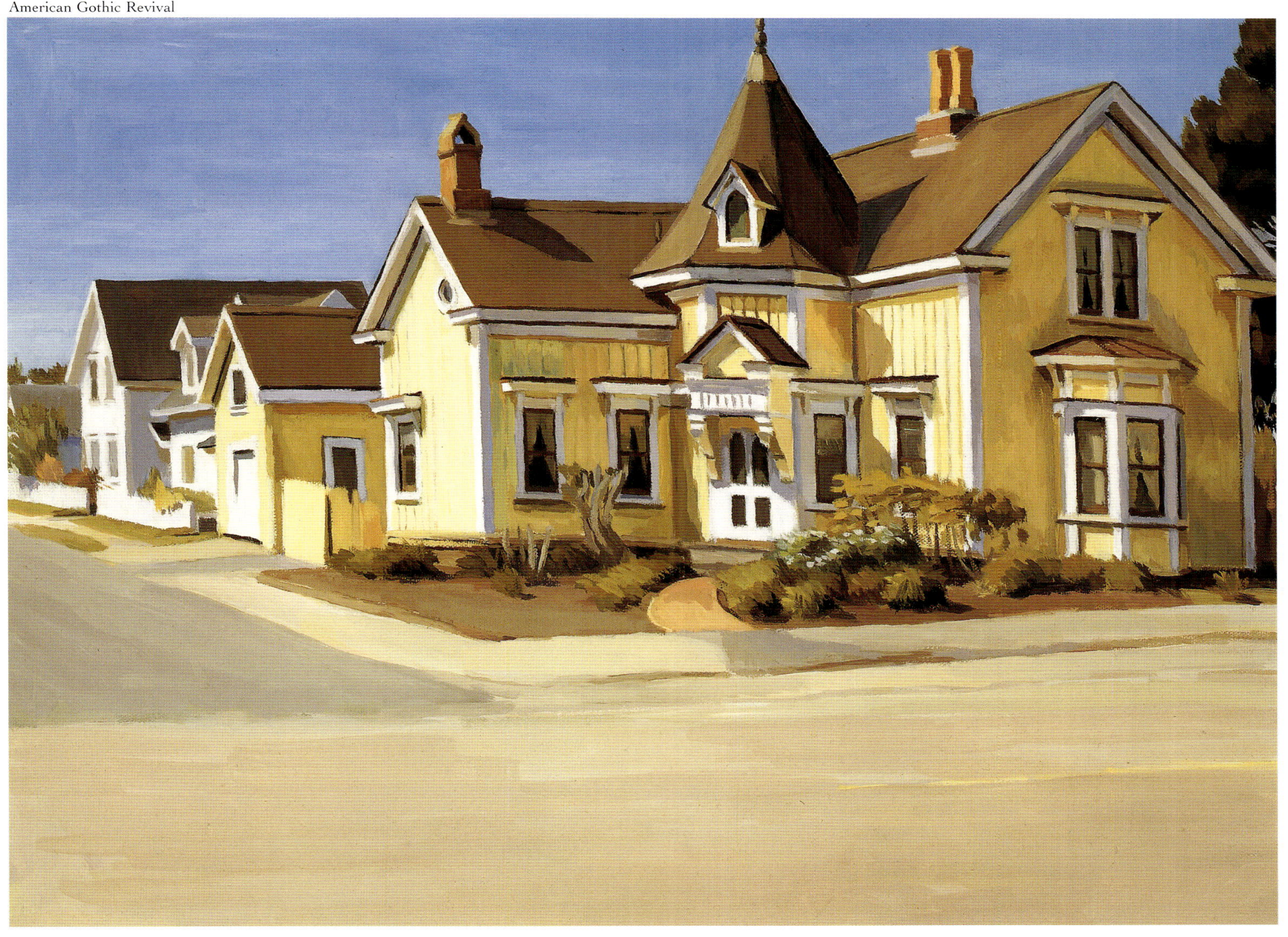

Denslow-Maxwell House 2002, Oil, 16" x 20"

Designed by C. W. Denslow in the American Gothic Revival style, and built by J. D. Johnson c.1880 on the corner of Kasten and Calpella Street, it's the only home in town to face across a corner. It has a distinctive windowed turret above an ornate portico over the front door. It was the home of Perley Maxwell (son of Albert and Jane), who married Joshua Grindle's stepdaughter Elsie Tobin Grindle in 1892. Perley, a builder like his father, was also an avid wet-plate photographer. In June 2000, Emery Escola donated to the Kelley House some 300 of Perley's 8" x 10" glass plate negatives showing local scenes from the first decades of the 20th Century. In a joint project with the Kelley House, Mendocino High photography students have now made positive prints, under the direction of teacher Bill Brazill, a descendant of Michael J. Byrnes [1841–1902], twenty years a constable and deputy sheriff for Mendocino.

Hayden and Denslow– Maxwell.

The latter two exemplify a more elaborate American Gothic Revival style. Denslow had training in architecture and was undoubtedly involved in the design of the homes he commissioned. Common features include vertical board-and-batten siding, second-story Gothic windows such as those in the Maxwell House's distinctive turret, and entryways that extend from the houses to create foyers. Pediments over the front doors are supported with corbels and repeat the gable pitch of the major roofline. This entryway feature was altered on the Denslow-Hayden around 1960 when a front porch was added. Like most Mendocino houses it rested on redwood sills rather than an actual foundation, but the woodwork of J. D. Johnson was so superior, constructed with thick floor beams dovetailed together for better support, that new owners of the house reported it still level more than 126 years later.

From a dormer added to the Captain Lansing home, second-story Gothic windows overlook the Presbyterian Church, which itself was built in the American Gothic Revival style. Its vertical board-and-batten siding and Gothic windows and doors are complemented by a windowed bell tower spire.

Several homes still retain the kind of embellishments called *gingerbread* or *carpenter's lace* though many others, like the Lansing House, have fallen victim to age, the weather or vandalism. One can still see intricate bargeboard trim outlining the roof of the MacCallum House. The Spenser Hills House and the Masonic Hall also display their original bargeboard trim, the very same pattern as once adorned the Ford House and the long-gone Chalfant House to the east of the Ford.

The McCornack House on Main Street, known as the "House of Doctors," stands out because of its gambrel roof punctuated by windows with projecting trim and finials on the gable points, as well as a balustered platform atop a bay window.

Other borrowed influences are Italianate details seen on such structures as the Morgan–Mullen House, the Maxwell–Jarvis House and the Odd Fellows Hall, currently the William Zimmer Gallery. These Italianate details imitate structural elements such as stone corners, under-eave supports and columns, but are mainly ornamental. Many houses have other decorative details such as pediments over windows, dentils under the eaves and brackets supporting the curb roofs of bay windows.

Spacious porches decorated with ornate balustrades grace a number of homes, like the Joshua Grindle and the MacCallum. Often the post corners are chamfered, creating beveled facets, with lamb's tongue detailing at each end. Elaborate brackets may decorate the angles between post and eaves.

These architectural details can also be seen, along with several remaining false fronts, on Main Street commercial buildings. The Jarvis–Nichols Store (now Gallery Books) combines false front, bay windows, dentils and other enhancements.

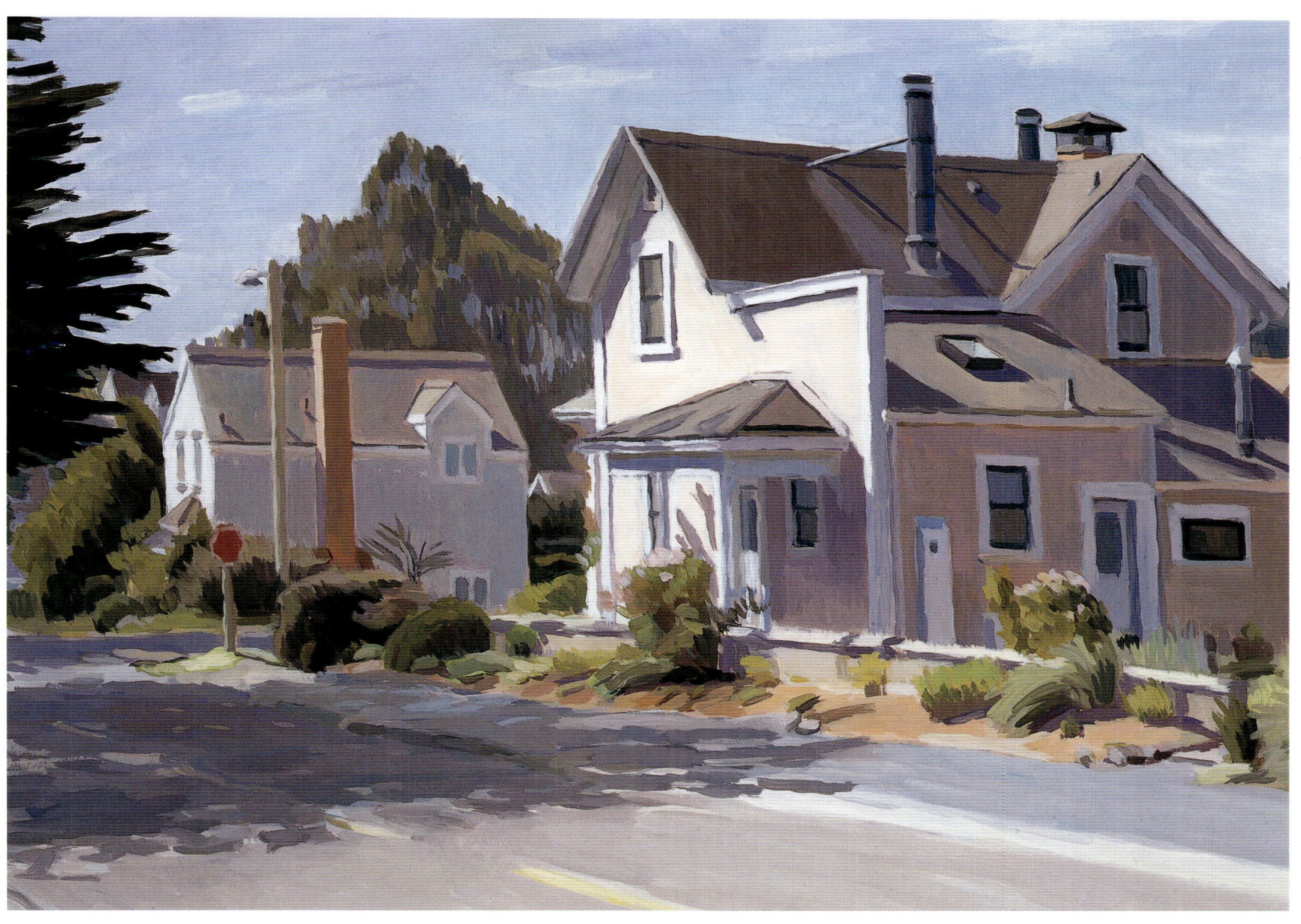

Walsh–Doolittle House 2000, Oil, 14" x 18"
In the collection of Tim and Laura Zadel; San Jose, California

William Riley Hamilton built this home c.1883 on the northwest corner of Ukiah and Howard Streets for the widow Mrs. Maria Walsh, mother of Mary Jane Walsh Paddleford. A lesser-known architect, contractor and builder, Hamilton constructed a number of other buildings on the eastern end of town between Ukiah and Little Lake Streets. In 1882, across from the Walsh House on Howard, north of the Bowman House, he erected a home for local photographer Ira C. Perry that no longer stands. In 1885 he built the town's second school, near the current Recreation Center, and in 1885–86 the four cottages on the north side of Pine between Howard and School Streets. He also sired 15 children. Later, this was the home of Dora Buck Doolittle (1896–1987), Honorary Life Member of Mendocino Historical Research, Inc., sister-in-law of Walter Jackson and aunt of Francis Jackson, both local author/historians.

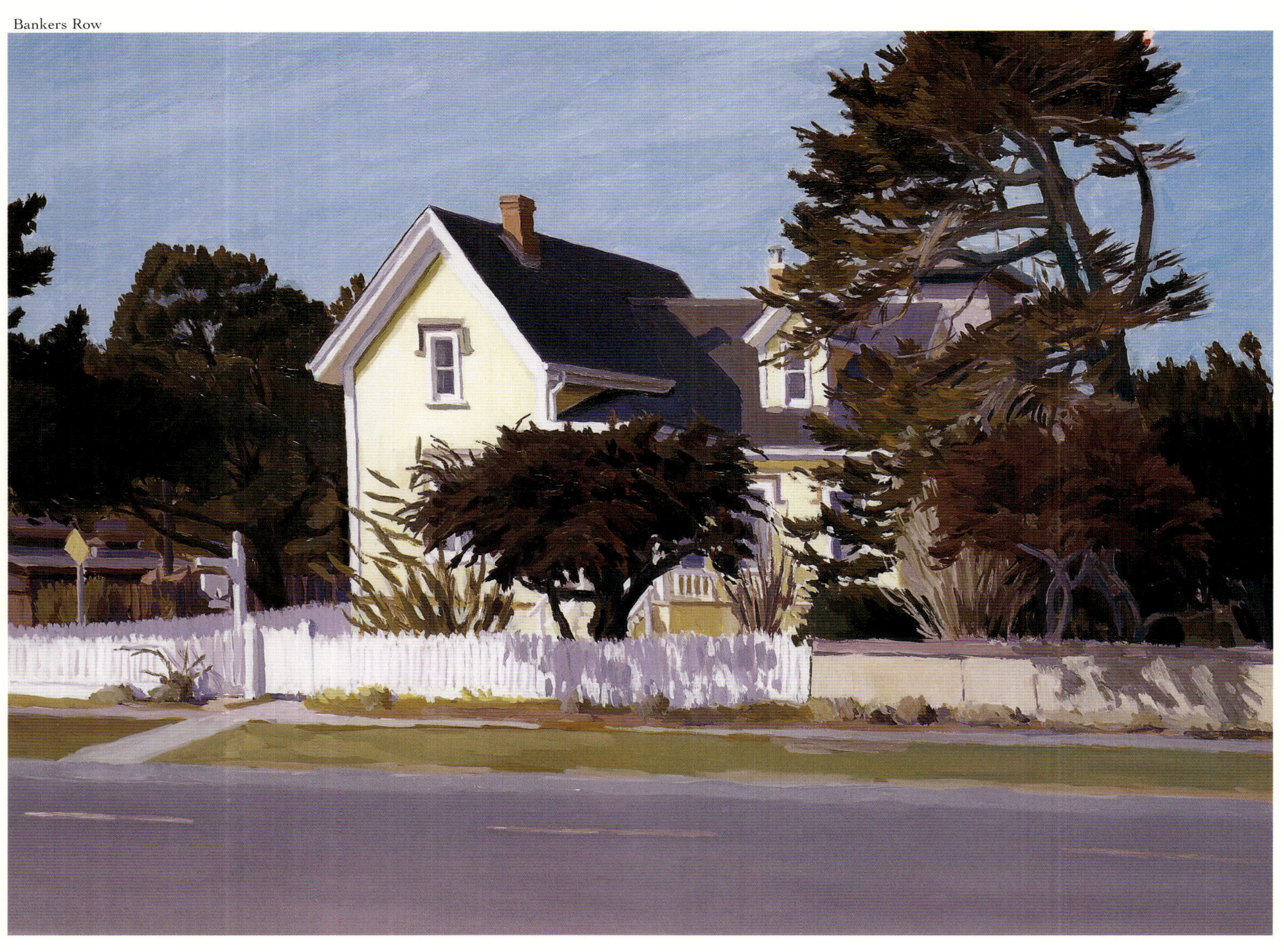

C. O. Packard House 1999–2001, Oil, 20" x 24"
In the collection of Andrew Hindman and Damien Wood; San Francisco, California

Charles Oscar Packard bought this house from L. A. Morgan, who built it in 1878. Here C. O. and Hannah reared eight children. According to one story, Packard had been a carpenter, but Dr. McCornack persuaded him to become a druggist, and it seems to have been a good choice, as he ran his drugstore from the same Main Street shop for some 35 years. Unlike his brother, J. E. Packard, who shared a business with him, Charles lived out his life in Mendocino. His grandchild Dorothy Morrison lived in the house with her grandparents from 1907–16. In 2000, she recalled, *"It was with great excitement that I would look from the second-story window and watch the S. S. Sea Foam sail into the Mendocino Bay bringing relatives and friends from San Francisco. We would rush down to The Point to greet them."* Today visitors can enjoy the same view, as the Packard House is now a Bed-and-Breakfast.

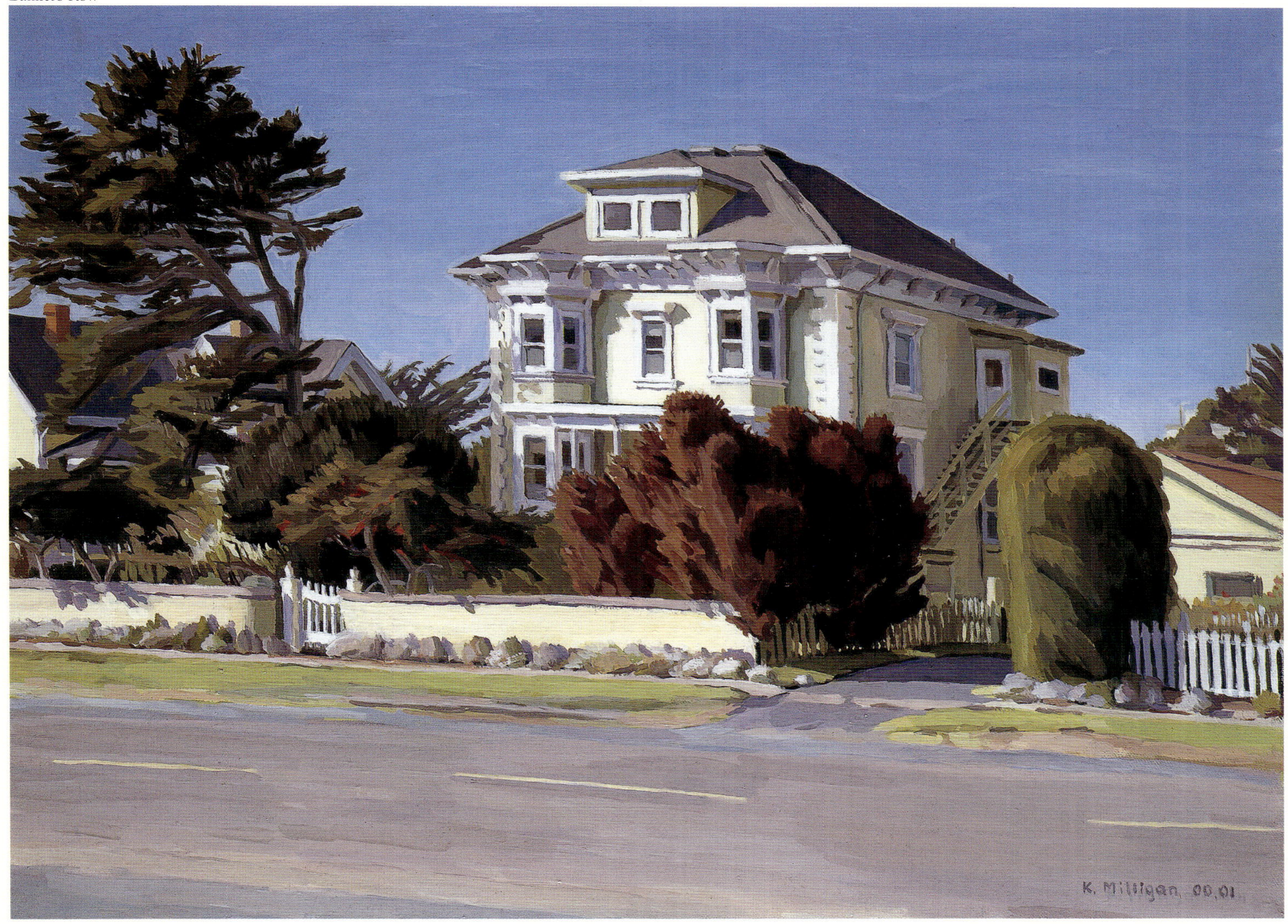

Maxwell–Jarvis House 2000–01, Oil, 18" x 24"

In 1878 Albert Maxwell designed and built this beautiful home, where he and his wife Jane lived with their son Perley. Their two daughters were already married. Ardell, the youngest, married Henry Jarvis, an up-and-coming Main Street merchant. Working as a building contractor, Albert Maxwell also constructed the Presbyterian Church, Central House Hotel and the Eugene Brown House. When he died at age 51 in 1880, his son-in-law Henry and Ardell Jarvis,moved in and took care of the widowed Jane and her son Perley Maxwell. Jarvis, along with various partners, owned a general merchandise store on the corner of Main and Kasten, currently Gallery Books, and served as Postmaster between 1877-1885.

The house has had few changes over the years and is known for the Italianate details: the quoins on the corners of the building and the corbels under the eaves.

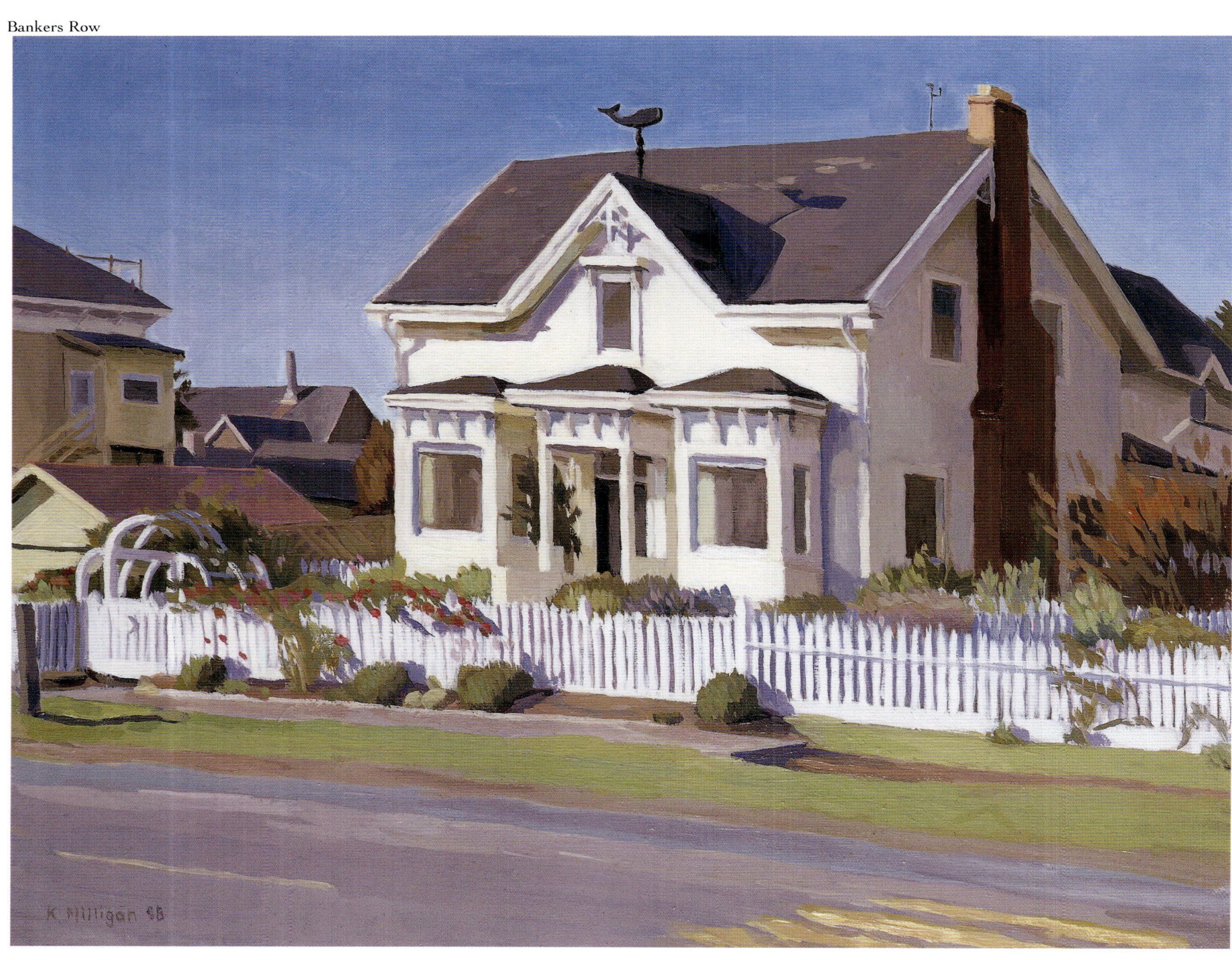

Albert Brown House 1998–2001, Oil, 14" x 18"
In the collection of Gary and Carrie Evans; Mendocino, California

Albert and Georgiana Brown reared their seven children in this home, built in 1880. He was a bookkeeper in the late 1800s and ran a hardware business in his cousin Eugene Brown's general store. Albert was also an inventor. Two of his creations, a paper bag holder and a machine that cut and wrapped paper, went to the 1885 World's Fair. Later he became an electrician and founded the Mendocino Electric Light and Power Company. In 1902, 1,300 lights were illuminated in the town using more than five miles of wiring. Besides becoming a banker and the commissioner of the Fire Company, he made contributions to Grindle Park and created deposit accounts for children with the Mendocino Discount Bank. From 1923 until his death in 1935, he owned the Mendocino Hotel.

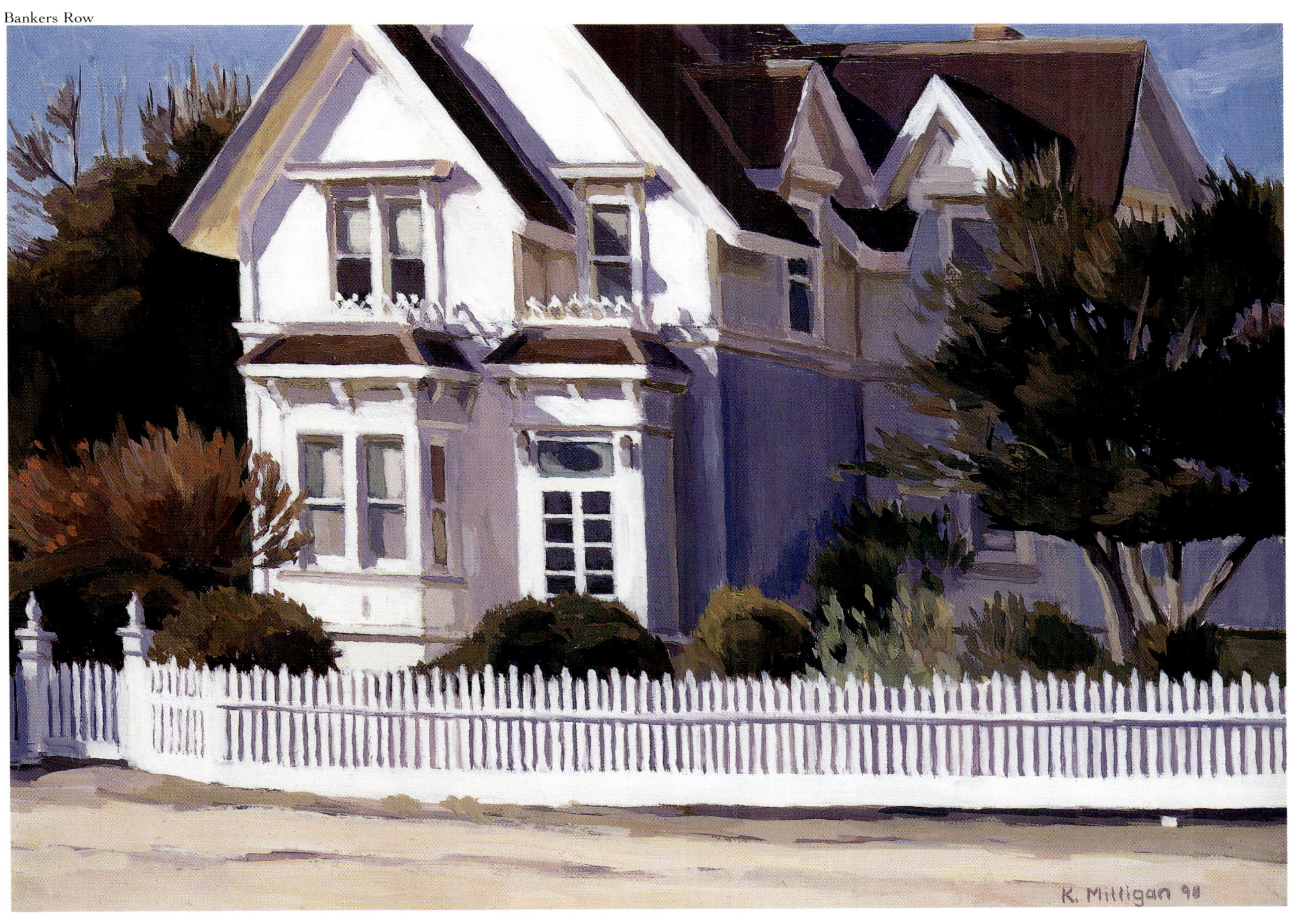

Elisha W. Blair House 1998–2001, Oil, 12" x 16"
In the collection of Ron and Gay Anderson; Madison, Mississippi

Renowned Mendocino carpenter J. D. Johnson built this house for Elisha and Hattie Blair. It was one of four homes side by side on Little Lake Street referred to by locals as "Bankers Row." They might have won the nickname because of their elegance and size, or because Albert Brown was in the banking business and Elisha Blair cashed mill orders. Blair worked out of an office in Packard's drugstore, and in this capacity he would have been known to many mill workers since he cashed their checks or money orders, and probably seemed like a banker to them. It may also have to do with the fact the houses faced the open field called the Bank Square. During the 20th century the Blair House became a popular Bed-and-Breakfast, having gained further prestige when the TV show *Murder She Wrote* used the dwelling as the home of the main character, Jessica Fletcher.

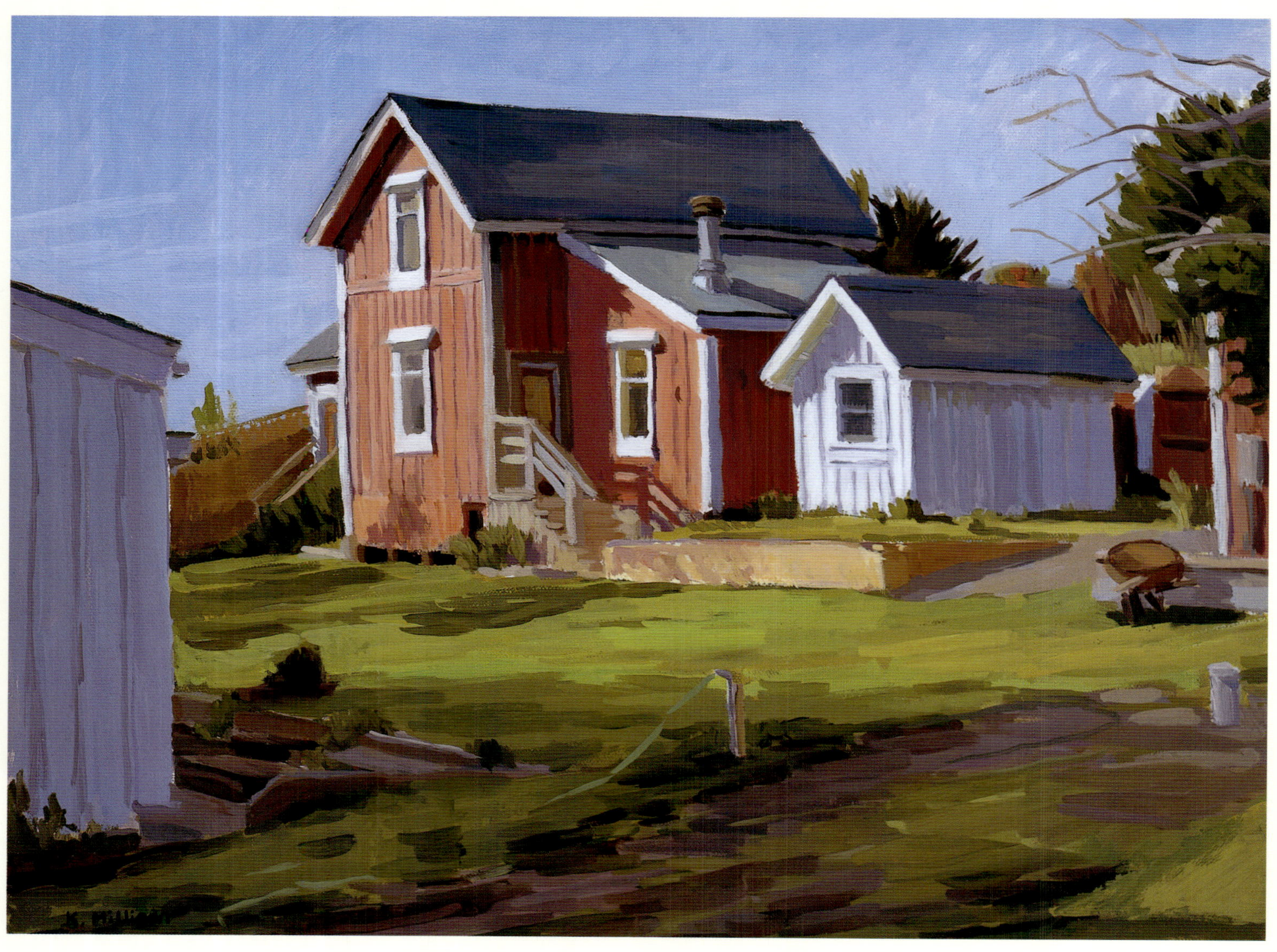

Red House behind Blair House 1998, Oil, 14" x 18"
In the collection of Edward Gordon and Joa Ginsburg; Mendocino, California

At a public auction in 1879, Elisha Blair paid $90 to purchase the former tollbooth at the north end of Big River Bridge for his wife Hattie, who had once been the toll-taker. It's not known where he moved it, but it wasn't behind his fine home on Banker's Row. The house, at left of frame above, wasn't built until 1888. Tragically, a year later, Blair was thrown violently to the ground when his team spooked crossing that same bridge. Attended by Drs. Milliken and Gallison, he appeared to recover but never fully regained his health. He died in May 1892, leaving Hattie with their 7-year-old daughter Florence. Accidents involving most types of horse-drawn vehicles were all too common and often deadly. Panicked animals, faulty equipment and treacherous roads claimed many casualties.

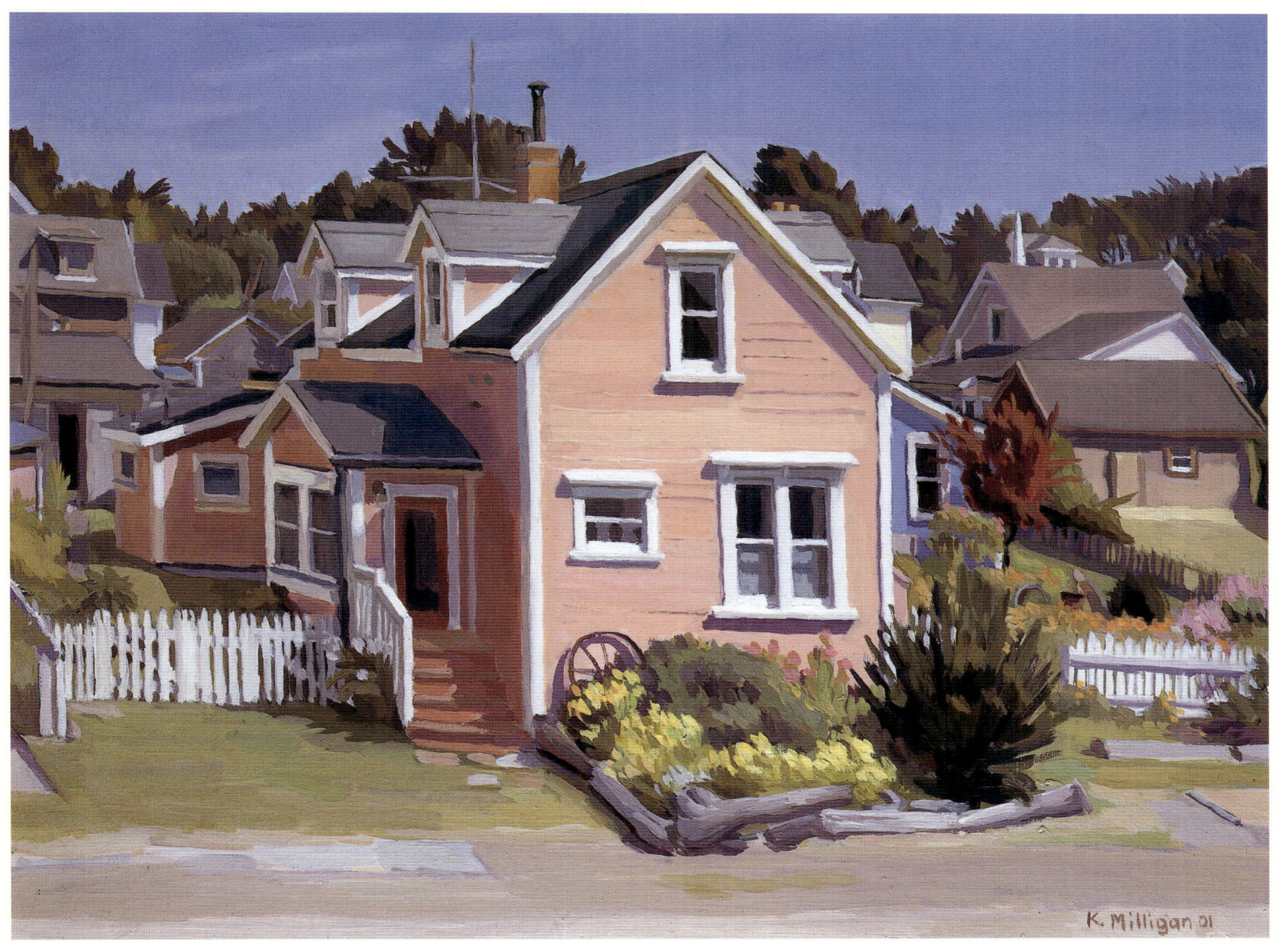

House on Ukiah Street from Lisbon House Porch 2001, Oil, 14" x 18"
In the collection of Michael and Diva Lawrence; Laguna Nigel, California

Elsewhere in this book are notes about several prominent Mendocino physicians, but they would not be complete without more than a passing mention of Dr. James Wallace Milliken (1850–1909). A relative of the early pioneer Daniel B. Milliken, J. W. came to Mendocino in 1883; his wife, son and daughter followed in 1884. Four more daughters were born between 1885–1900. Originally a dentist (his innovative dental chair is still treasured by his descendants), he practiced locally as a physician, surgeon and gynecologist. He wrote treatises on his common-sense approach to good health and about his opinions that the Chinese were being unfairly treated. He was a frequent orator at July 4th gatherings. In 1903 he bought the "House of the Doctors" from W. A. McCornack, but before that, the Millikens lived on Ukiah Street in a home just to the left of the one pictured above, which was probably once a millinery store.

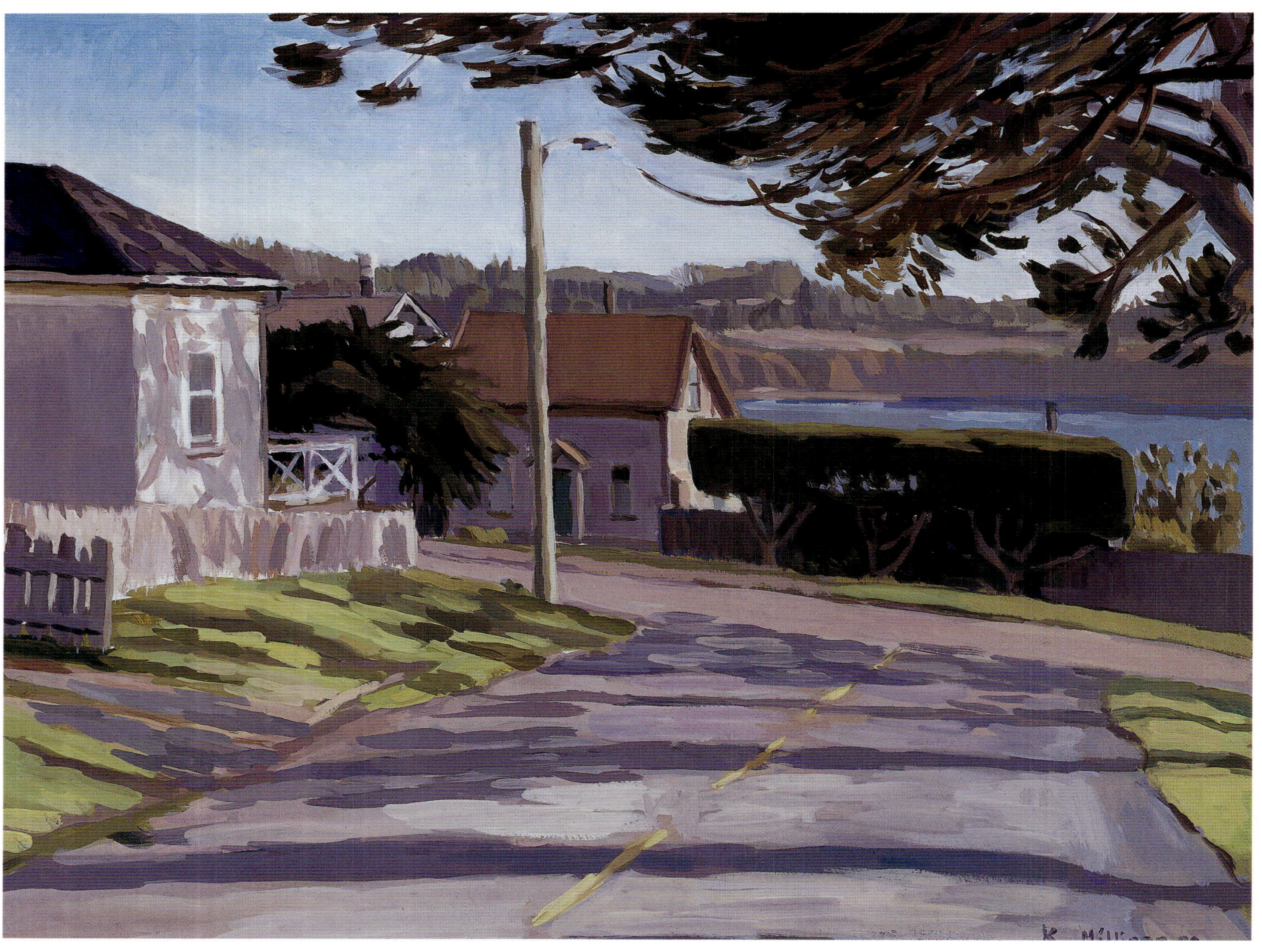

Golgert House from Williams Street 2001, Oil, 14" x 18"
In the collection of Tim and Laura Zadel; San Jose, California

On the south side of Ukiah Street west of the old Lisbon Hotel, the Golgert House, built c.1890, has four rooms downstairs and two upstairs over the front. Displaying the expected long, sloped roof, it takes a new twist on the classic saltbox. The back part of the building is also lower than the front, following the natural incline of the landscape. Additionally, there's a handsome storm entrance on the north side.

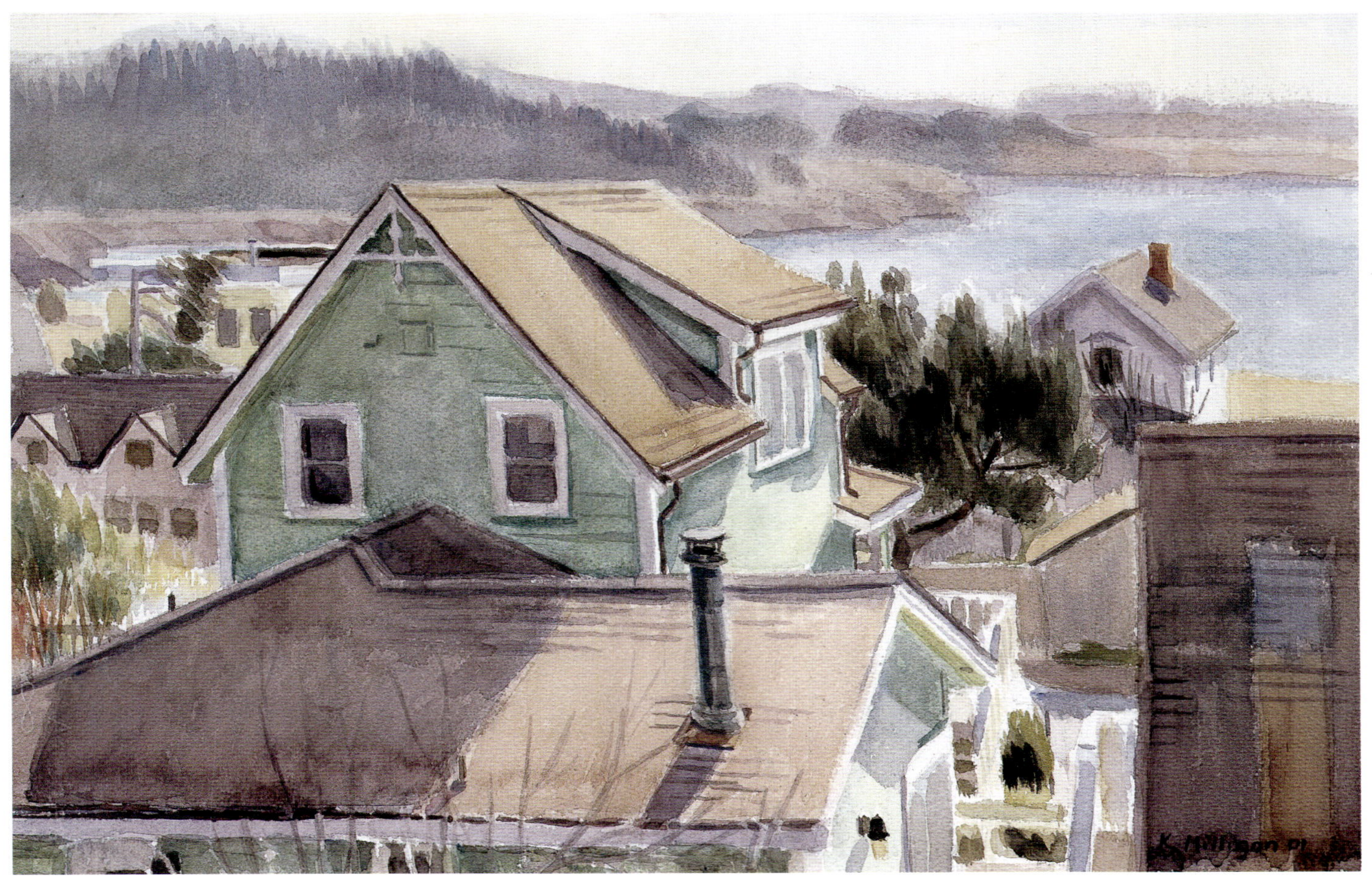

Albion Street House from Lisbon House Porch   2001, Water color, 15" x 22"
In the collection of Don Pollard and Ann Bruce Campbell; Mendocino, California

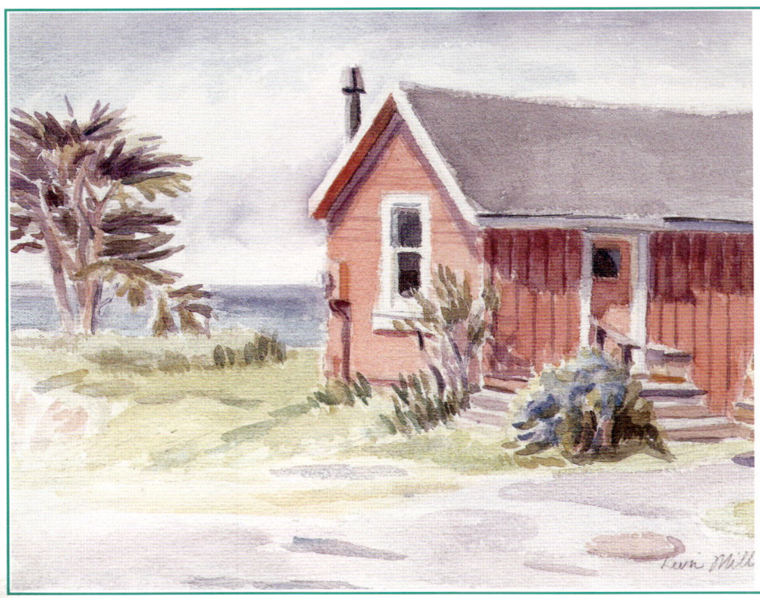

Joe King, son of Joaquina Thomas King, stepson of Joseph King, had a varied career. He worked as a cook in a logging camp and for a time ran the Mendocino Hotel, as did John Silvia, brother of Mary Julia Ramus, a relative of Joe King's by marriage through the Thomas sisters. Joe dabbled in several food and beverage businesses, including a bar on the northeast corner of Ukiah and Lansing, which is currently a barbershop. In November 1932 he was elected first treasurer of the newly formed Mendocino Coast Chamber of Commerce. Joe King married Florence Lawrence, daughter of Joseph Lawrence and niece of Manuel Lawrence.

Joseph King House   1999, Watercolor, 11" x 15"

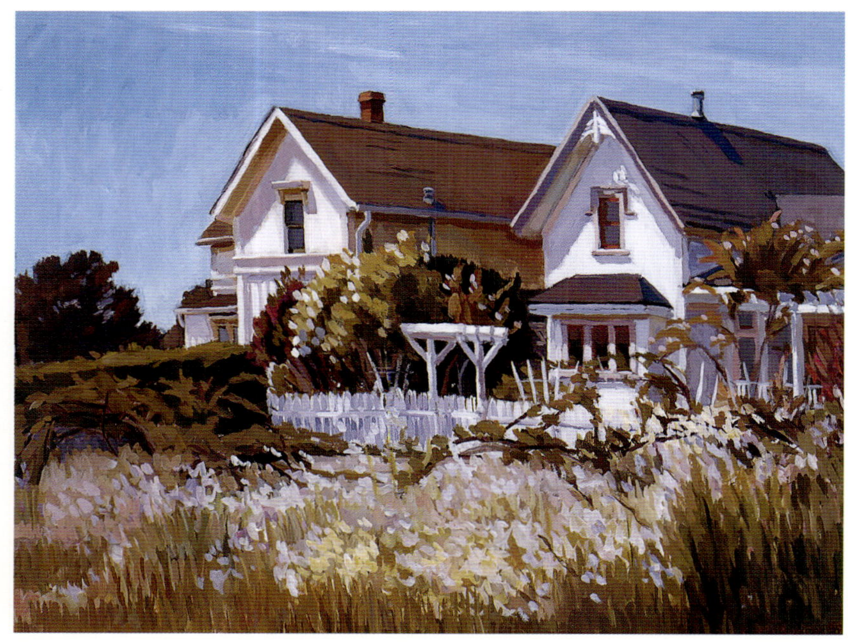

Calpella Street Houses with Flowers
1999, Oil, 14" x 18"
In the collection of Russ Christoff and
Genie O'Toole; Antioch, California

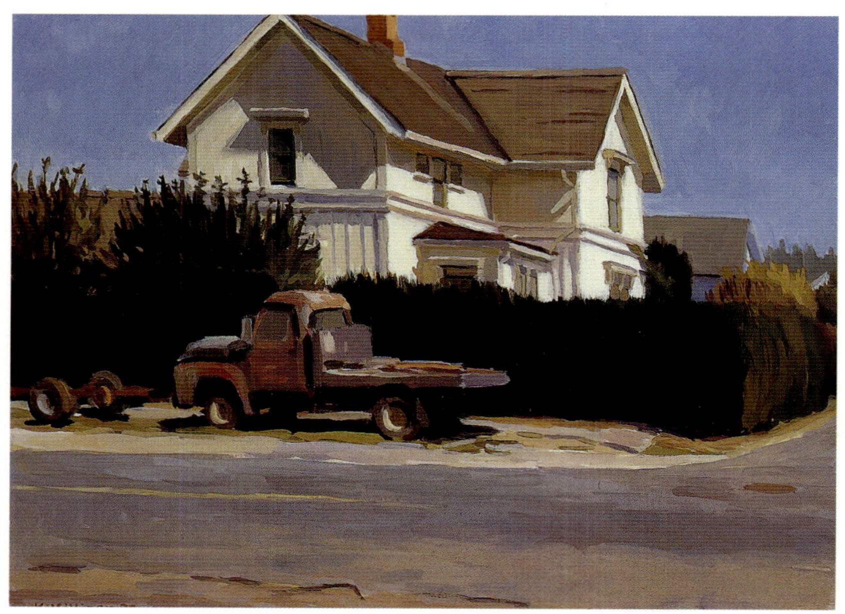

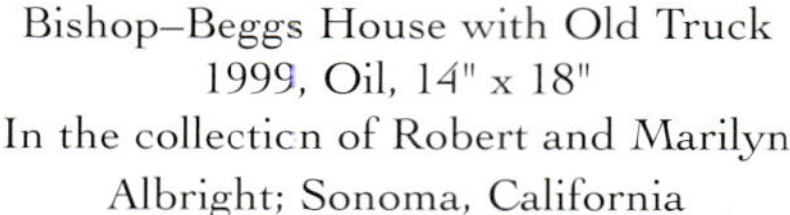

Bishop–Beggs House with Old Truck
1999, Oil, 14" x 18"
In the collection of Robert and Marilyn
Albright; Sonoma, California

The Beggs family was one of the earliest to reside in this house on Calpella Street. Tom Beggs, who owned a butcher shop on Main Street, lived here in the early 1900s with his wife Florence, of the prominent Jarvis family, and their daughter. Although there were other owners, the Bishop Family was in residence from the 1920s into the later part of the century. The upstairs room with the T-shaped windows was used as Hermie's bedroom in the 1970 Warner Brothers film, *The Summer of '42.*

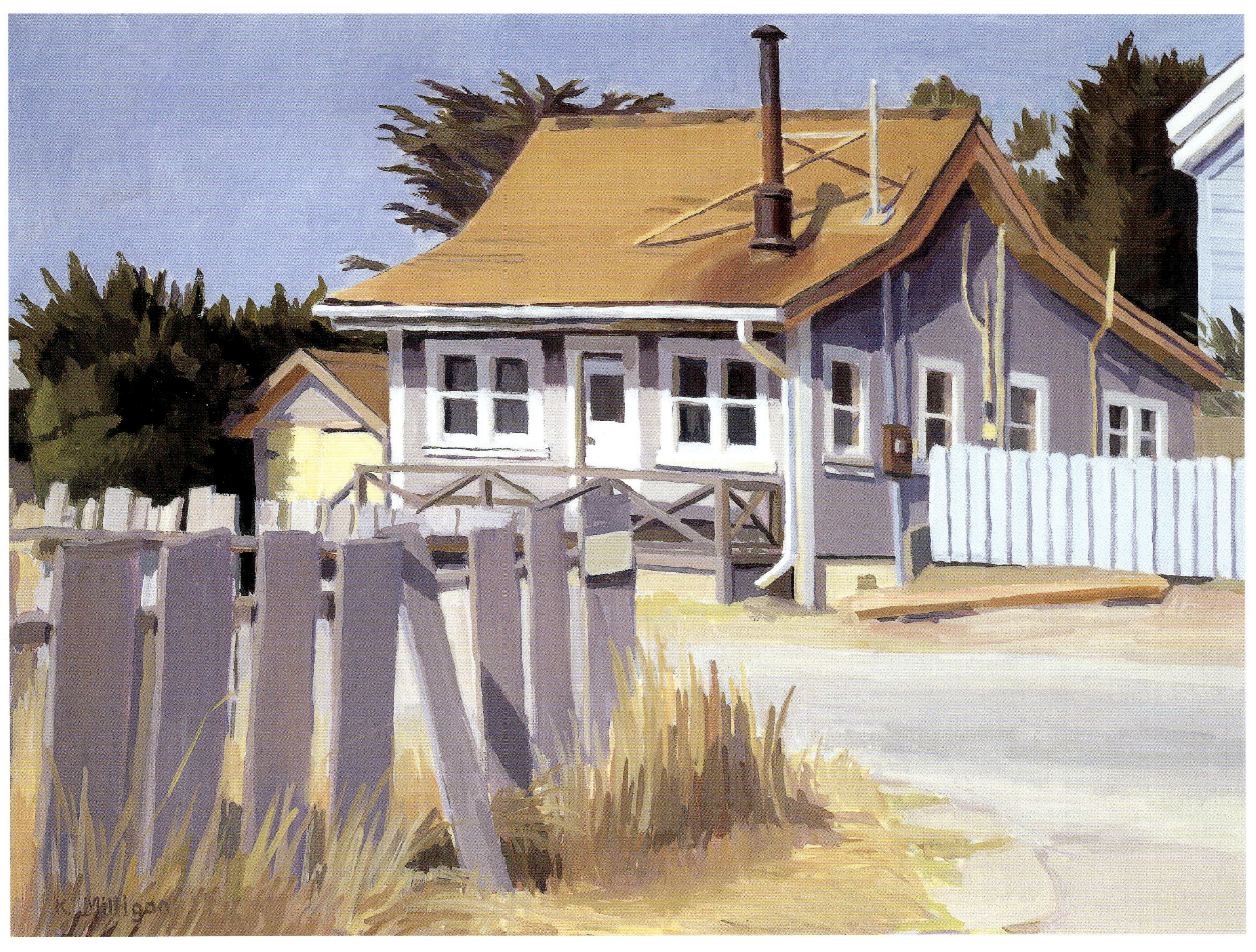

Cottage with Stovepipe from Osborn Street 1998, Oil, 14" x 18"

This scene was painted while standing on Osborn Street, though the street sign may say Woodward. It is north of Main and just south of Albion St., which runs in front of the cottage. Beginning as an alley between Silas Osborn's property and the City Hotel, Osborn Street only runs for two blocks, up to Ukiah St., where Crown Hall, seen at the upper right of this painting, is located. The "Osborn" spelling is shown on all early maps, but through the years an "e" was added, making it Osborne Street on many later maps. Since this street runs through a section of largely Portuguese population, perhaps later citizens unaware of Silas Osborn thought that naming it thusly honored William Osborne. Osborne, one of Mendocino's original settlers was also known as Mattias Fraga, the first husband of Annie Thomas. Woodward Street does not go through to Main, but ends at Ukiah Street.

Most know this building as the White Gate Inn, a well-manicured Bed-and-Breakfast, but it was built as a family home in 1883 for William T. Wilson, proprietor of Wilson's Oyster & Coffee Saloon next door to Jarvis & Nichols Store on Main Street at Kasten. In 1887, Dr. William McCornack rented this house on the southeast corner of Howard and Ukiah Streets, to create the community's first in-patient facility—The Mendocino Hospital Company—which served the town for ten years. A local could buy a certificate entitling the holder to admission, treatment, medicine and board in the hospital while suffering from wounds, injuries, diseases or illness incapacitating him for labor, but not to exceed 30 weeks for any one disease or injury. Cost: $10 a year.

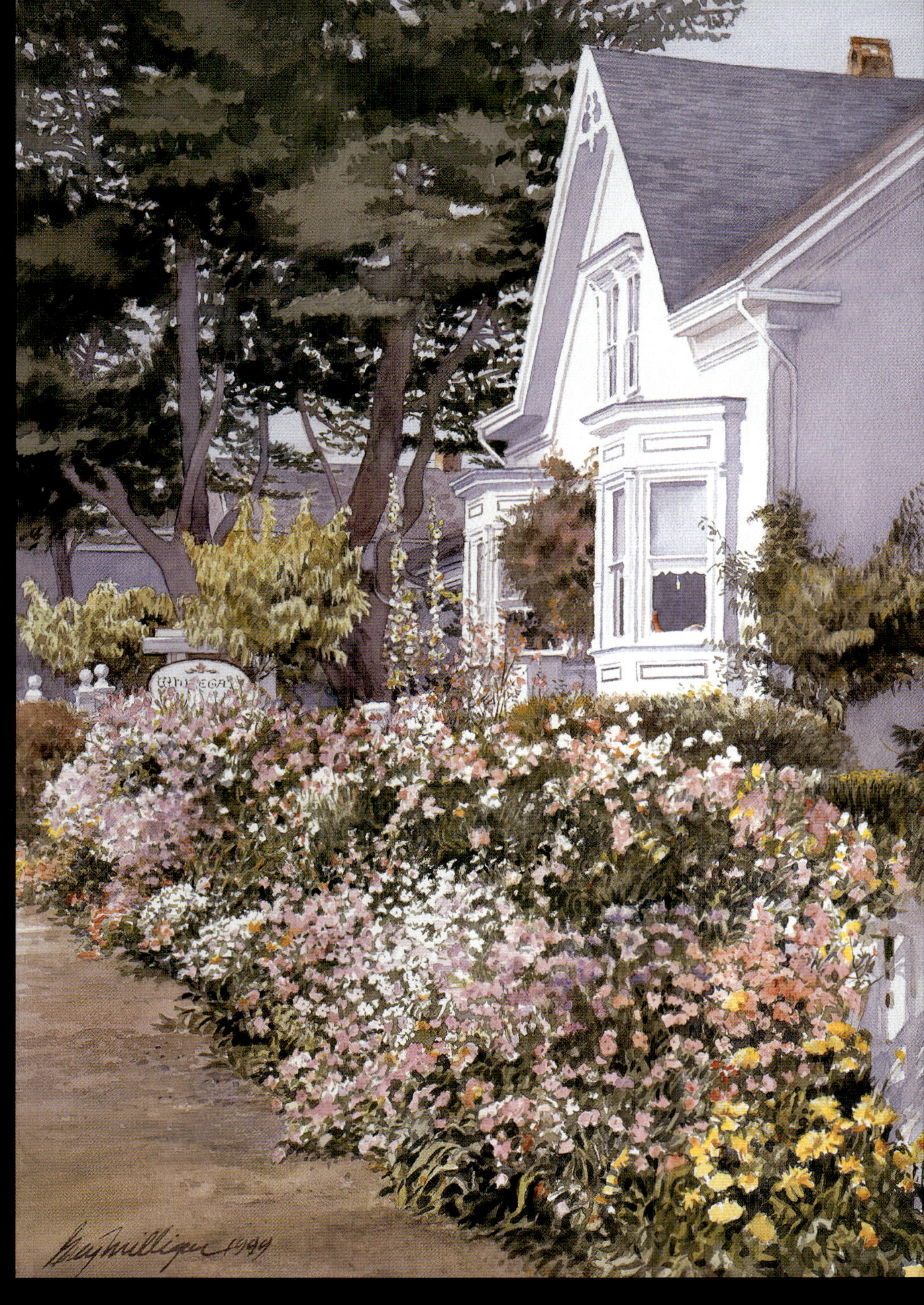

White Gate Inn 1998, Watercolor, 22" x 15"
In the collection of Kevin Milligan; Mendocino, California
By Guy Milligan

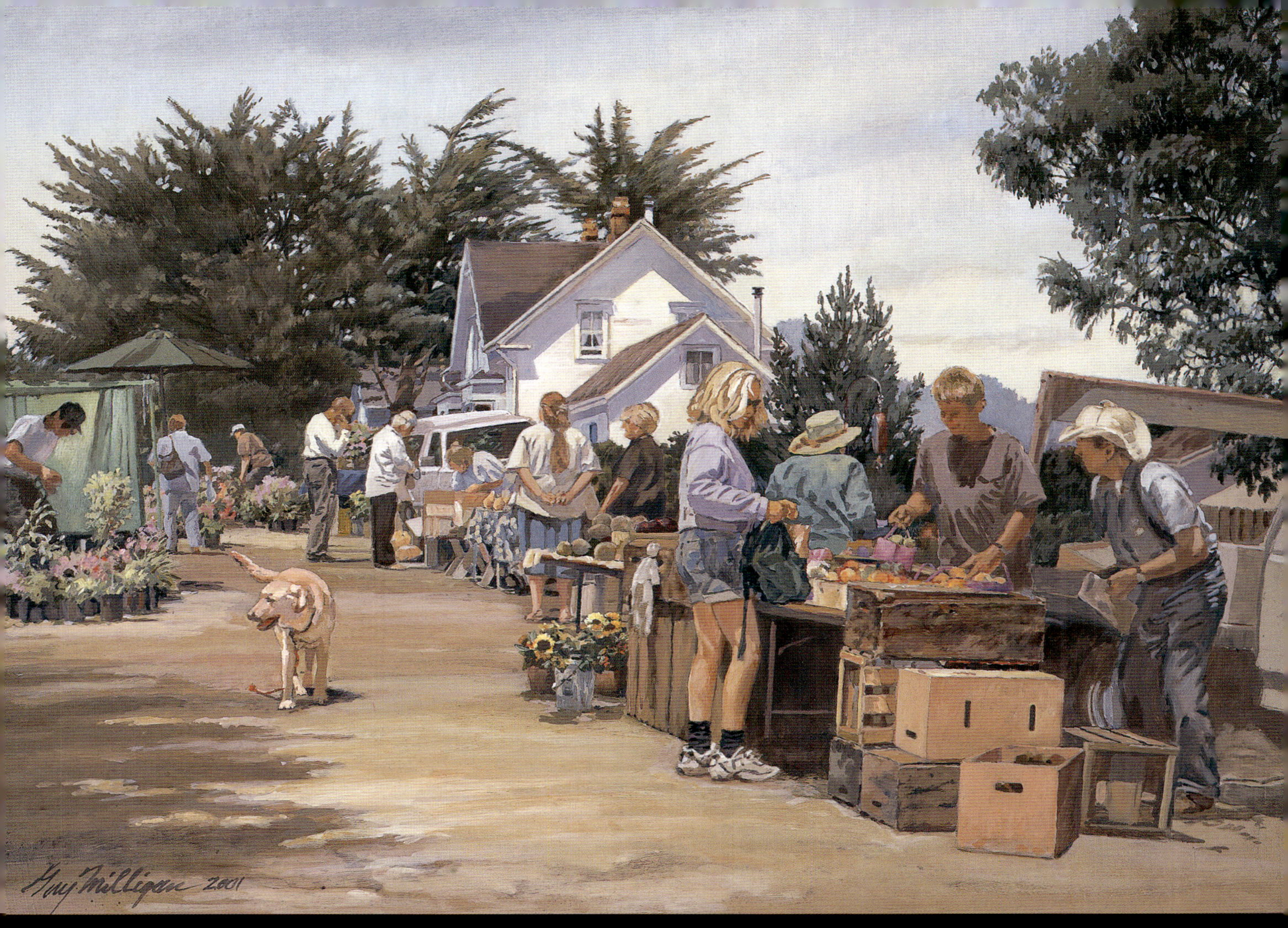

Farmers' Market Today 2001, Oil, 18" x 24" by Guy Milligan
In the collection of Gary and Margaret McCray; Rancho Palos Verdes, California

This painting by Guy Milligan, Kevin's father, depicts the Mendocino farmers' market that takes place Friday afternoons on Howard Street. The White Gate Inn can be seen in the background. The public has the opportunity to buy fresh produce and flowers brought by local growers, represented here by the Gowan family of Philo. From left to right, Josephine (in hat), Daniel and Jim stand at the far righthand side of the picture

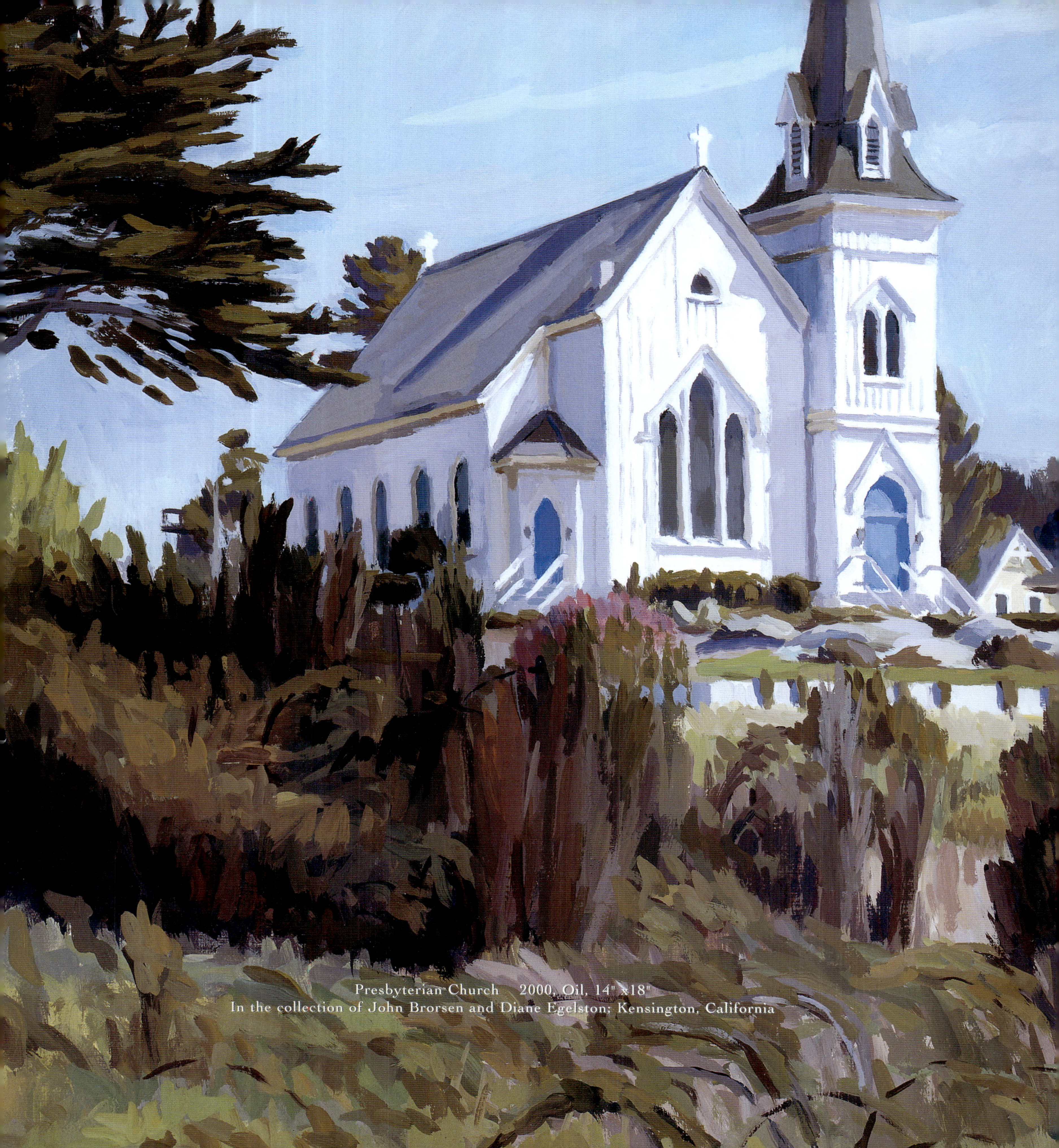

Presbyterian Church 2000, Oil, 14" x 18"
In the collection of John Brorsen and Diane Egelston; Kensington, California

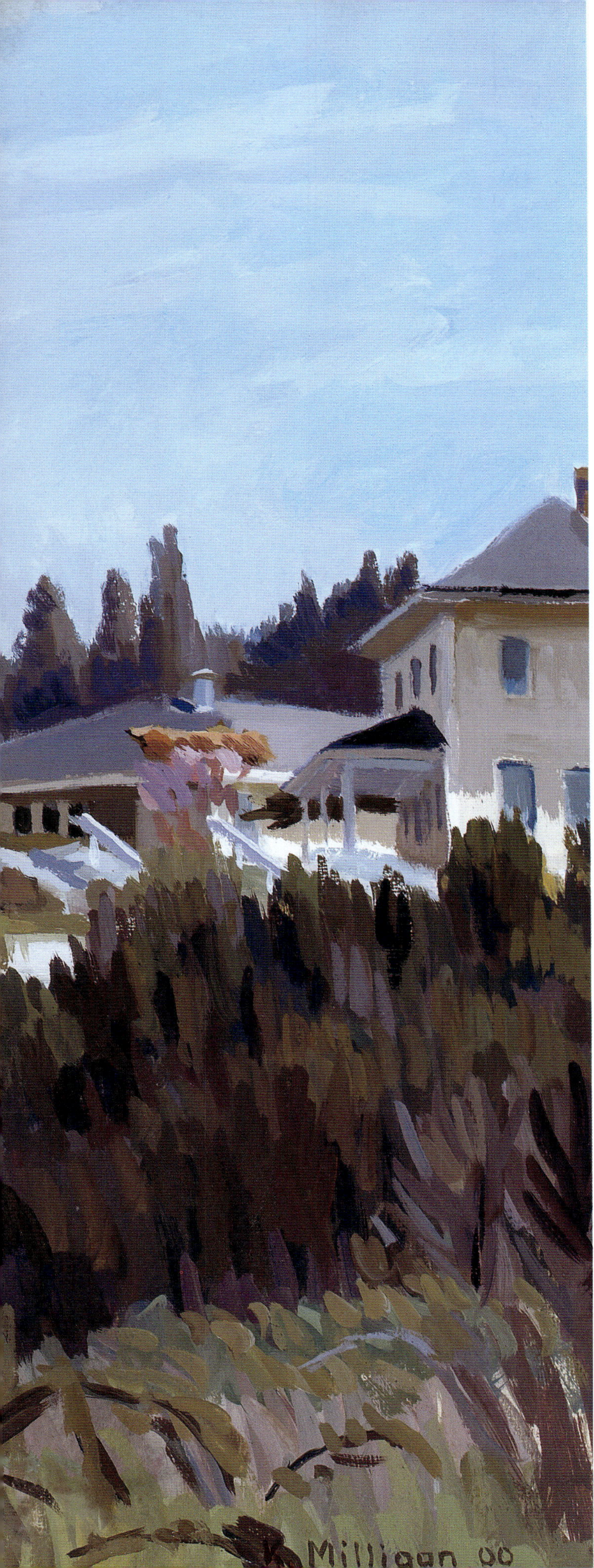

Churches

Presbyterian Church

California Historical Landmark #714

This most famous Mendocino Church, built in 1868, was the third in the town. Facing south toward the Bay on Bridge Street (once the Old Coast Road and the main route through town) gives the impression the church is "backwards" on Main Street. This lovely Gothic building has been photographed countless times, and has also appeared in numerous films, such as *Johnny Belinda.* Its Preston Hall serves as a community venue for cultural and educational events.

Churches

The first house of worship in Mendocino was a non-denominational Protestant church built in 1858, facing south near the corner of Lansing and Ukiah Streets. (In 1862 the first school was constructed a bit east of the church, and by 1868 the Masonic Lodge was finished across Lansing.) Previous to that, prayer meetings were held in private homes and in the dining room of the lumberyard cookhouse. While searching for a permanent minister, services were conducted by William Kelly's father, Peter. He was an experienced preacher and an Elder in the Presbyterian faith back on Prince Edward Island where they originated. This was largely the reason Mendocino's Protestant congregation officially became Presbyterian in November 1859.

The second church in town, St. Vincent's Catholic Church, was erected in 1864 on the north side of Little Lake Road at the top of Howard Street, about where the white cross is now in the Catholic Cemetery on the hill. From 1860 until Father Bernadine Sheehan was able to get the church finished, Catholics took him into their homes, providing his room and board, as well as a place for all to gather in worship. The first Catholic Church in Mendocino County, it was designated the home Parish, so that other churches built later became Mission churches of St. Vincent's of Mendocino. The building itself had an interesting three-story windowed tower with a spire reaching 50 feet. For many years the Government Coast and Geodetic Survey used it as a sighting point.

In 1868, to accommodate the growing Protestant population, the new Presbyterian Church was built between Main Street and Bridge Street, once a major route between the Flats and town. The scale of the new structure's windows, roof and spire are large and in perfect proportion. The bell tower and spire extend impressively to the heavens. Since the old bell could no longer be heard so close to the ocean, it was donated to a church in the next county, and Jerome B. Ford paid $500 to provide a new bell weighing 1000 pounds.

At that time, the now-vacant First Church building allowed the also-growing school population to expand into its space. In 1874, the old school building was moved closer and attached to the church. By 1884 classes had to spill over into the downstairs of the Masonic Lodge. The opening of a brand-new school in 1885 emptied out the old combination building. In 1890 Reverend J. M. Clark leased it for a Methodist Church, a congregation usually overlooked in histories of the town.

The fourth Mendocino church to be erected was the architecturally distinctive Baptist chapel that William Kelly built on Ukiah Street for his wife Eliza in 1894. Fortunately, it still stands today. Now a health food store, Eliza's chapel has been modified a bit. Instead of its current barn-red coloring, early photos show it was painted a light color, probably yellow or tan with dark trim, possibly brown. The bell tower opening has been boarded up, and an extension was added on the back of the building. The bell tower and stained glass windows remain its best architectural aspects. The pulpit has been moved to the foyer of the MacCallum House Inn, where it holds the dinner reservation book instead of the Bible Eliza Kelly and Reverend John Ross used for their sermons.

Meanwhile, the Catholic population was growing as well. The Portuguese community built Crown Hall in 1901, and for some years services were held there as well as at the increasingly crowded St. Vincent's. Thus, Crown Hall was the town's sixth Christian house of worship, and the seventh would be the second Catholic Church, St. Anthony's. It was completed and opened for its first services in September 1906, despite delays from April's famous earthquake. This much larger building was situated on the west side of Lansing and farther up the hill. Just to the west of it stood a three-story monastery or seminary of the Friars Minor Capuchin in California. Mendocino had become the first home of the Friars Minor Capuchin in California. With considerable sadness, the original church was dismantled in 1921. Then in December 1930, disaster struck. St. Anthony's and the monastery were engulfed and destroyed in a terrible fire. Both Catholics and non-Catholics risked their lives to save treasures from inside the church such as the historic Crucifix. But the worst was yet to come. With no place to live, the priests had to relocate to Fort Bragg, which became the Parish, making Mendocino the Mission. And with the area already in the Depression, the Archdiocese at first refused to replace the church. However, due to the persistence of a few determined women who trekked more than once to San Francisco to plead their case, they finally received permission and began the process of fund-raising and building. The first regular mass in the new St. Anthony's was said March 15, 1931. The Hall and Rectory were built in 1967–69. Tragically, the Crucifix rescued from the 1930 fire, which had hung in all three Catholic churches, was damaged beyond repair when another fire gutted the interior of St. Anthony's on November 30, 1999. Once again the Catholic community pulled together to restore the church and replace the Crucifix.

Although the Masonic Lodge is not a church, it is considered a Temple with many interesting architectural details, both inside and out. The sculpture atop this Hall is regarded as a folk art classic. Carved from a single block of redwood over a period of several years, it depicts "Father Time and the Maiden," a Masonic allegory about life lost at a young age.

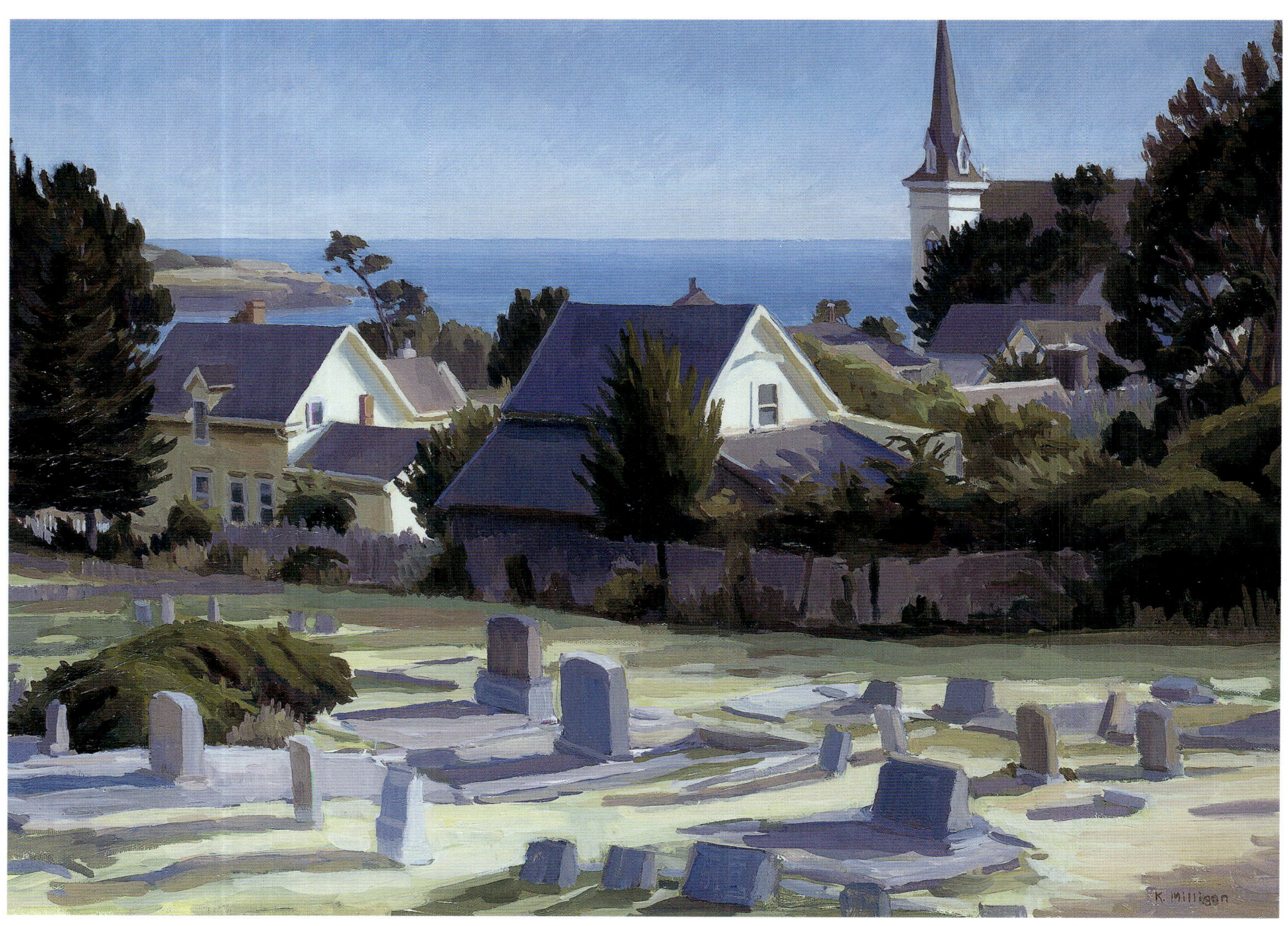

Rooftops from Evergreen Cemetery 1997–99, Oil, 18" x 24"
In the collection of Mike and Terri Phelps; Lafayette, California

Kevin Milligan's First Mendocino Painting

Against the summer sun, buildings and gravestones cast evening shadows onto the field of Evergreen Cemetery. Beyond the steeple and shingled rooftops, Mendocino Bay and the Pacific Ocean lie gleaming in the distance.

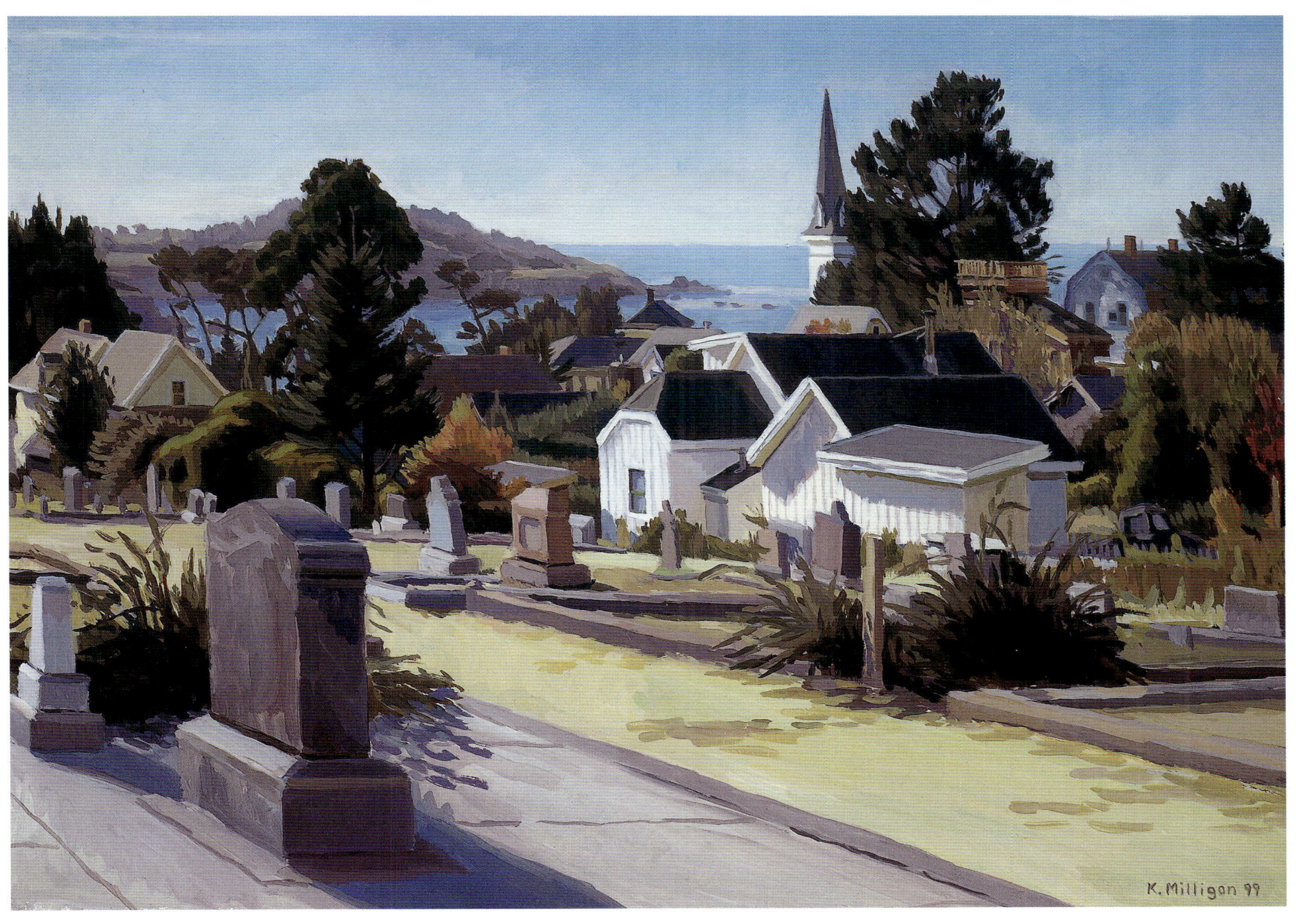

Headstones at Evergreen Cemetery 1999, Oil, 18" x 24"
In the collection of William and Theresa Brodsley; Carmel Valley, California

The Headstone of William McLein reads:

Died at Mendocino Cal, March 10, 1895

We can not tell who next may fall
Beneath thy chastening rod,
One must be first,
But let us all
Prepare to meet our God.

The headstone of Prentiss McKenna reads:

Died Nov 7 1888, 8 yrs 9 mos 25 days

Rest little Prentiss, in happiness rest
Mingling with angels we know thou are blest,
Far from the trials that tempt us to stray,
God in his mercy has called thee away.

Eliza Kelly, a Baptist from Prince Edward Island, found a kindred spirit in the Rev. John Simpson Ross, who also came from Canada. Meeting her very shortly after his arrival on the Mendocino Coast, in the fall of 1869, he and his wife Jane became Eliza's lifetime friends. Over forty years Ross attended to the duties of his ministry, preaching in many churches from Gualala to Westport, marrying nearly 300 couples and burying 350 people. Of Eliza Kelly he said, *"Her friendship was always warm, her kindness never relaxed, and her generosity was always at high tide flow. She was the succorer of many, and of me also."* —Excerpt from *Footprints on the Mendocino Coast: A biography of Reverend John Simpson Ross*, edited by Julia L. Moungovan.

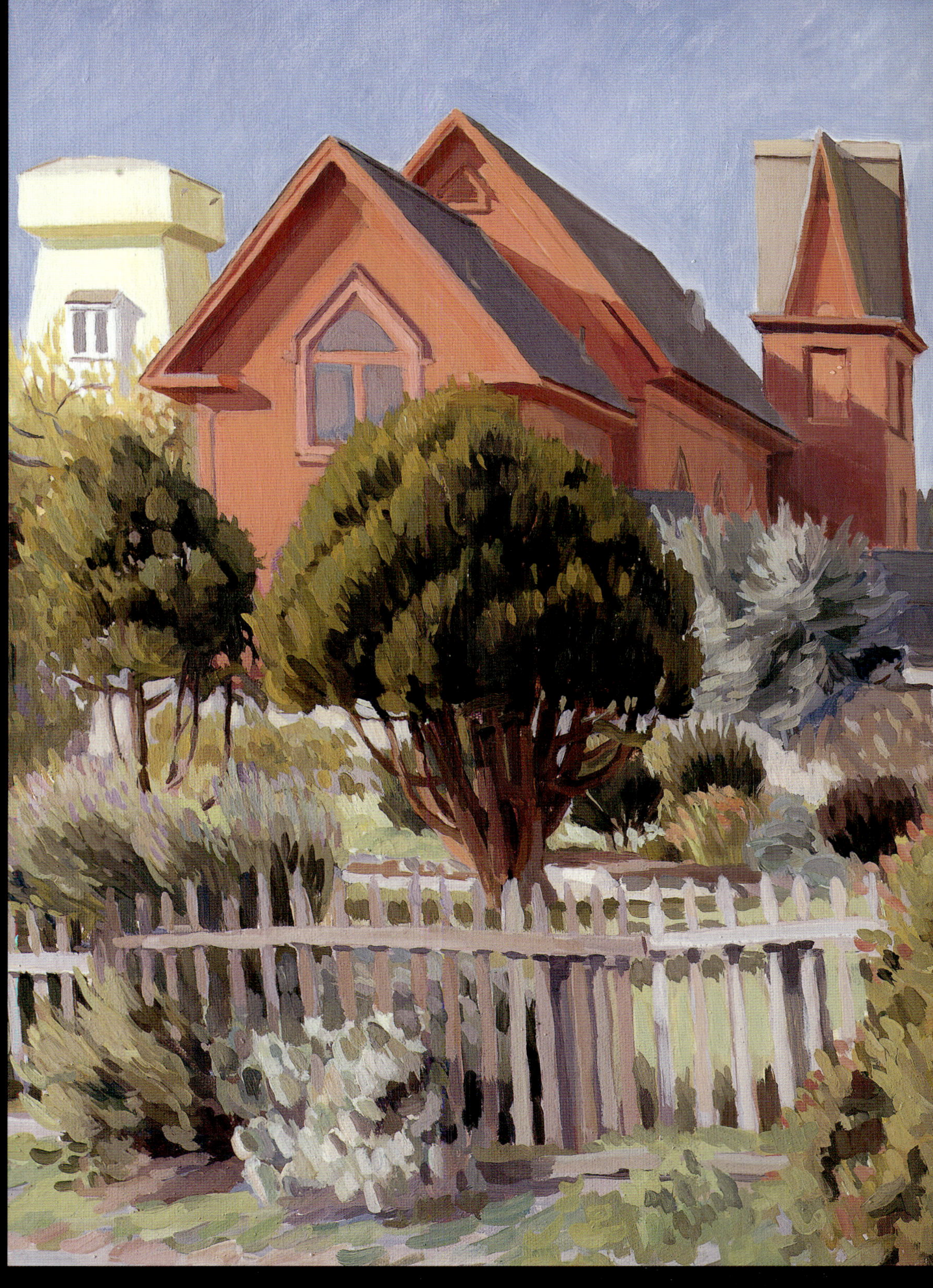

Baptist Church from Albion Street 1998, Oil, 18" x 14"
In the collection of Dr. and Mrs.Wolfgang Lederer; California

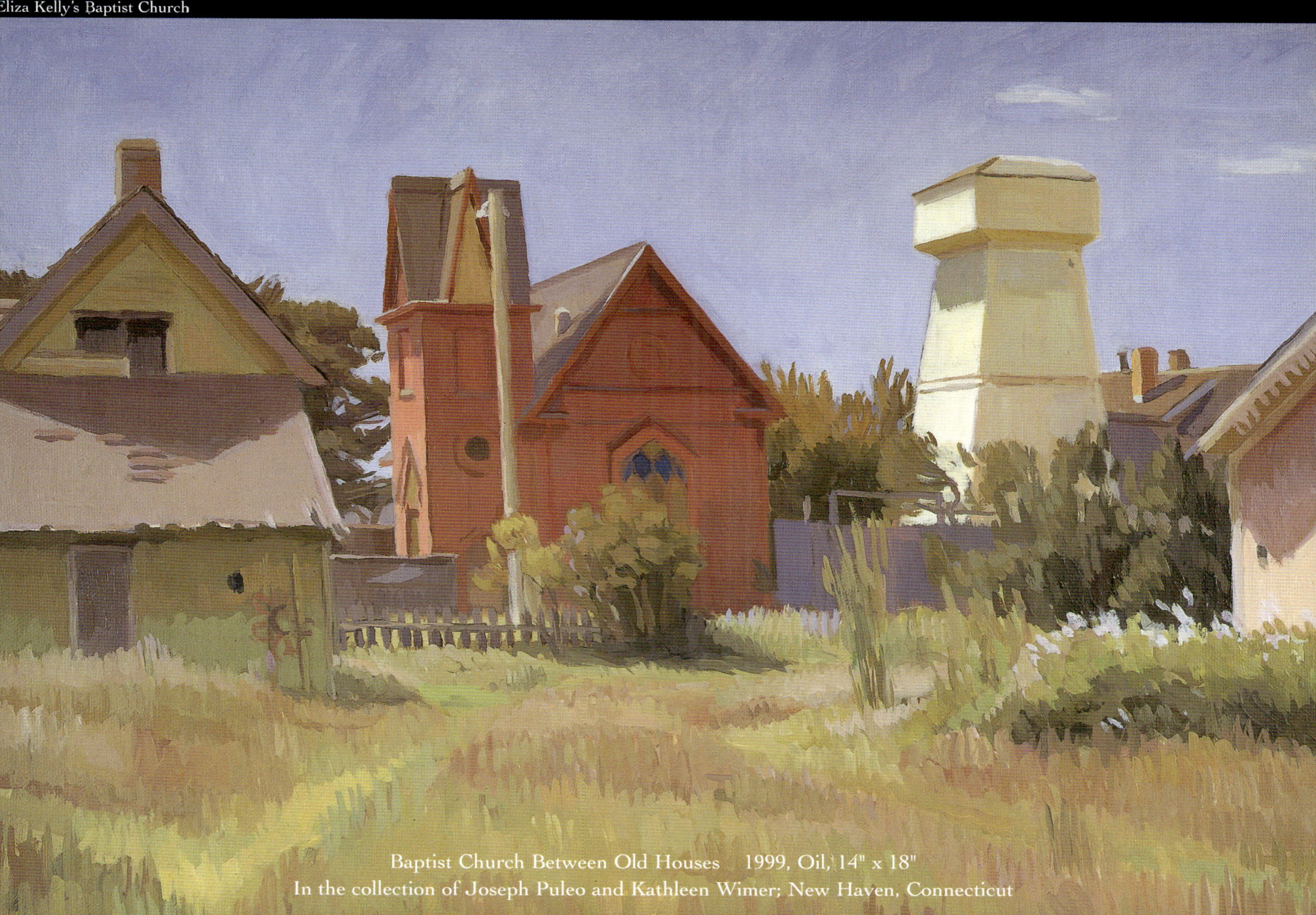

Baptist Church Between Old Houses 1999, Oil, 14" x 18"
In the collection of Joseph Puleo and Kathleen Wimer; New Haven, Connecticut

The fourth church built in Mendocino was dedicated in 1894 by Rev. John Simpson Ross, who officiated at marriages, baptisms and funerals all along the Mendocino Coast between 1869–1909. He was well-loved and had great compassion for the working class man. In his diary, he wrote, *"Fourteen hours consisted a day's work. Men were fairly exhausted. Goaded on for six successive days at this high pressure and speed they were completely exhausted with fatigue. Single men largely in excess of those who were married. Each lived in isolation, in his own cabin . . . I saw my fellow men busy at their daily avocation, many toiling hard, with no bright prospect of any future reward, and I who had a good hope through faith in Christ: why should I not faithfully persevere in my high calling, rest in the Lord, and wait patiently for him?*

"If others can endure hardship, meet difficulties, and enlist their physical powers in order to gratify their own personal desires and personal enjoyment, why should I not try with all my might to please God, benefit men, and bless those who are outside the ranks of saved men and women?" — *Excerpts from Footprints on the Mendocino Coast: A biography of Reverend John Simpson Ross*

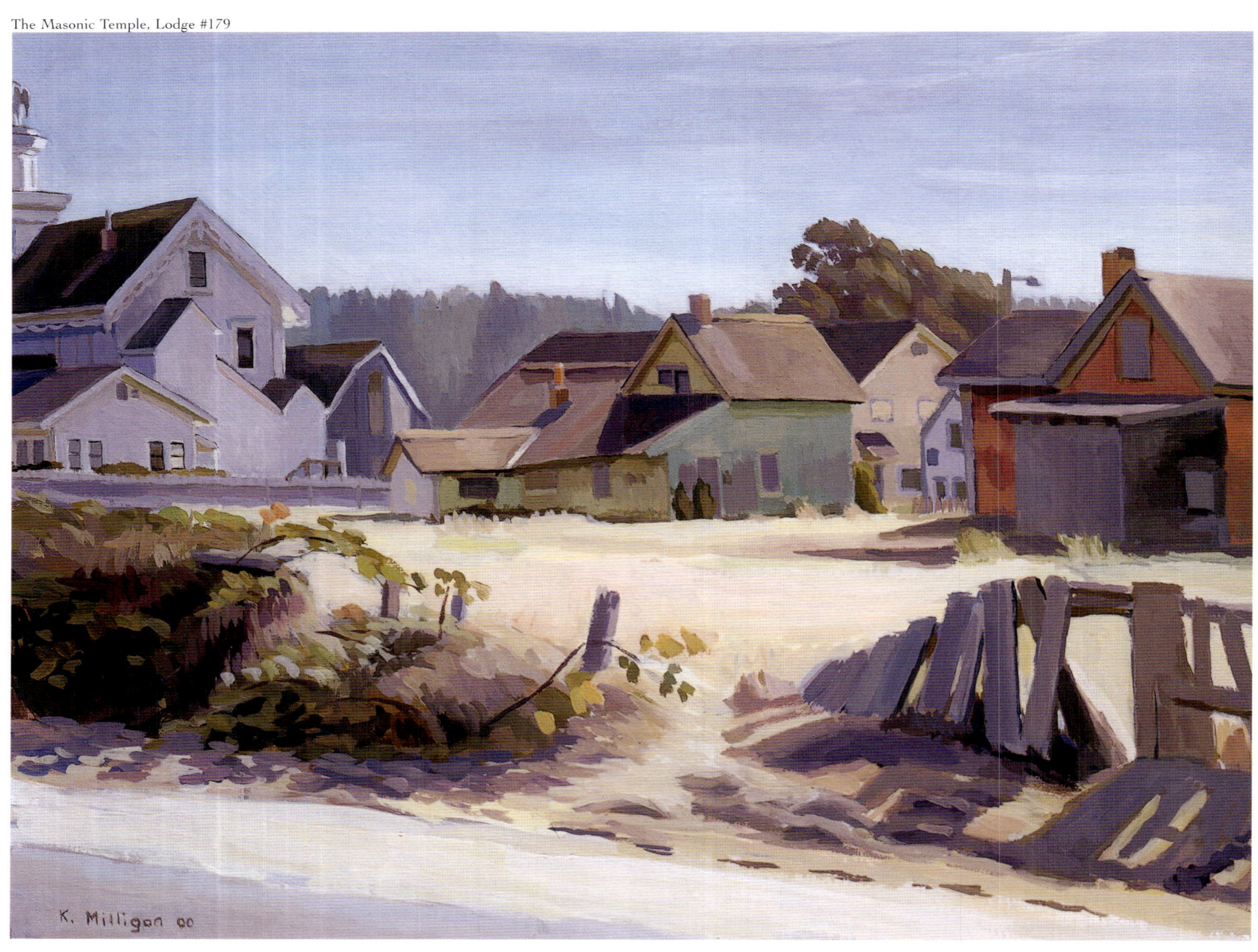

Masonic Hall with Old Fence and Houses 2000, Oil, 14" x 18"
In the collection of Ian McNeill and Laurie Miller; Danville, California

Beginning in 1866, Erick Albertson built the Masonic Hall over the course of nearly seven years. A charter member and the first Worshpful Master, he was selected for the contract at a cost of $1,000. The members paid dues five years in advance in order to fund the project. During the hard times that followed the Civil War, many of the members had to cash in their shares. Albertson created the statue on top of the building and also intricate carvings of columns, arches and ceiling decorations on the inside of the building. Today the lower floor houses the town's only bank.

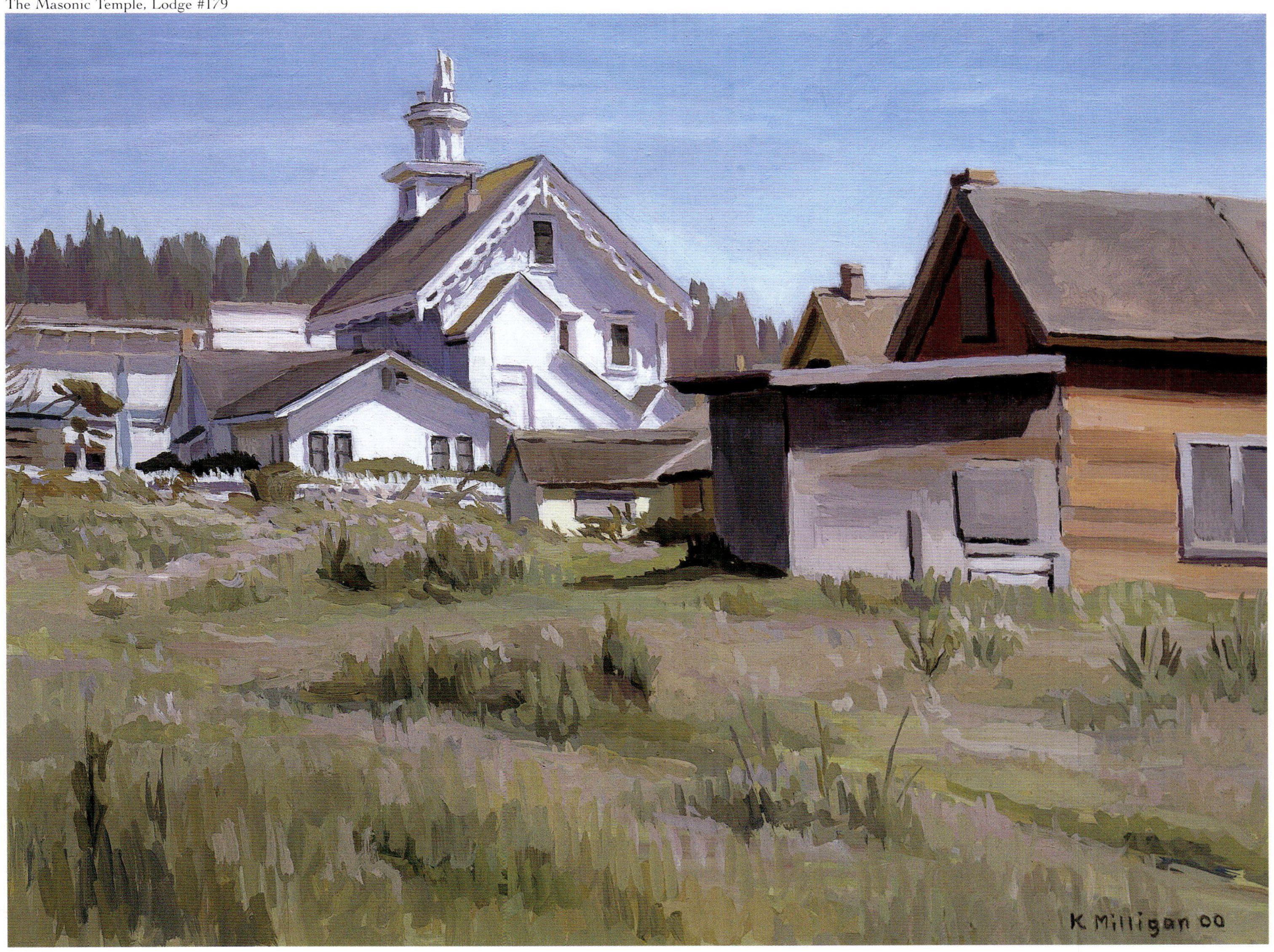

Masonic Hall with Old Red House 2000, Oil, 14" x 18"
In the collection of Edward and Rochell Letasi; Windsor, California

Erick Albertson carved the figures atop the Masonic Hall from a single redwood log. Symbolic of a particular rite of passage from one of the 33 Masonic degrees to another, the wooden sculpture depicts images from ancient mythology: the Angel of Death (also called Father Time), the Hourglass of Transience, the Weeping Maiden, the annointment of her hair as she holds an acacia branch, and the Sacred Urn with the Book of Light resting atop the Sundered Column.

Another distinctive feature of the building is the bargeboard trim, identical to that still present on the Spencer Hills House, with pendant finials at the four corners.

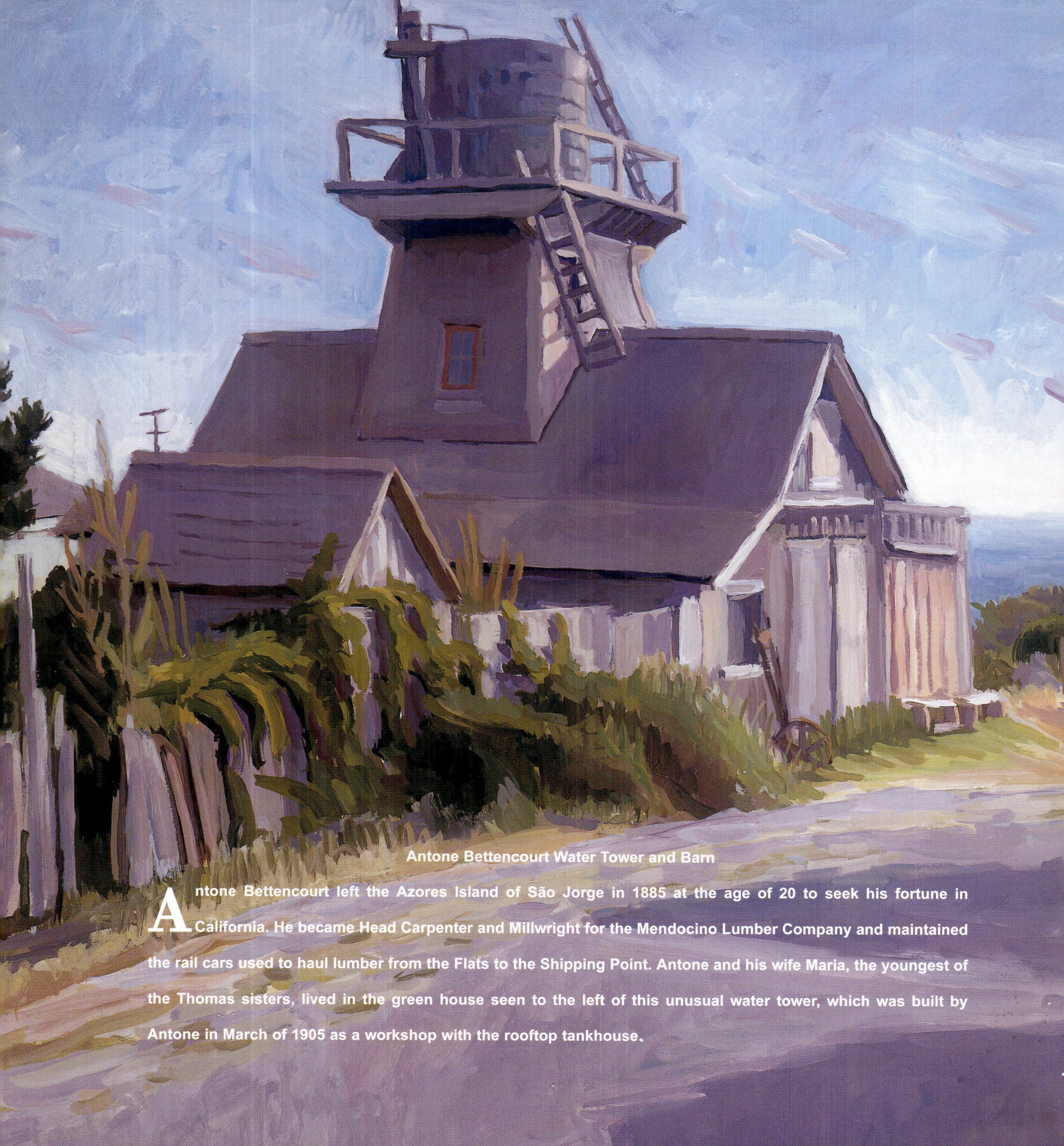

Antone Bettencourt Water Tower and Barn

Antone Bettencourt left the Azores Island of São Jorge in 1885 at the age of 20 to seek his fortune in California. He became Head Carpenter and Millwright for the Mendocino Lumber Company and maintained the rail cars used to haul lumber from the Flats to the Shipping Point. Antone and his wife Maria, the youngest of the Thomas sisters, lived in the green house seen to the left of this unusual water tower, which was built by Antone in March of 1905 as a workshop with the rooftop tankhouse.

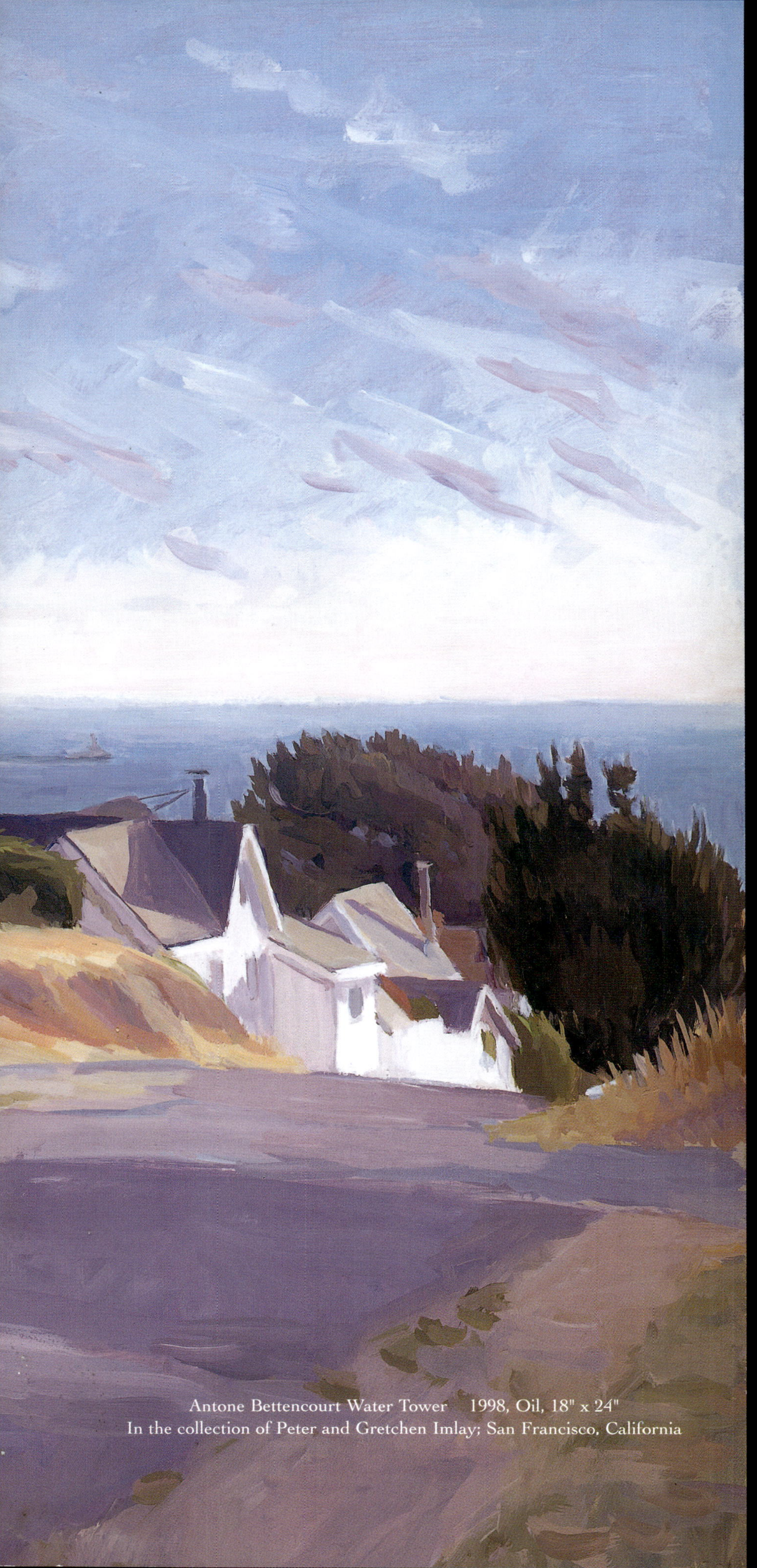
Antone Bettencourt Water Tower 1998, Oil, 18" x 24"
In the collection of Peter and Gretchen Imlay; San Francisco, California

Barns & Water Towers

Important as houses, churches, halls and commercial establishments might be, many other buildings were vital to existence a century ago, especially in rural and frontier communities. Outbuildings including privies, wash houses for laundry, tool sheds, chicken coops, storage sheds, carriage houses and the like served important purposes, but it's the barns and water towers that stand out in Mendocino History.

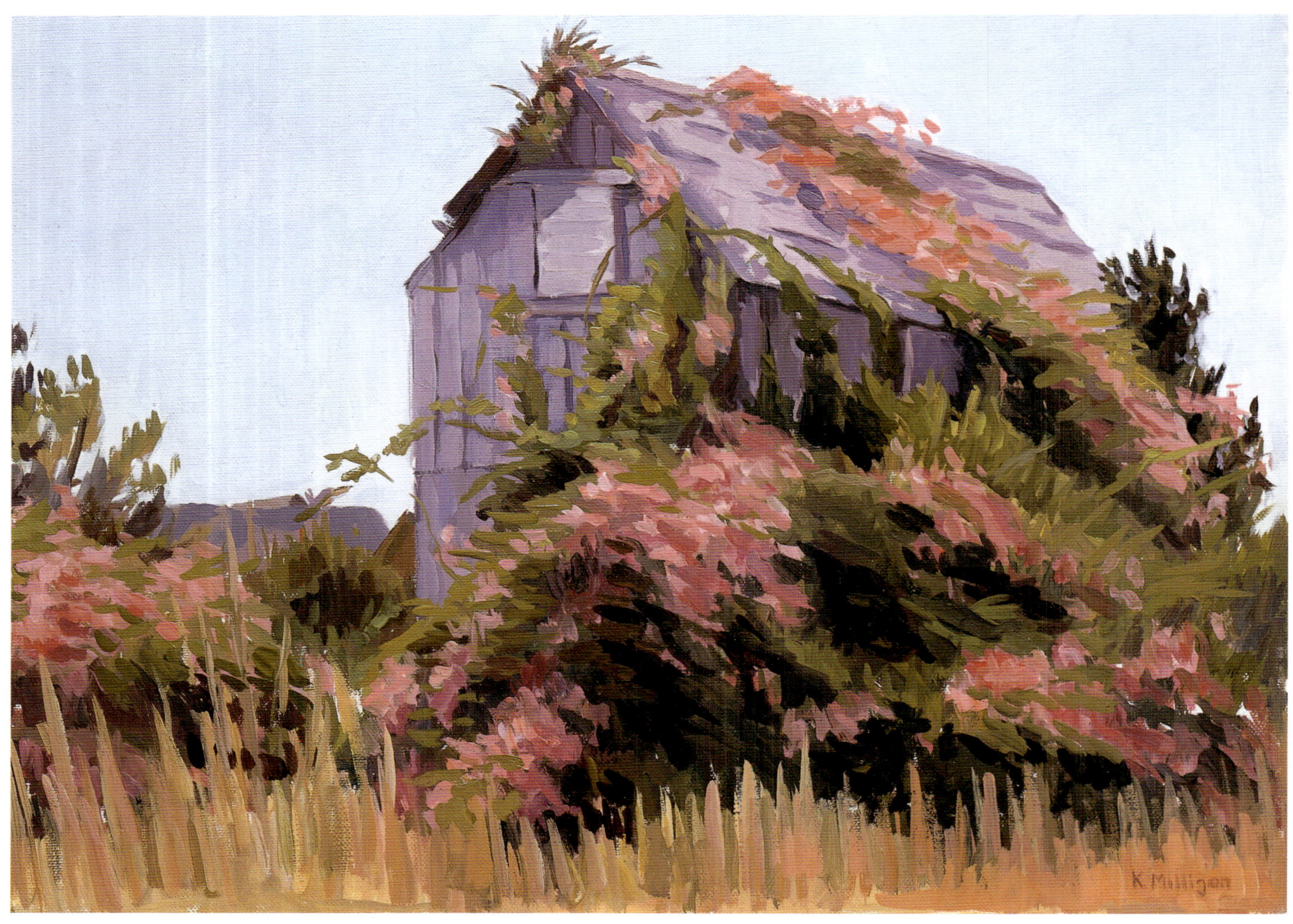

Rose-Covered Barn 1998, Oil, 14" x 18"
In the collection of Patricia Dillon; El Granada, California

Barns

Most of Mendocino's historic barns are long gone, but a few picturesque structures survive. Though often overlooked, they are well worth viewing to appreciate their workmanship and distinctive features. Gambrel roofs, hayloft door hoods and ventilator cupolas may be seen on barns like that of the Ocean View Dairy. Some beams still bear chip marks from the carpenter's adz.

The most imaginative combination of functional elements is displayed in the Bettencourt barn-water tower. While creating his own woodworking shop, Antone Bettencourt cleverly incorporated a water tower, windmill and water storage tank on the roof. From its hillside perch the structure's distinctive profile is set against the blue Pacific.

Barns were an essential part of frontier life. Besides sheltering livestock, hay and grain, they protected wagons, car-

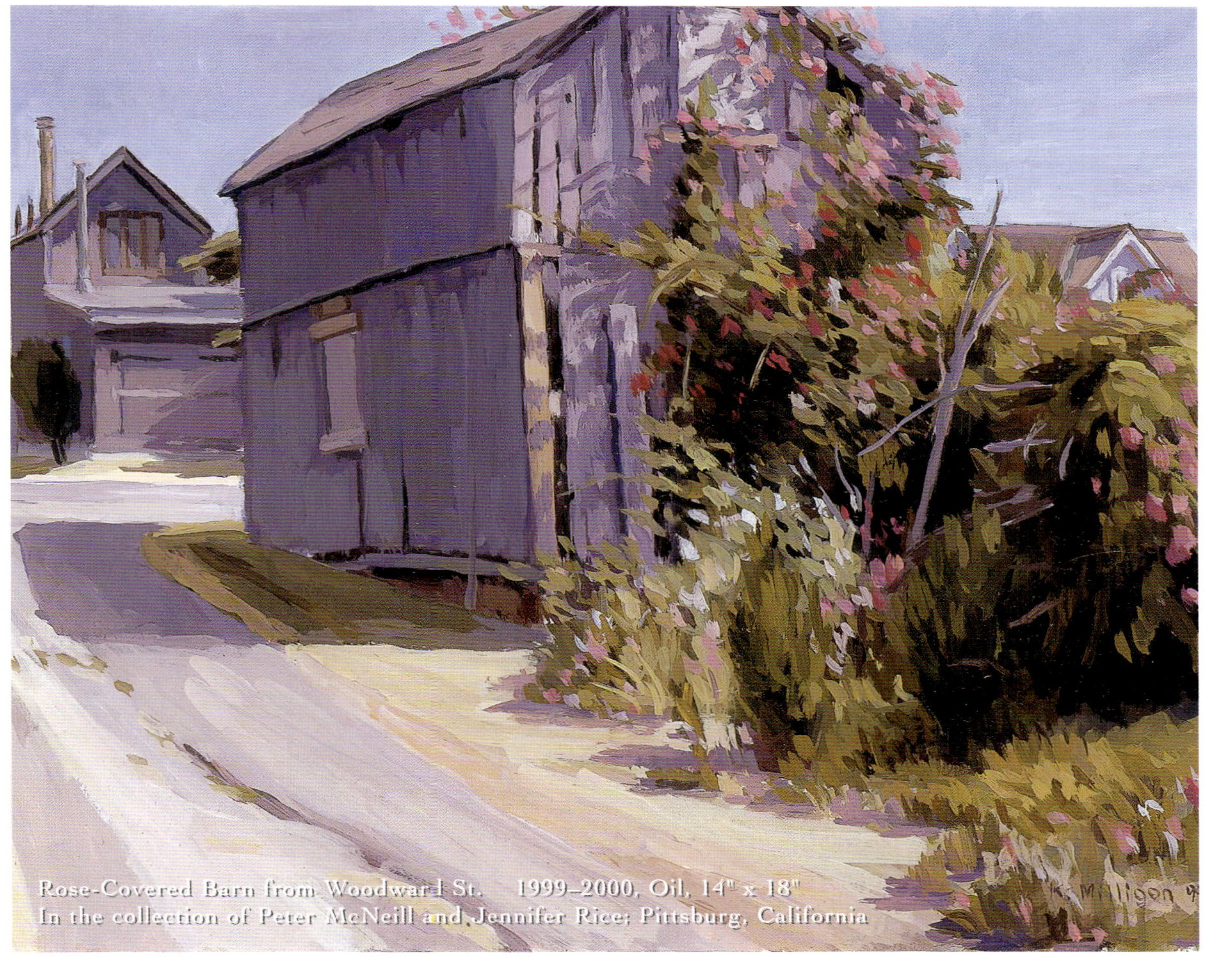

Rose-Covered Barn from Woodward St. 1999–2000, Oil, 14" x 18"
In the collection of Peter McNeill and Jennifer Rice; Pittsburg, California

riages and farm equipment. Despite a mild climate, the Coast's continual dampness leads quickly to the rusting of metal. Additionally, certain farms such as dairies needed structures large enough to house equipment used to gather and process milk.

Like all wooden structures in Mendocino, barns were susceptible to fire, especially when filled with stored hay. On June 2, 1895 William Heeser lost his Ukiah Street barn, six horses and ten tons of hay in just such a blaze. A July 1936 fire took the historic structure called the Company Barn. It was located at the southeast corner of Lansing and Bridge Streets, east of the Ford House. Over the years it had served as a bull barn, a bark mill, a storage facility, a dance hall and a skating rink.

Uncounted barns burned; others were dismantled for their lumber or fell victim to the elements and vandalism. Inevitably, some became garages. Many were remodeled into homes and shops and storehouses still in use today. Along Mendocino's back streets, a last few may be found slowly sinking beneath their burden of blooming roses.

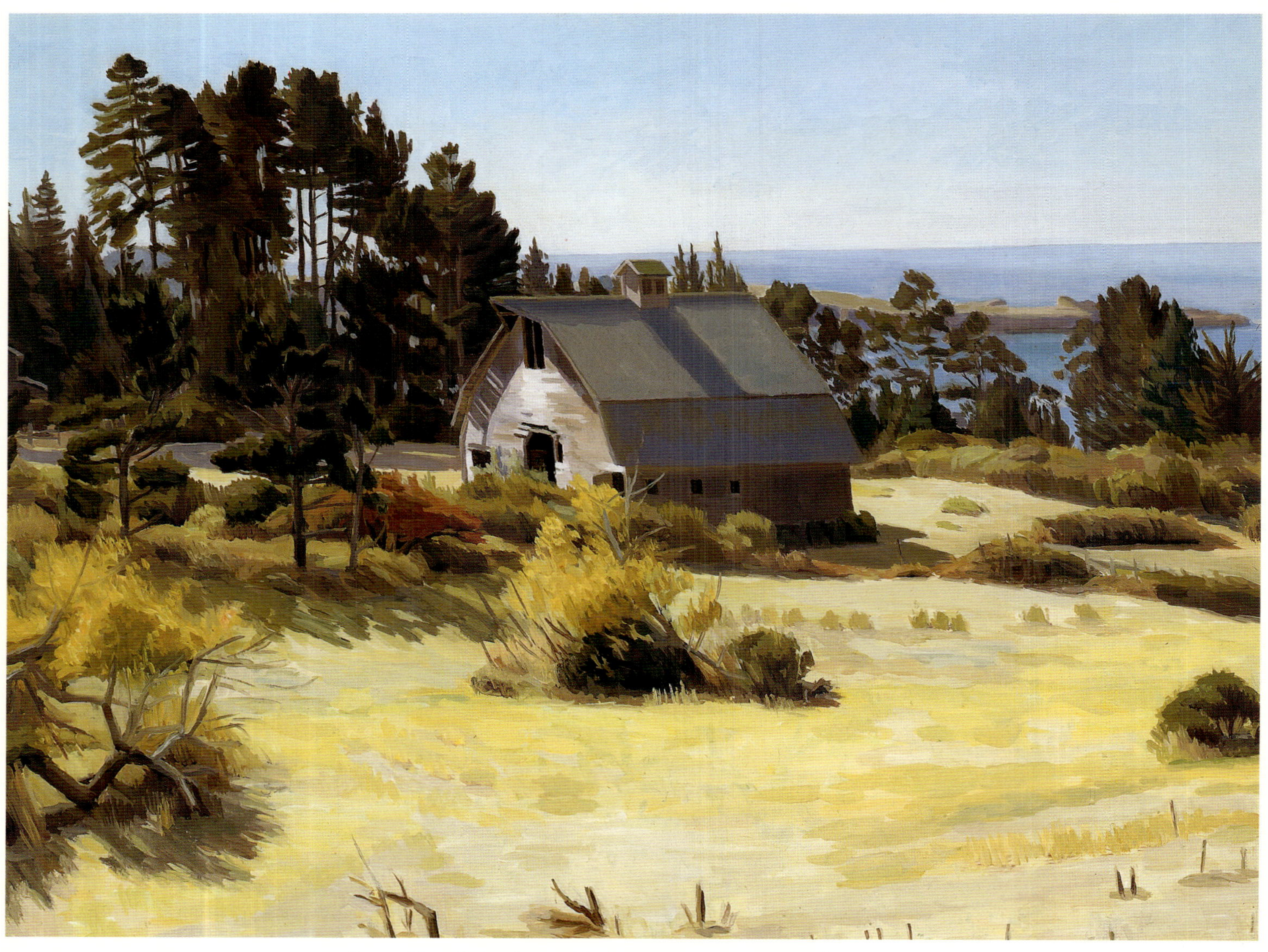

Ocean View Dairy Barn with Agate Cove 2000-01, Oil, 22" x 28"
In the collection of Patricia Dillon; El Granada, California

Ocean View Dairy was owned and operated by the Donoho Family from 1914–39 (prior to that by the Joy Family). Before they came to Mendocino, Peter R. Donoho worked for the government at Ft. Barry and ran a dairy on the Marin Headlands. First child, daughter Bonita, was born to Pete and wife Lillian there and named after nearby Point Bonita. The family of three came from Marin when Lillian was pregnant with their second child. Shortly after arriving in Mendocino in 1912, she gave birth to son Raymond Preston Donoho. The family of four worked together to run one of the main dairies supplying milk to the town of Mendocino. Located one mile north of town, it was near Agate Cove, where a brewery also flourished for many years.

Bonita Donoho reminisces about her childhood spent in the idyllic setting of the Ocean View Dairy in the following excerpts from *My Life Story on the Mendocino Coast* by Bonita Donoho, lent to Mendocino Historical Research, Inc. by Merna Brown, Bonita's friend and classmate.

When I was six to nine years old, I drove the dairy herd down as far as the Catholic Church where they would wander off for the day to feed on the high grass as far as the lumber yard below the Heeser place. Then, after school I would have to get them and bring them home. That is where the teachers started to complain because I was not getting enough rest and too many miles of walking. Later I would go home and get my horse and go after them, ready for my Dad to milk them by hand in those days.

During the Apple Fair everyone participated that could. Of course, my Dad had a large hog he displayed near Apple Hall as well as a brown bear he captured up the Russian Gulch. At the time he was advertising Bear Brand shoes. I rode a bay horse when only six or seven. While parading I would place my hand on his back and make him buck, which frightened the people, thinking I would get bucked off, but I knew when to stop before it happened.

They had races at that time near the ocean bluff on the Heeser Ranch so I had a chance to race one of our running horses but he was too much for me to handle. Dad had to take over, racing against some Point Arena horses.

One year in my high school term, I rode to Comptche to the Rasmussen Home where Addie Rasmussen and I rode from there to Willits on our horses to attend the rodeo. While there I was asked to go into the girls' race, so I took a chance, knowing my horse could run. The horse had no experience on a track so I came in second with an Indian girl crowding me into the fence. That is when I clashed with her, and told her she better watch out.

According to a local bus driver who attended the event, Bonita won the next two races against the Pomo girl.

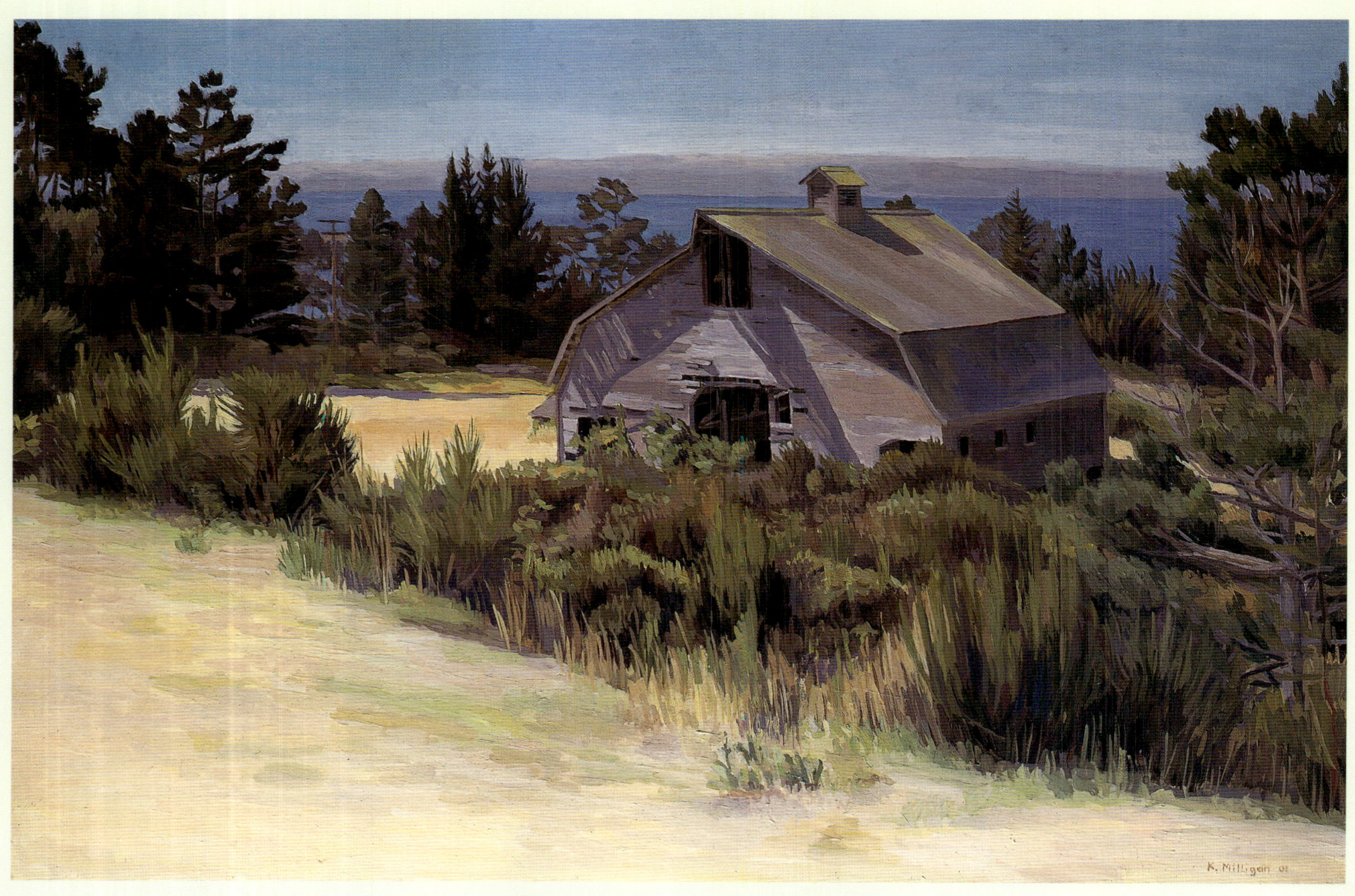

Ocean View Dairy Barn 2000-01, Oil, 24" x 36"

Barns sometimes performed an additional function, serving as early billboards. At one time around 1920, a large advertisement for the Hotel Alhambra was painted on the south side of this structure. Years ago Coast Highway 1 took a more easterly route and passed right by this huge barn. The Hotel Alhambra, also known as the Alhambra Hotel and Seavey's Hotel, was built on Main Street c.1885 by Hiram B. Seavey. The Alhambra once boasted an elaborate lamp post in front of the building until the place was enlarged in 1891. Situated several doors east of the Mendocino Hotel, it rivaled that establishment, offering spacious and sunny rooms, first-rate food, and retail liquor sales. It was demolished in 1923, but the word BAR engraved in the cement sidewalk on Main Street still shows where it was located.

The Donoho Family

The following is quoted from a letter Ray Preston Donoho wrote to Dorothy Bear, dated March 9, 1974. The Dr. Preston mentioned was Dr. Russell W. Preston (1879-1954), well-loved by the community he served for many years and especially remembered for his tireless care during 1918's terrible influenza epidemic. He lived in several homes, but is best known for the Denslow–Morgan–Preston mansion where scenes from *East of Eden* were filmed and where the Art Center now stands. He willed this property to the Presbyterian Church. With its sale, Preston Hall was built and dedicated to him in 1957.

"My middle name is Preston, named after Dr. Preston of Mendocino, who saved my life. When I was first born, my mother's milk, goat or cow milk and formulas did not agree with me. I was slowly dying till Dr. Preston told my father there was an Italian lady in Fort Bragg that just had a baby and had plenty of milk. As a last resort he could go and see if she would come to the ranch and see if her milk would work. Well he jumped in the buggy, drove that horse like mad to Fort Bragg, to see Mrs. Pedrotti. Her husband gave her permission to return with him to the ranch (well, I guess it agreed with me because I am here). I was so near gone I could not leave the ranch house, that is why she had to come to the ranch with her baby, and stay till I got well."

In November 1934, Peter R. Donoho donated a whole veal to the Father and Son Banquet held at the Foresters Hall (old Odd Fellows Hall).

In the August 23, 1957 *Mendocino Beacon*, Editor-Owner, August Heeser, wrote about the passing of Pete R. Donoho, a man who—despite many adversities in his early life—always remained a positive force in his community:

"He was a good neighbor [and] stood many losses from unpaid bills [but] a family with a shortage of funds was never denied milk. . . . His experience with stock made him an excellent veterinarian and he would answer any call, day or night to attend to ailing horses and cattle."

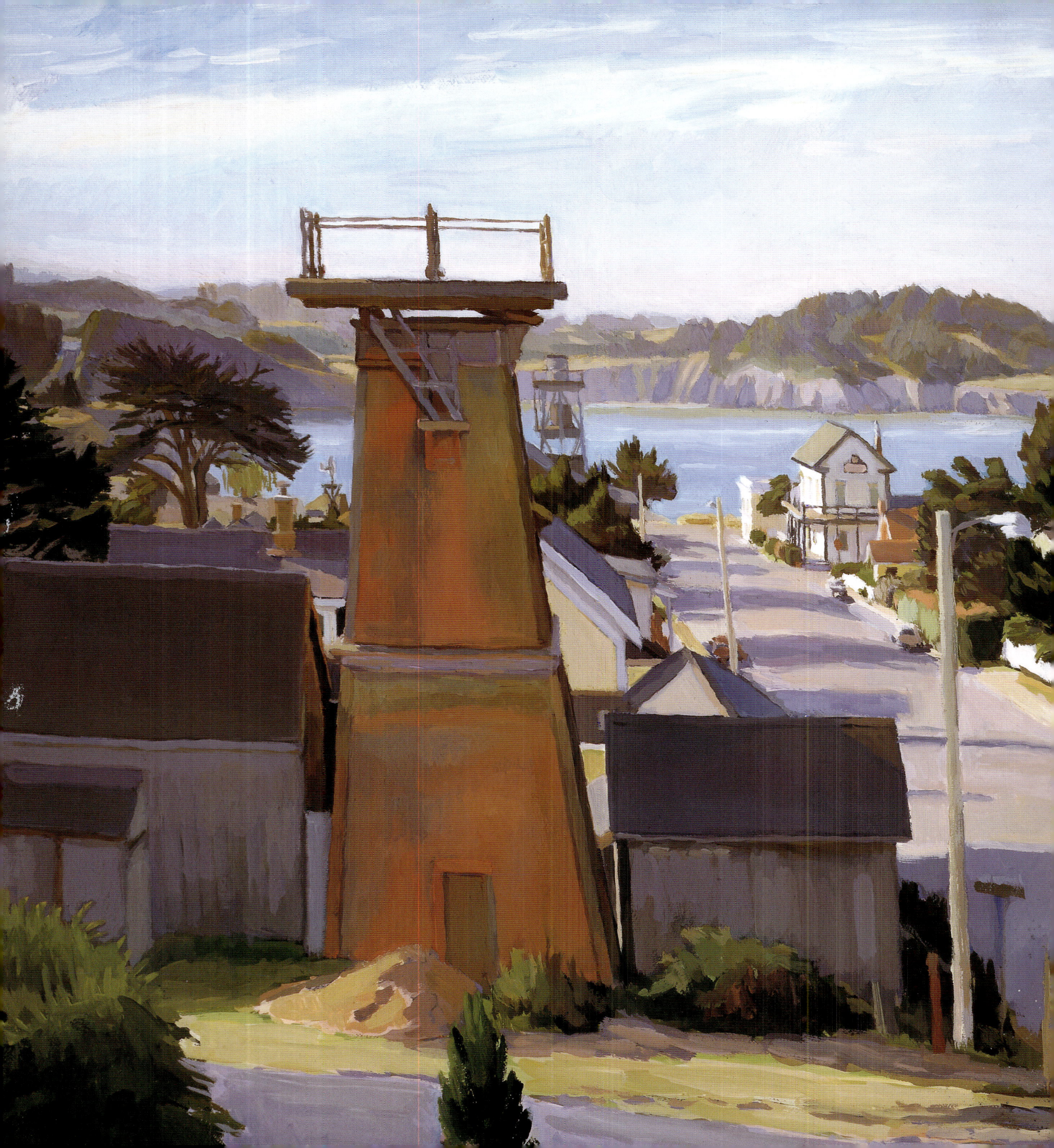

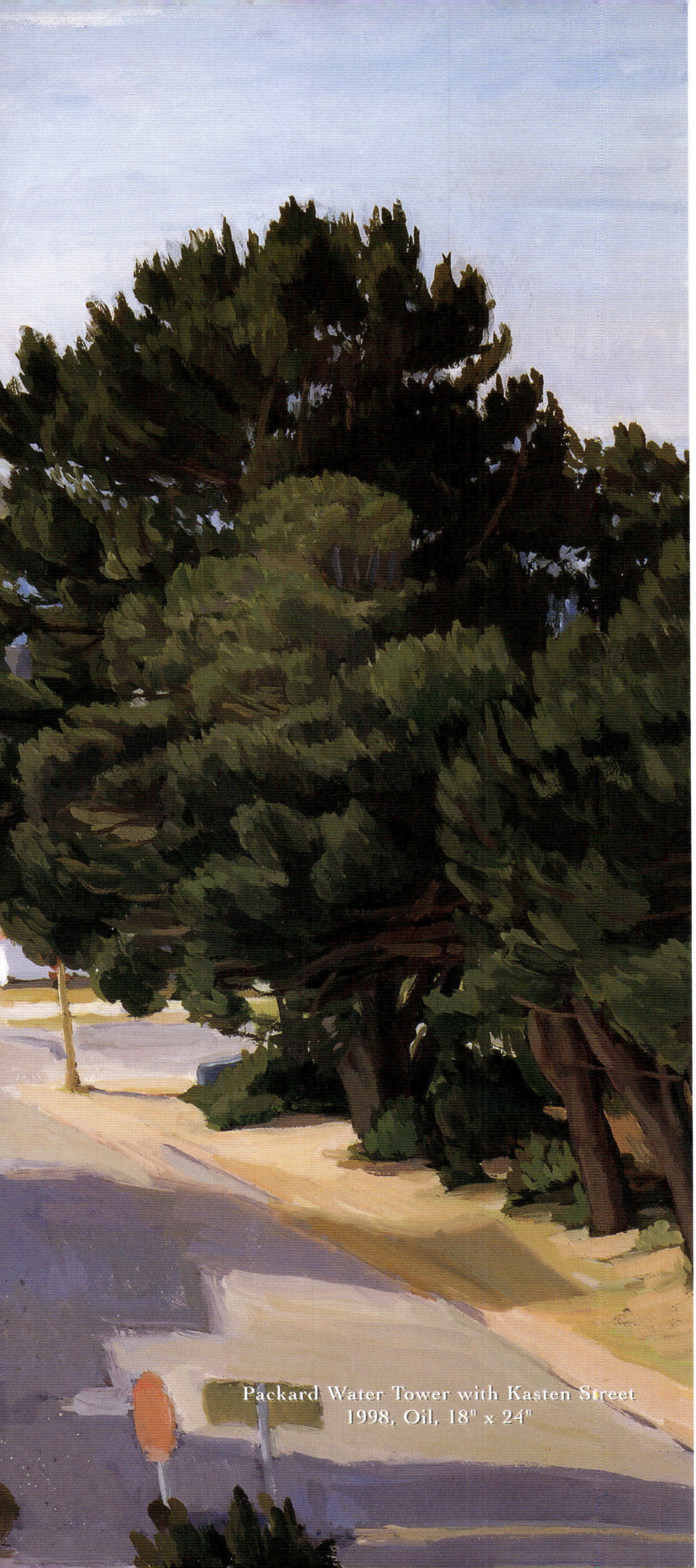
Packard Water Tower with Kasten Street
1998, Oil, 18" x 24"

Water Towers

In the early 1900s, Dorothy Morrison, granddaughter of druggist Charles O. Packard, spent part of her childhood living with her grandparents in their stately home on the corner of Little Lake and Kasten Streets. In an August 2000 conversation at age 93, she recalled those times:

> *I wish that I had never left Mendocino. They were the happiest days of my life. . . . We had a cow, chickens and a potato patch in our backyard. A weekly favorite was going to get candy down at my grandfather's drug store on Main Street.*

The water tower is the signature structure of Mendocino Transplanted New Englanders took the same pride in the style of their three-to-four-story water towers as they did with their homes. Most of the towers were built in the 1800s with tapered sides to help support a heavy water tank on the top level known as the tank deck. These uppermost areas could be used as viewing points and were often railed or paneled for protection, decoration, or sometimes to disguise the tanks. Many others had additional storage tanks on second and even third-story platforms. Sometimes these were located inside enclosed towers. Each water tower marked the site of a well. Windmills located on the top story drew water out of the ground to the tanks above, from which it flowed downward into homes for use. Gravity flow produced about 15 lbs. per square inch of water pressure for a tower 30 feet high. The ratio was half-a-pound per square inch after a certain height was attained.

Two of the most interesting and elaborate water towers were at the Kelly House and at the Blair House. Both were enclosed with siding and painted. Both had storage tanks inside with an exposed tank and a windmill on top. The four-story Kelly tower had a lower floor with arched supports large enough for a horse and carriage to pull underneath during stormy weather. The Blair House tower was an unusual three-story structure with the top two floors displaying a tapered eight-sided design atop a square, windowed ground story. These two structures were quite stylish but, unfortunately, they are gone. The Kelly blew down in 1886 and was not rebuilt. To the southeast of the house, a large stilt-style tower served the Kelly-MacCallum Store on the corner of Lansing and Main. Since this structure stands between Kelly's home and store, it appears to have supplied both, and it may be seen there today.

Other examples of the enclosed style are the MacCallum, Packard, Lansing, Hegenmeyer and Carlson tankhouses, each still standing. Only the bottom story is left of the once five-story, 60-foot Hegenmeyer tower. The oldest remaining water tower in town, the Carlson, leans severely with a steel support brace added in 1999. The Lansing Tower also leaned steeply that year due to major structural damage, which resulted in its being condemned. It was restored in 2001 with the tank returned to the top, but not the window. The C. O. Packard tower no longer is painted to match the home and is used for storage. Since the MacCallum House was moved down to Albion Street, its tankhouse stands beside the Baptist Church, about 40 feet to the west. Painted the yellow of the MacCallum House Inn, the tower's bay window on the south side gives a lovely view to Inn guests who stay in this unit.

Several of the enclosed towers had windows and some even had gingerbread trim. But more common were towers

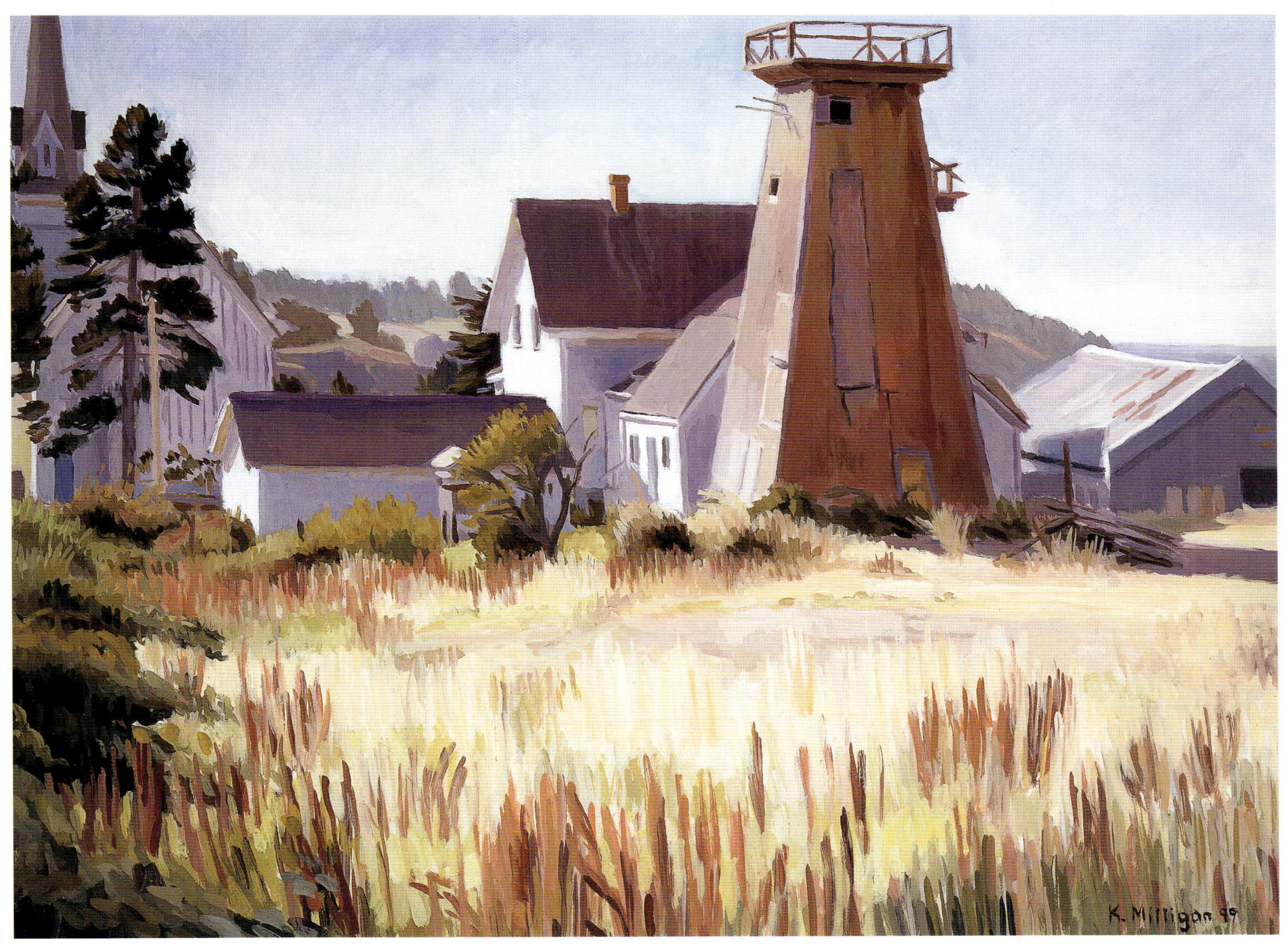

Captain David Lansing House and Water Tower 1999, Oil, 14" x 18"
In the collection of Russ Christoff and Genie O'Toole; Antioch, California

constructed of large timbers left exposed in an open or stilt style.

Unfortunately, the most notable characteristics of the towers were often their downfall. Many wooden structures were lost to fire and weathering, although redwood holds up to the elements quite well. The aspects that made water towers most useful, their height and ability to catch the wind, also made them vulnerable. Harsh storms and violent gusts ripped away windmill blades, siding and whole tank platforms. Many times the tanks and towers simply collapsed against the battering gales. Just before Christmas in 1892, a record storm—the *Beacon* called it "a perfect hurricane" with "torrents" of rain—took out a dozen windmills and parts of towers, including those belonging to the Jarvis and Nichols store, the Lisbon House, Manuel Ramus, J. D. Johnson, L. A. Morgan and the widows Blair and Maxwell. Surprisingly, a full tank was good for stability and made it more likely that towers would survive the windy conditions common on the peninsula.

For more than half a century water towers and windmills were essential to everyday life, but as gasoline engines and electric pumps took over their chores, the space where they stood could be used to expand homes and businesses. Most towers were neglected and ultimately lost to the elements or a need for easily harvested building materials.

However, some survived well into the 20th century when renovation was necessary in order to keep the last of them standing. Barry Cusick, who came to Mendocino in 1974, has rebuilt three of the town's notable water towers, including the one that forms a stairway for the Bay View Café. This was originally Frank Mendosa's tower on Lansing Street. Cusick's second renovated tower housed the Wind & Weather shop on Albion Street. He also built a new tower next to the site of a former 1800s tankhouse. This tower, located at Pine and Evergreen Street, has a working tank and windmill on the top. It is also used for a living accommodation.

The skyline of Mendocino was once filled with these structures, and it echoed with their voices, as noted by visiting journalist Ninetta Eames in an *Overland Monthly* account of 1892:

> *Viewed from a distance on shore or at sea (Mendocino City) seems to have an imposing array of cupolas, which are in reality water tanks, with windmills of every known pattern. There is in fact individuality about the water works of this town not found in any other place of its size.*
>
> *Every family or group of families has its separate well and windmill, thus obviating the necessity of a general source of water supply. One sees windmills painted in red, white, or blue, or dark shades of maroon and yellow, and still others so ancient and wind tortured that their distinctive color can only be guessed.*
>
> *When the wind blows, and there is rarely a day here it does not, these diverse windmills set up a medley of discordant creaks and groans, each pitched in a different key, and whether heard singly or collectively, all equally nerve-rending. It is presumable that one could get used to the constant slapping, straining, and screeching, for nowhere are there people more serene, healthy, and home-loving than in this breezy town of Mendocino.*

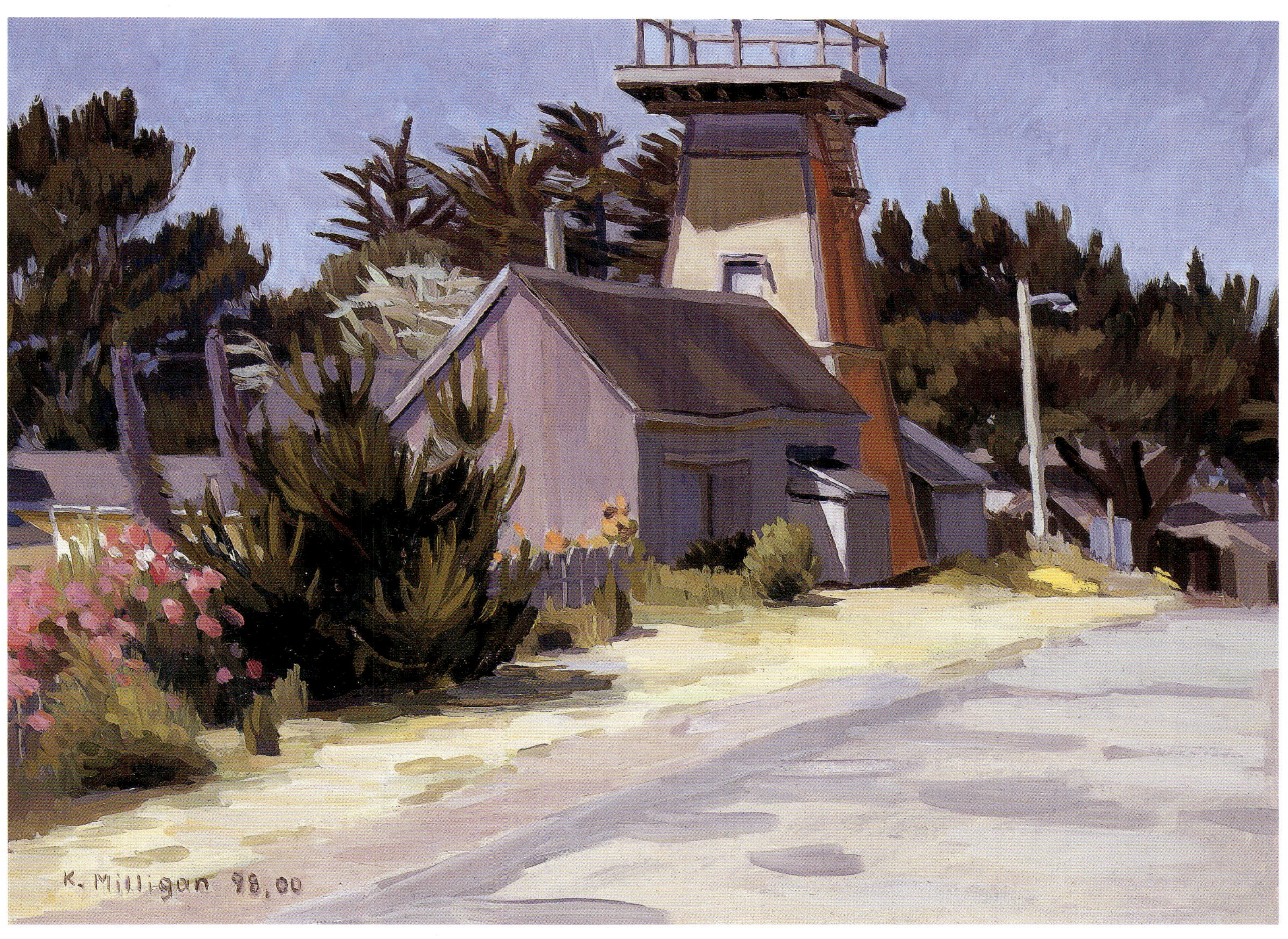

Packard Water Tower from Covelo Street 1998–2000, Oil, 14" x 18"
In the collection of Chris and Connie Gordon; Diamond Springs, California

C. O. Packard came to town with his brother Justin E. Packard. Together they bought out the Witherell Drug and Jewelry Store on Main Street. C. O. became the druggist; J. E. handled the jewelry and watch-making. His home was on the east end of Main Street next to the cemetery. Nearby Evergreen Street was once called Packard Ave. after him. It led to the Soda Bottling Works, in which he was a partner with L. H. Bither. J. E. had some unhappy times, including two divorces and the death of his young son, who drowned in the family's water trough. He left town around 1891. His first wife was Zella Young, sister of Eliza Young Tobin Grindle, whose daughter Elsie Tobin married Perley Maxwell. Justin's second wife, Cora, was the sister of his partner L. H. Bither. J. E. married again after leaving Mendocino.

Paddleford–Peirsol–Fraga House's Water Tower and the Peirsol Family

In 1904 Dr. Frank C. Peirsol and his wife Edith bought the Paddleford House *"on Calpella Street three doors east of the Beggs home on the west corner."* Before that, they lived above Bert Stone's jewelry store on the south side of western Main, and it was there their first son, James, was born in 1898. In *My Boyhood in Mendocino,* James reveals yet another interesting advantage of water towers:

> *If Don Quixote could have waited until the beginning of the twentieth century to start out on his windmill tilting crusades, he would have found enough windmills in Mendocino to keep him jousting for a lifetime. Since there was no central water plant, almost every home had its own well, windmill, and tankhouse. It was those tankhouses some of them three stories high, which provided the necessary water pressure, and it was tankhouses, particularly those where the third story room could only be reached by a steep, ladder-like stairway outside the building, which provided young boys areas of safety their mothers could not reach.*
>
> *It was there that they stashed away their Bicycle Playing Cards; and it was there that they would go to play casino, pinochle, rummy, hearts, and sometimes even poker. They were forced to seek the safety of those tankhouse hide-aways because playing cards were sinful and were not allowed in better homes in Mendocino. Parents were very adamant about the evils inherent in a deck of Bicycle Playing Cards. Such things were "tools of the devil" and were only used by gamblers, loafers, cardsharps, and fast women. So, in better homes in Mendocino, you found "Lobby" decks. "Lobby" playing cards used the numbers 11, 12, and 13 in place of the Jack, Queen, and King. With them you could enjoy any game played by the gamblers, loafers, cardsharps, and fast women but because you were playing with "Lobby" cards you would still go to heaven when you died. Being young and sinful, we preferred the evil thrill of Bicycle Playing Cards with their attendant risk of eternal damnation, and those third story tankhouse bastions were ideal places to pursue our sinful vice. They were also excellent places in which to practice the art of cigarette smoking. There was a time when only a mother knew what was going on up there, and she was afraid to climb the outside stairway to prove it.*
>
> *After the 1906 earthquake, our tankhouse had to be rebuilt. When it was remodeled, a new more easily negotiated stairway was installed to the third floor. At last even my mother could climb it. An impenetrable hide-away was lost forever.*

Later that same year, Dr. Peirsol bought a house in the same block on Covelo and added on to it, providing accommodation for his family in the west wing and an eight-bed hospital in the east wing with the kitchen in between. In 1912, when the Fort Bragg Hospital opened, Peirsol closed his facility and moved his family to the McCornack House on Main Street. The house is nicknamed the "House of Doctors" because it was built by Dr. McCornack (in 1882), and three other doctors lived in the house: Dr. James Milliken, Dr. Roy Moore and Dr. Frank Peirsol—father of James, Madge, Clayton and little Edith. James grew up to be a newspaperman, and it was his sister Madge who became a second-generation physician. In March 2000, 100-year-old Madge Peirsol, M.D., returned to Mendocino for a visit. She recalled the years she and her family spent in the town, remembering how she *"played cards with my brothers in the yellow water tower (where) we were able to escape parental supervision."* She also revealed, *"While living on Main Street, I took my mother's diamond ring out of her apron pocket and scratched my name in a bedroom window upstairs. . . . I did not get in trouble for doing it."* Her name *Madge*, written in cursive, may still be seen etched in the second-story back window of the McCornack House.

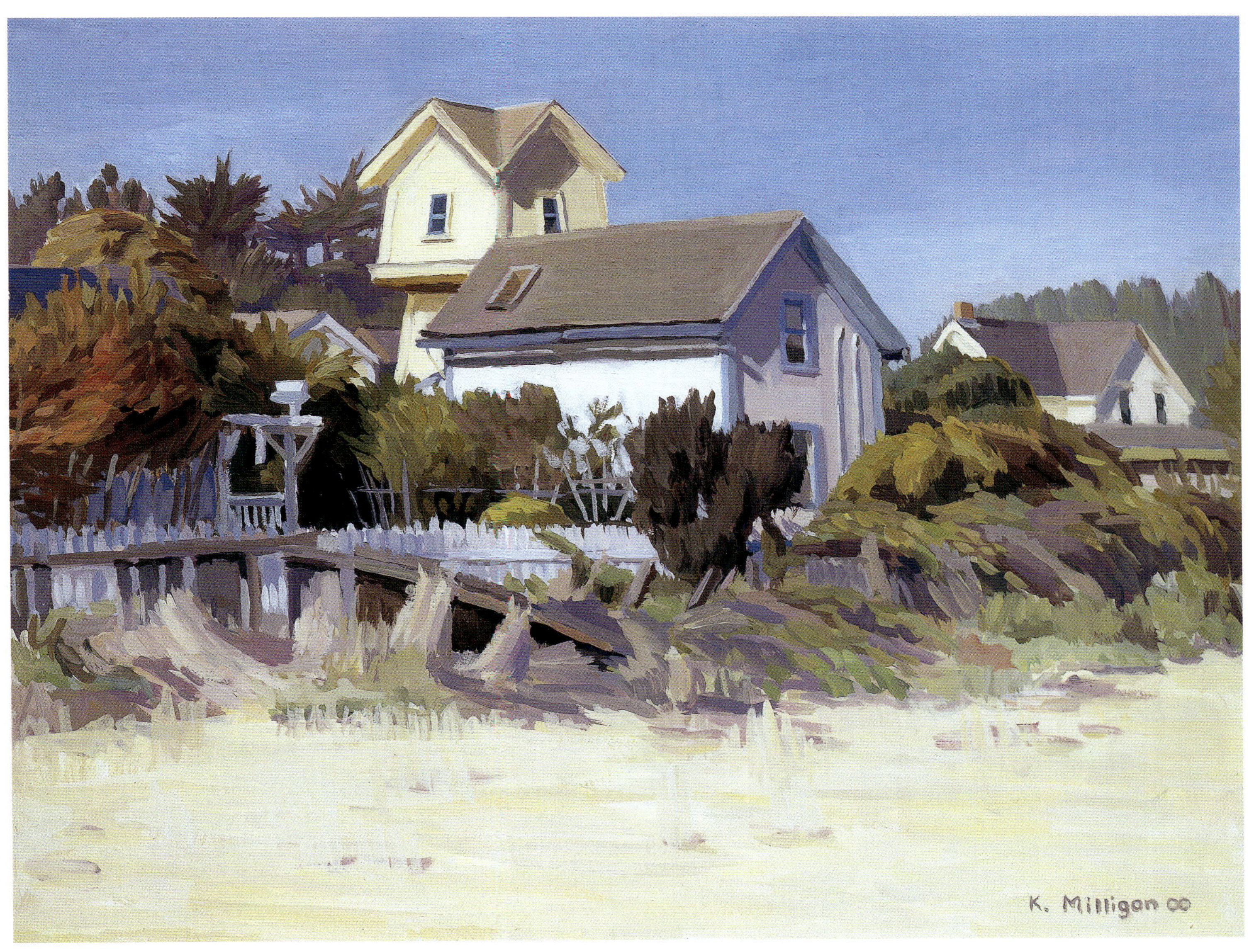

Paddleford–Fraga House and Water Tower 2000, Oil, 14" x 18"
In the collection of Bryan and Kara Uegawachi; Aurora, Colorado

Benjamin Almon Paddleford was one of the earliest settlers and served as Mill Foreman for 20–25 years. Later he ran a hardware and plumbing business. He and his family were very active in the town's social societies—his wife was Mary Jane Walsh. They had two sons, and their daughter Nettie May married Horace Nichols, who bought C. O. Packard's drugstore in 1917. The Peirsols lived in the Paddleford House 1904–1906 but must have retained ownership after they moved to Covelo Street and then Main, because an heir, Alice Peirsol, sold the home to Fernando and Elise Fraga in 1923. The Fragas moved from their smaller house on Ukiah Street, probably to gain space for their seven children. Fernando gave fifty years of service to the Mendocino Volunteer Fire Department.

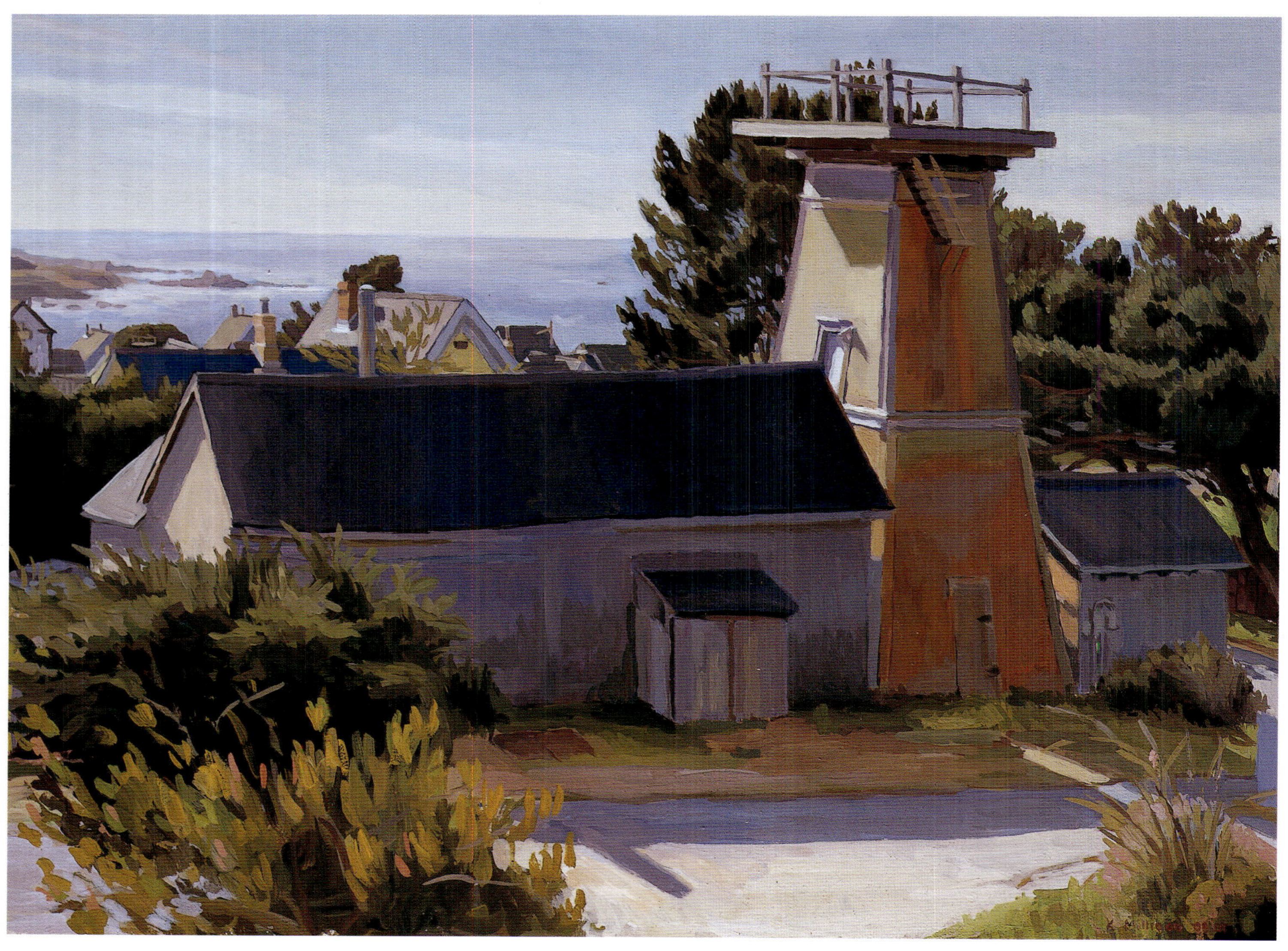

Packard Water Tower 2000-01, Oil, 18" x 24"
In the collection of Andrew Hindman and Damien Wood; San Francisco, California

Druggist Charles O. Packard was also a founding vice president of the Mendocino Debating Society (1878), a founding director of the Mendocino Electric Light & Power Co (1896), founding member and treasurer of the Mendocino City Game Protective Society (1901), elected treasurer of the fire department (1903), and sat on the Board of Trustees for the Grammar School at the time of a bond election in 1907. He also had the distinction of being the first person arrested for violating Mendocino's Dry Law in 1909. At arraignment, he said, *"I do not deny selling the liquor but do deny violating* the law." Ultimately, the trial ended in a hung jury unable to answer the question: *"Was the 50¢ flask of whiskey purchased by Percy Daniels a whiskey or a drug?"*

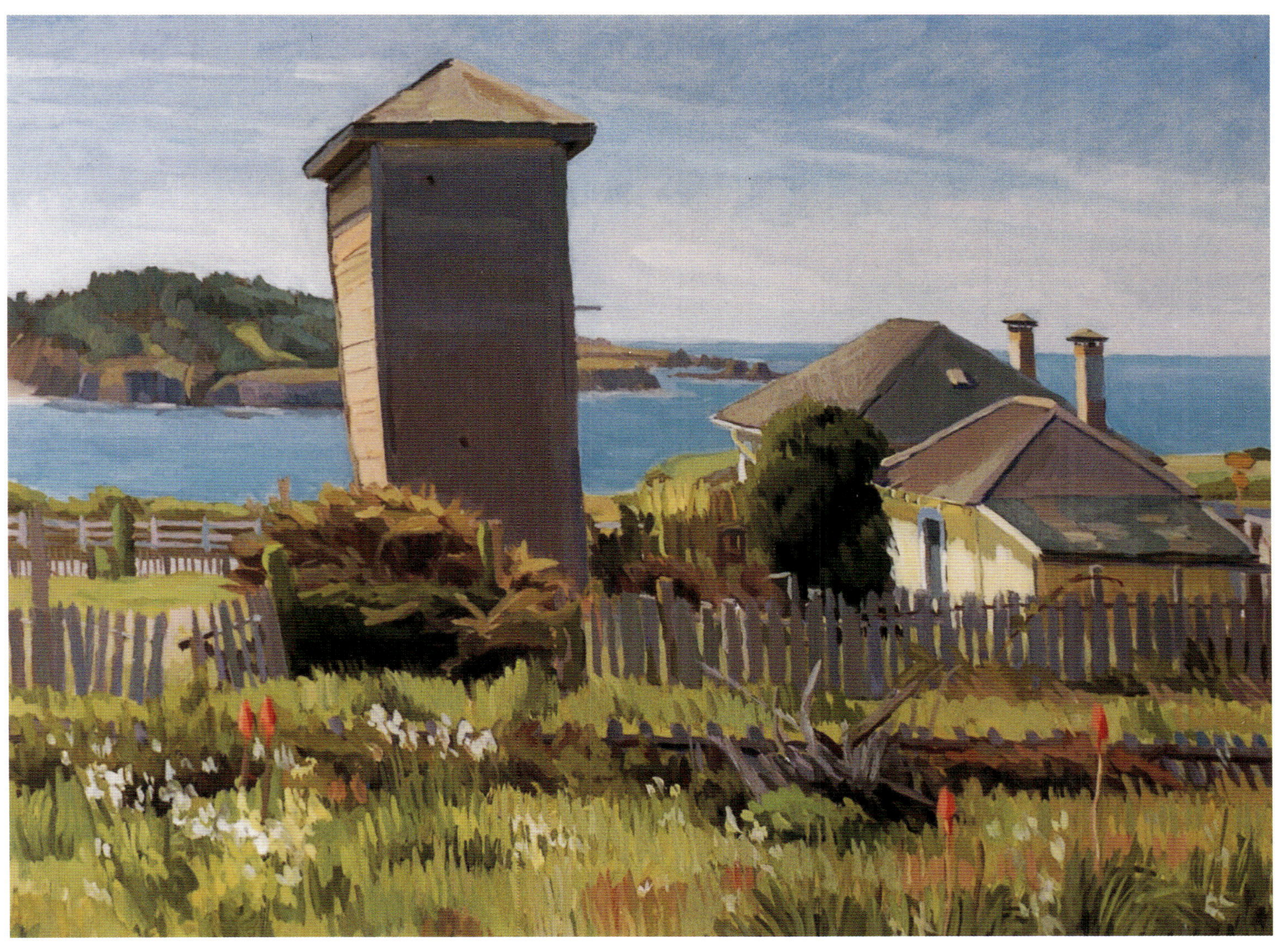

Carlson's City Hotel Water Tower 1999, Oil, 14" x 18"
In the collection of Jeffery Combs and Alice Cadogan; Oak Park, California

Carlson's City Hotel & Water Tower

The original City Hotel was built in 1858 by J. E. Carlson, one of Mendocino's founders, but was destroyed in 1870 by fire along with 24 other buildings including its neighbor, Silas Osborn's hotel, saloon and stables across Osborn Street. Carlson rebuilt his City Hotel larger and more luxurious than before. Its three-story splendor with a wide, railed balcony porch around the second floor, was an impressive first glimpse of the town for passengers arriving by ship.

This water tower—the oldest still standing in Mendocino—was built in 1875. A steel brace had to be added in 1999 to support the historic structure and keep it from falling and being lost.

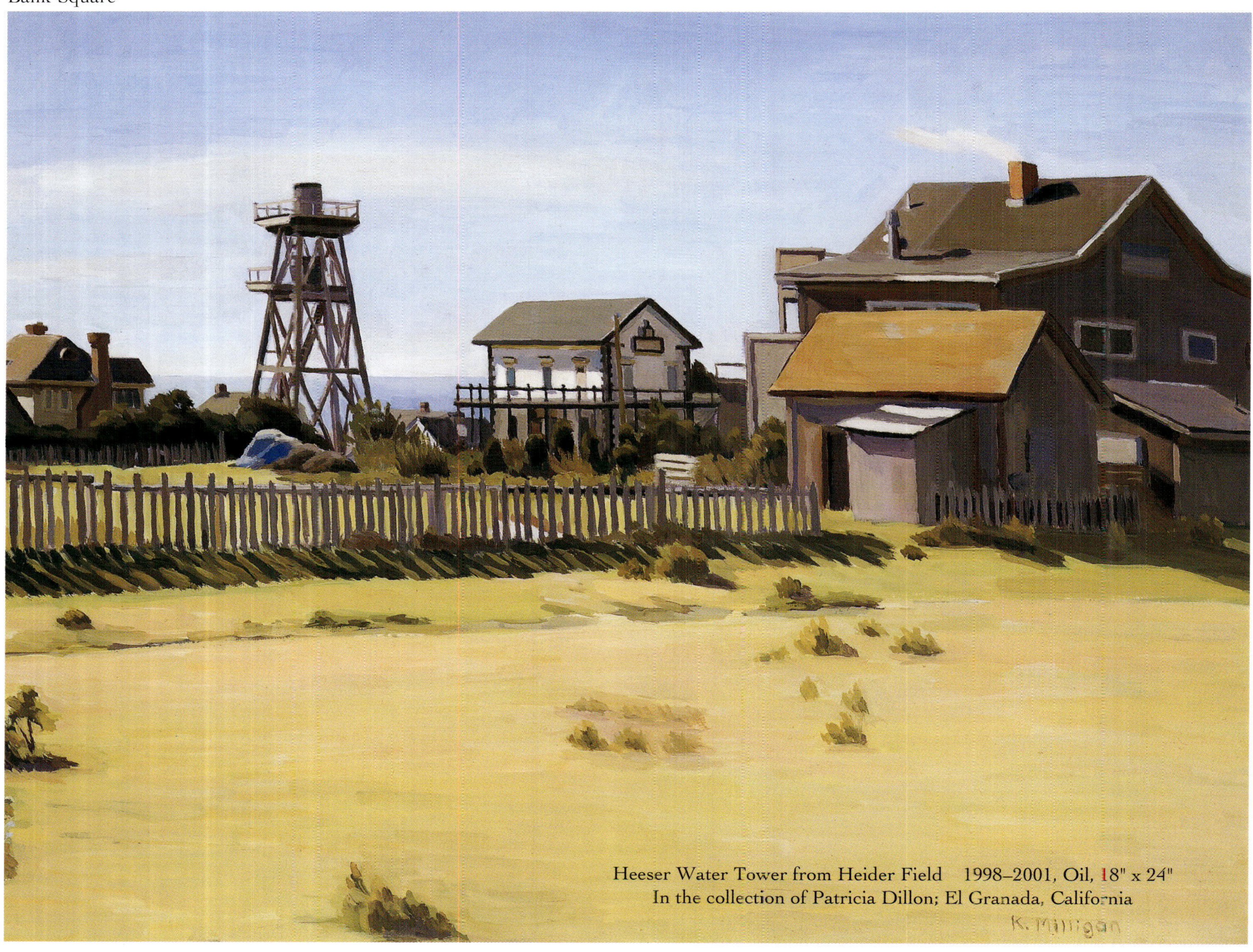

Heeser Water Tower from Heider Field 1998–2001, Oil, 18" x 24"
In the collection of Patricia Dillon; El Granada, California

In 1894 an Odd Fellows Hall was constructed on the southwest corner of the field known as Bank Square. In 1912 Auggie Heeser donated land on the northwest corner where the picturesque Apple Hall was built to house annual exhibits, dances and speeches sponsored by the Farmers' and Apple Growers' Association. Both buildings were replaced. The remaining 1.18 acre piece of open field narrowly avoided development. As a result of 12 years of meetings, a generous gift from John Heider, a State Assembly Bill and a complicated land swap and General Plan amendment, it is now officially Heider Field—part of Mendocino Headlands State Park. It was also the catalyst for the creation of the Mendocino Land Trust, which since 1976 has enjoyed numerous successes in conserving properties, including most recently the purchase and preservation of the Big River Estuary.

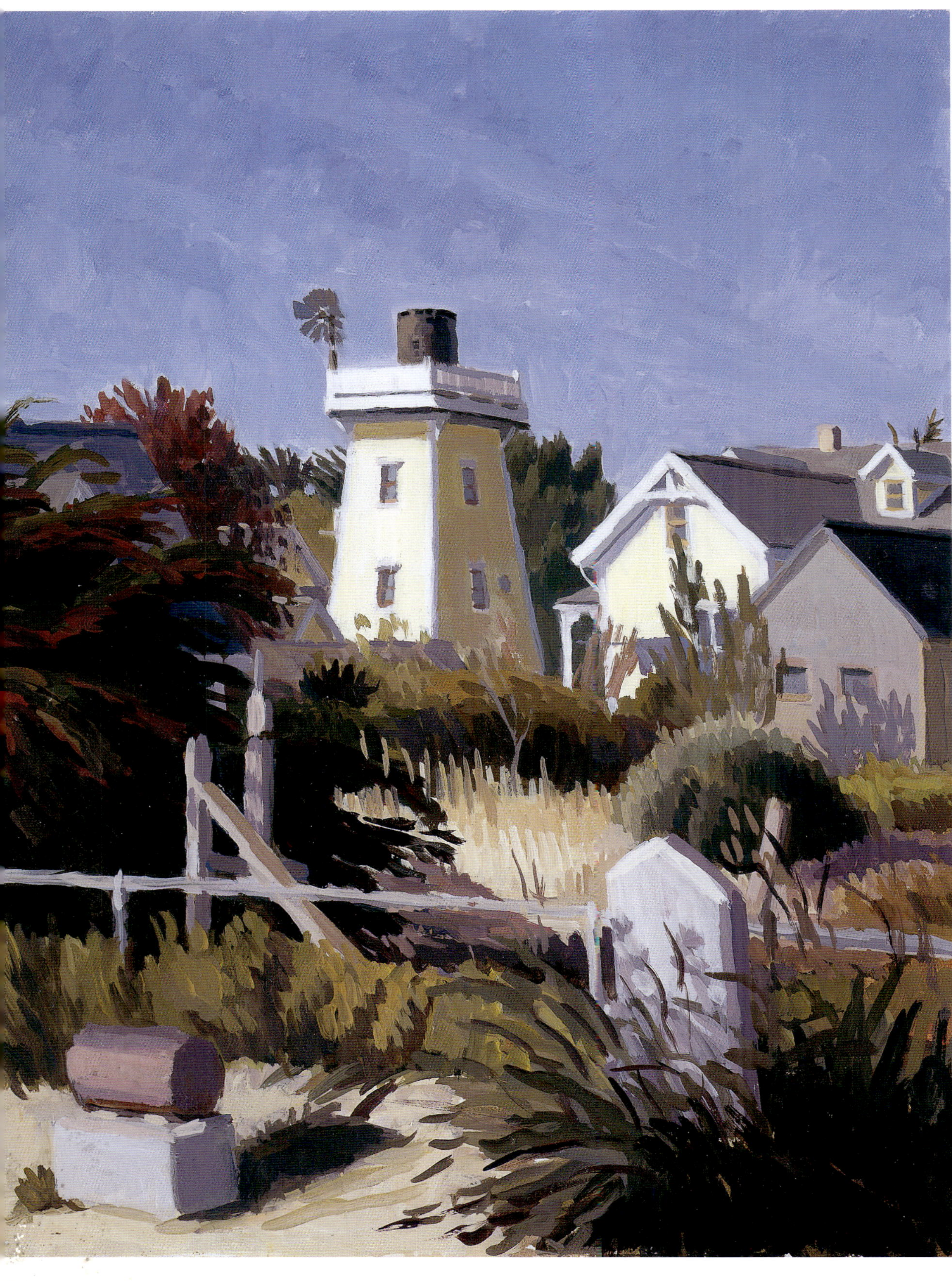

This water tower was built by its current owner Barry Cusick in 1988, replacing an older tankhouse. He also helped rebuild or restore water towers on both Main and Albion Streets. When Barry's son Brendan Cusick was 15, he and fellow classmate Susan Spring created an award-winning high school history project "Mendocino Water Storage and Movement," which featured not only text and photos, but also a working scale model of a water tower, windmill and storage tank.

Cusick Water Tower with Headstones
1999, Oil, 18" x 14"
In the collection of Edward Reagan and Tom Schrader; Southlake, Texas

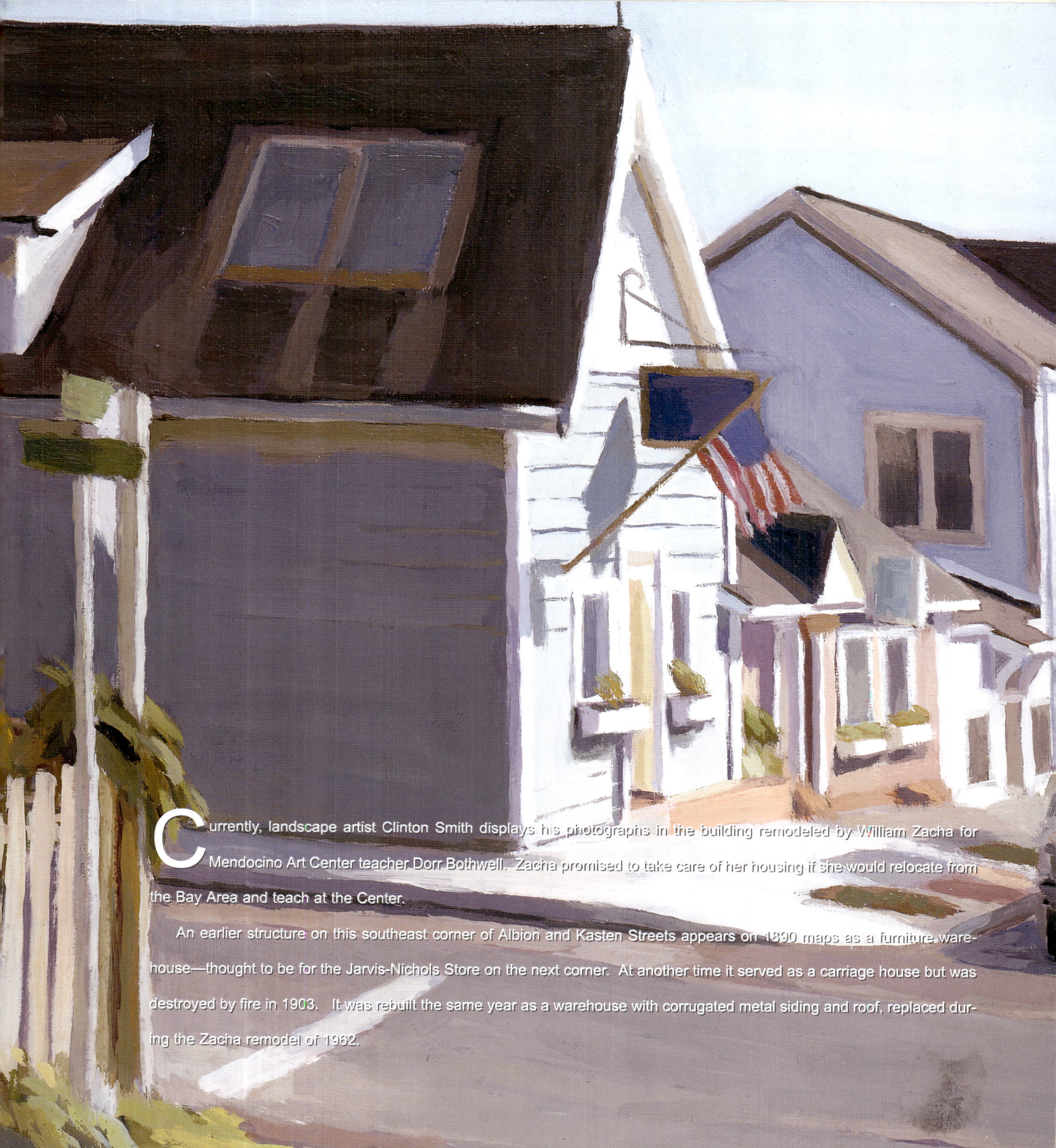

Currently, landscape artist Clinton Smith displays his photographs in the building remodeled by William Zacha for Mendocino Art Center teacher Dorr Bothwell. Zacha promised to take care of her housing if she would relocate from the Bay Area and teach at the Center.

An earlier structure on this southeast corner of Albion and Kasten Streets appears on 1890 maps as a furniture warehouse—thought to be for the Jarvis-Nichols Store on the next corner. At another time it served as a carriage house but was destroyed by fire in 1903. It was rebuilt the same year as a warehouse with corrugated metal siding and roof, replaced during the Zacha remodel of 1962.

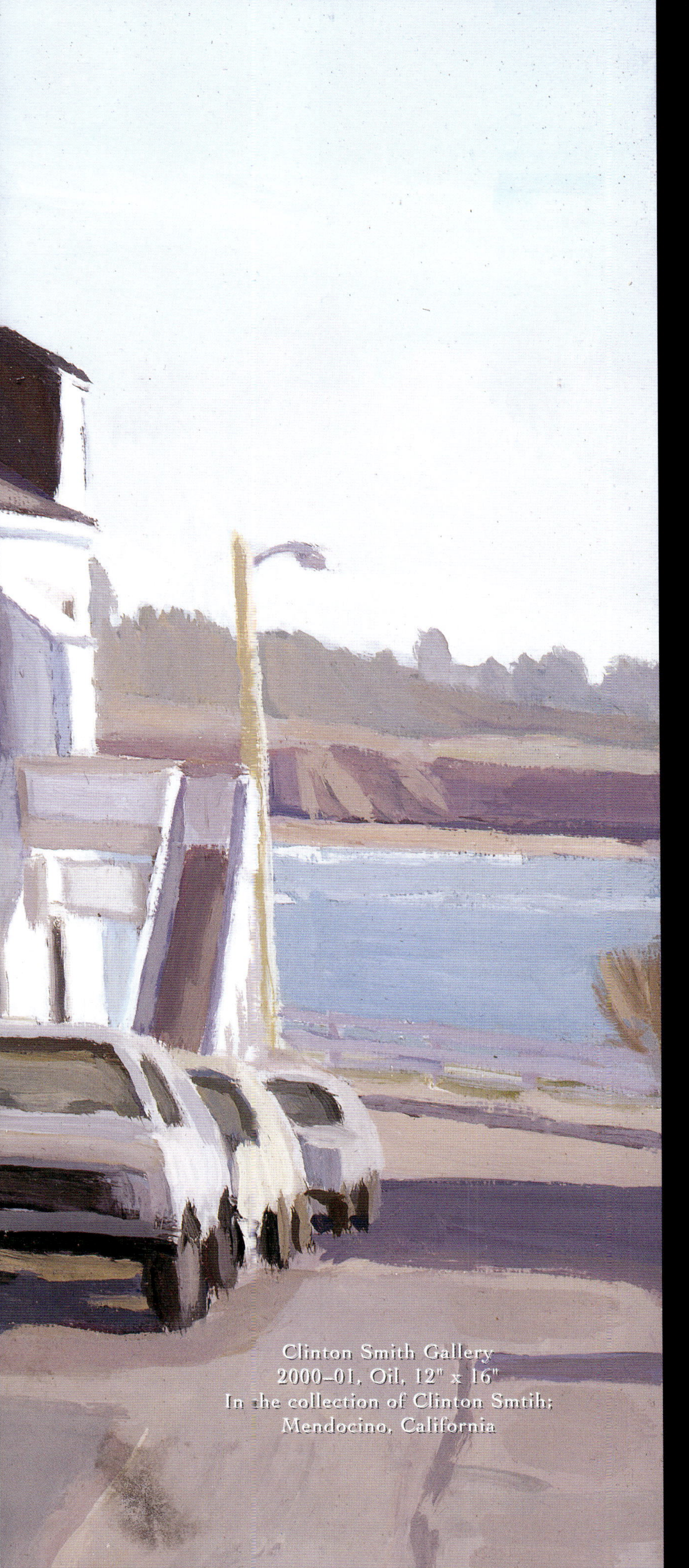
Clinton Smith Gallery
2000–01, Oil, 12" x 16"
In the collection of Clinton Smtih;
Mendocino, California

An Artist's Community

Writers and historians often refer to the two decades in the middle of the 20th century, between the mill's closing and the town's rebirth, as a time of slumber for Mendocino City; it seems an apt image. The Depression hit especially hard, and when economic recovery began elsewhere after World War II, Mendocino was too isolated and rural to benefit. Jobs were hard to find in town. In order to work in the timber industry, men had to go inland or north to Fort Bragg. Many young adults left for areas with better opportunities. The town languished, and many despaired. But that strong and independent spirit of Mendocino did not flicker out; rather it was like banked embers, waiting for a spark and proper fuel to rekindle it.

Then in the late 1950s—just over 100 years after the town was founded—the next wave of settlers began to arrive. William and Jennie Zacha, among the first and most

Bill and Jennie's daughter, Lucia Zacha, remembers, *"I grew up at the Art Center—climbing all the trees and up in the rafters, sneaking in the back door before I was ten to look into the Rhododendron Ball and watch the grownups dancing."* (This formal-dress, fund-raising event was a highlight each spring for some 20 years but became sporadic and then seldom occurred. Now, due to Lucia's fond memories and informed efforts, The Rhododendron Ball is again an annual event, beginning in 2001. For information about the Art Center, see *www.mendocinoartcenter.org*). Lucia continued:

> *I didn't rebel against my parents. It seemed more interesting to do what my dad thought up. They afforded me great opportunities to travel and try so many new things.*

Years before coming to Mendocino, Bill went to visit an ill aunt and, attempting to cheer her, showed her a drawing of his cabin on Mount Tamalpais. She told him to plant a rosebush beside it, saying, *"Your life is to be like a rosebush with lots of blossoms, and enough thorns to make you careful."* She died the next day. The event had such an effect on him that he *did* plant a rosebush next to the cabin. When he moved to Mendocino, he brought the rosebush with him, planting it at his new residence, the Albert Brown House. That rosebush grew well in its new environment, and so did Zacha and the Art Center, an enterprise that has enriched the lives of the hundreds of students, teachers, performers and patrons who have come to take part in Zacha's coastside vision. They would surely agree his life had far more blossoms than thorns.

The impact of these new citizens cannot be overstated. Because of their hard work and vision, countless people came to study or buy the resulting artwork. More visual and performing artists, more craftsmen gravitated to the area and settled. In the "outside world" it was a time of social and political upheaval; people came to find a quieter, cleaner, less stressful environment where they could be themselves and live their values.

Through the late 1960s–70s Mendocino attracted members of the "Counterculture" fleeing the cities looking for peace and love and freedom (not to mention cheap land for those who could swing it). Many of them dressed and spoke flamboyantly; many drank, many took drugs or as panhandlers became a public nuisance. Some were lost souls or mentally ill. Mendocino has long drawn those in search of healing and a new life. Inevitably, there were conflicts with the town's original residents who felt invaded by forces (sometimes negative) that could not be controlled, yet breathed new life and money into the community. Ironically, today some of the most solid citizens were once newcomers called *"beatnik"* and *"hippie"* and *"freak."*

As word got out about the place, it became a popular and fashionable vacation spot. Tourism was born. The wealthy bought up properties and in many cases, restored the town's buildings to a former splendor. Famous musi-

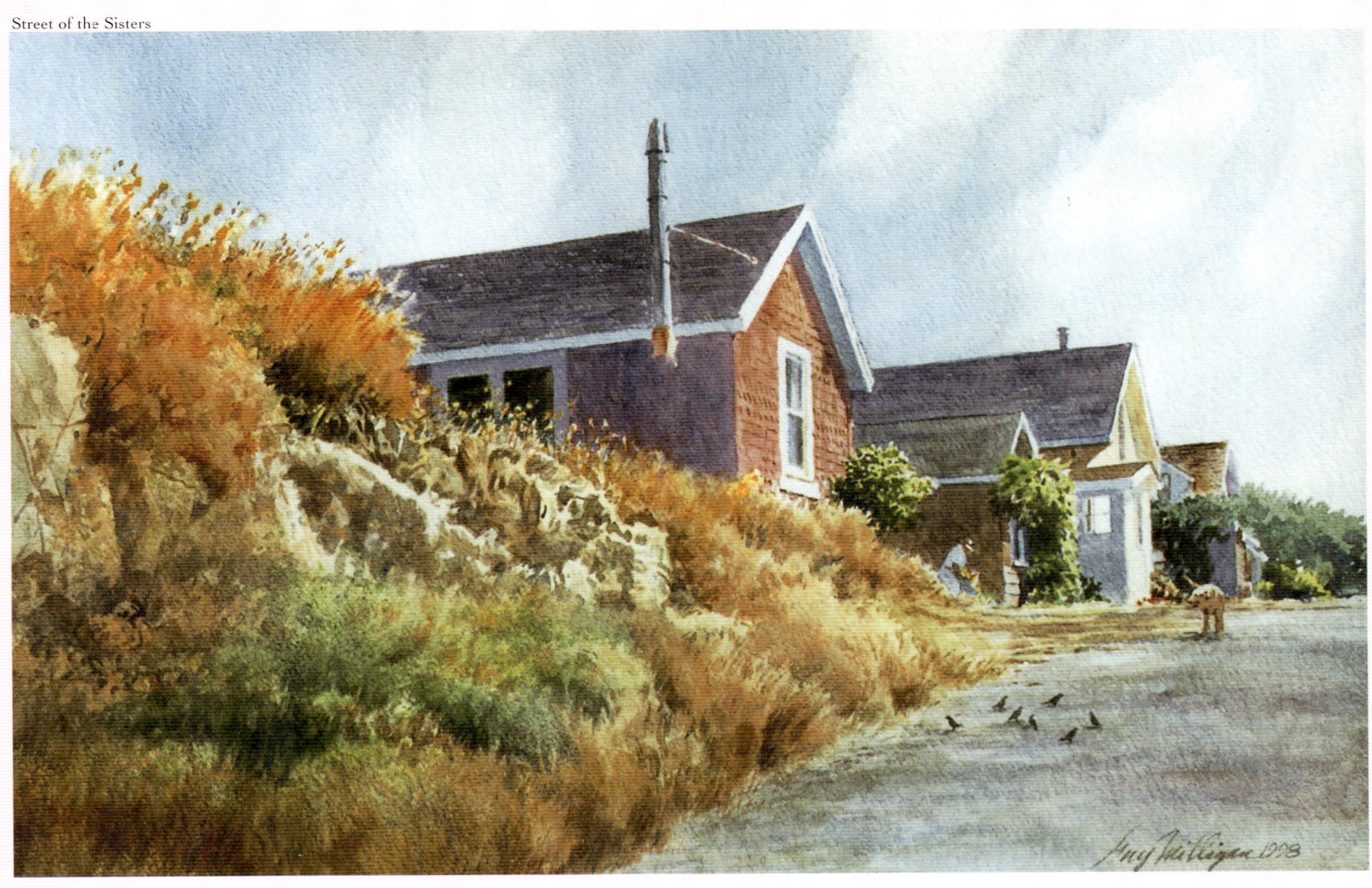

King–Rice House 1998, Water color, 15" x 22"
In the collection of Kevin Milligan; Mendocino, California
By Guy Milligan

For years this small wooden house on the crest of a hill overlooking the Pacific Ocean was the home of artists Ray and Miriam Rice. Mendocino Art Center founder Bill Zacha personally invited the Rices to come teach there, and after returning each year for several summers, they decided to stay and make Mendocino their home. Ray, known for his painting and drawing, passed away at his easel in 2001, but Miriam—famous for her sculpture and books on mushroom dyes used for textiles—still lives in their historic home (the Joseph King House).

Francis "Al" Alfred Nichols (Auggie's cousin by marriage), who inherited the Heeser holdings in 1966.

Beginning in 1969, artist Emmy Lou Packard proved a guiding force in preserving the southern strip of headlands which at the time were owned by the lumber industry. There were plans to build condominiums. By 1972 after much hard work, effort and negotiation, directed largely by Mildred Benioff, this area became part of Mendocino Headlands State Park. In 1971 the town was placed on the National Register of Historic Places. The passing of the Coastal Zoning Conservation Act in 1972 protected the natural environment while preserving both public access and the rights of landowners. Named a Historic Preservation District in 1973, the town now has strict guidelines aimed at protecting and preserving its charm and distinctive character, though these, too, are not without controversy. The Mendocino Land Trust (created in 1976 and having accomplished a number of goals conserving local open spaces) has just succeeded in purchasing Big River, which is the longest undeveloped estuary in Northern California and where the saga of the Mendocino lumber industry began. Currently, the Trust continues to work on numerous other preservation projects *(www.mendocinolandtrust.org)*.

William Zacha passed away in March 1998, but in a 1962 interview for *Look* magazine, he reflected on the pivotal role he played in the rebirth of Mendocino:

> *Towns have souls and needs like other living things. People forget this. When I first saw Mendocino, I became excited. It had an unusual, almost unearthly quality about it—pure, quiet, and unsullied—but it was dying. I knew I could help it, help it get back on its feet and make it a place where people would get simple but profound satisfaction out of living.*

The original residents might argue whether or not the town was dying; old-timers may lament some of the changes, especially the traffic and the strain of tourism on the water table, but we can be thankful it was artists who led the evolution, and that Mendocino continues to be populated by so many people who sincerely care about its past, its present and its future.

Detail Blair House

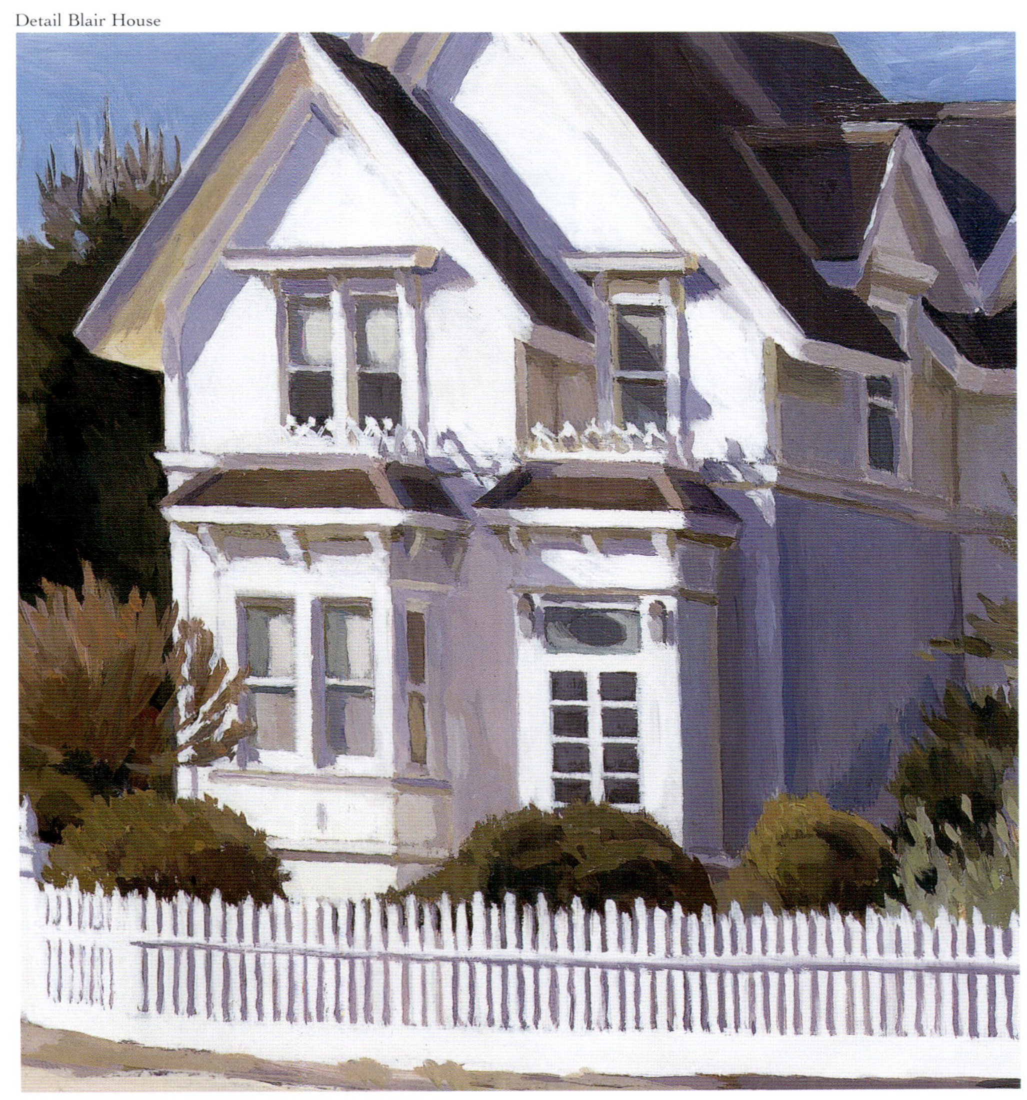

The Blair House, one of many locations to appear in a movie or on TV, "starred" in the *Murder She Wrote* TV series. Some of the better-known productions include:

Johnny Belinda, 1947 – Lew Ayres, Jane Wyman

East of Eden, 1954 – James Dean, Jo Van Fleet, Julie Harris

The Russians are Coming, 1965 – Alan Arkin, Carl Reiner, Eva Marie Saint, Brian Keith, Jonathan Winters

Summer of '42, 1970 – Jennifer O' Neill, Gary Grimes

Dying Young, 1990 – Julia Roberts, Campbell Scott

Strangers: The Story of a Mother and a Daughter, 1979 – Bette Davis, Gena Rowlands

Murder She Wrote, 1984-89 – Angela Lansbury

The Majestic, 2001 – Jim Carrey, Martin Landau

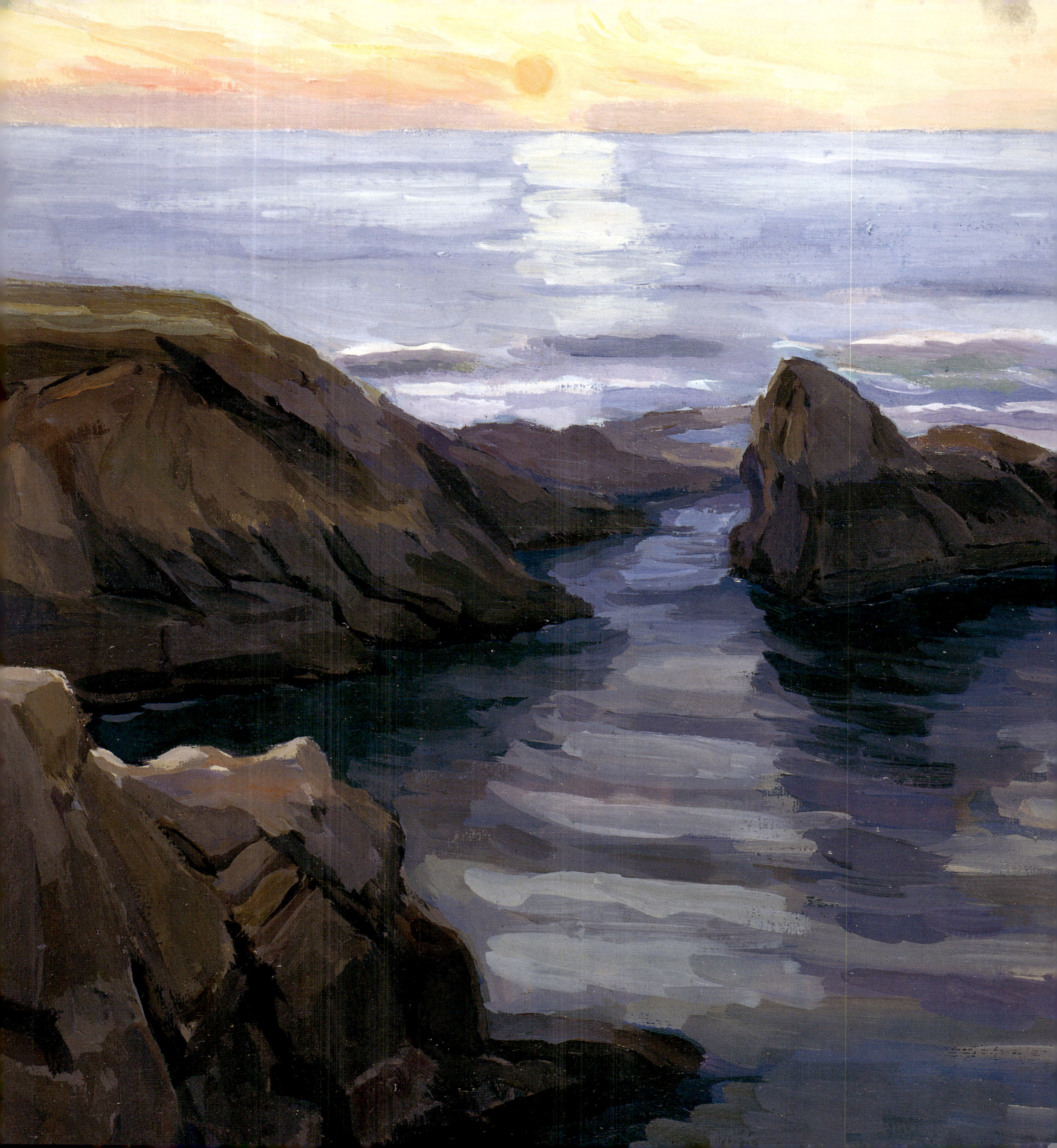

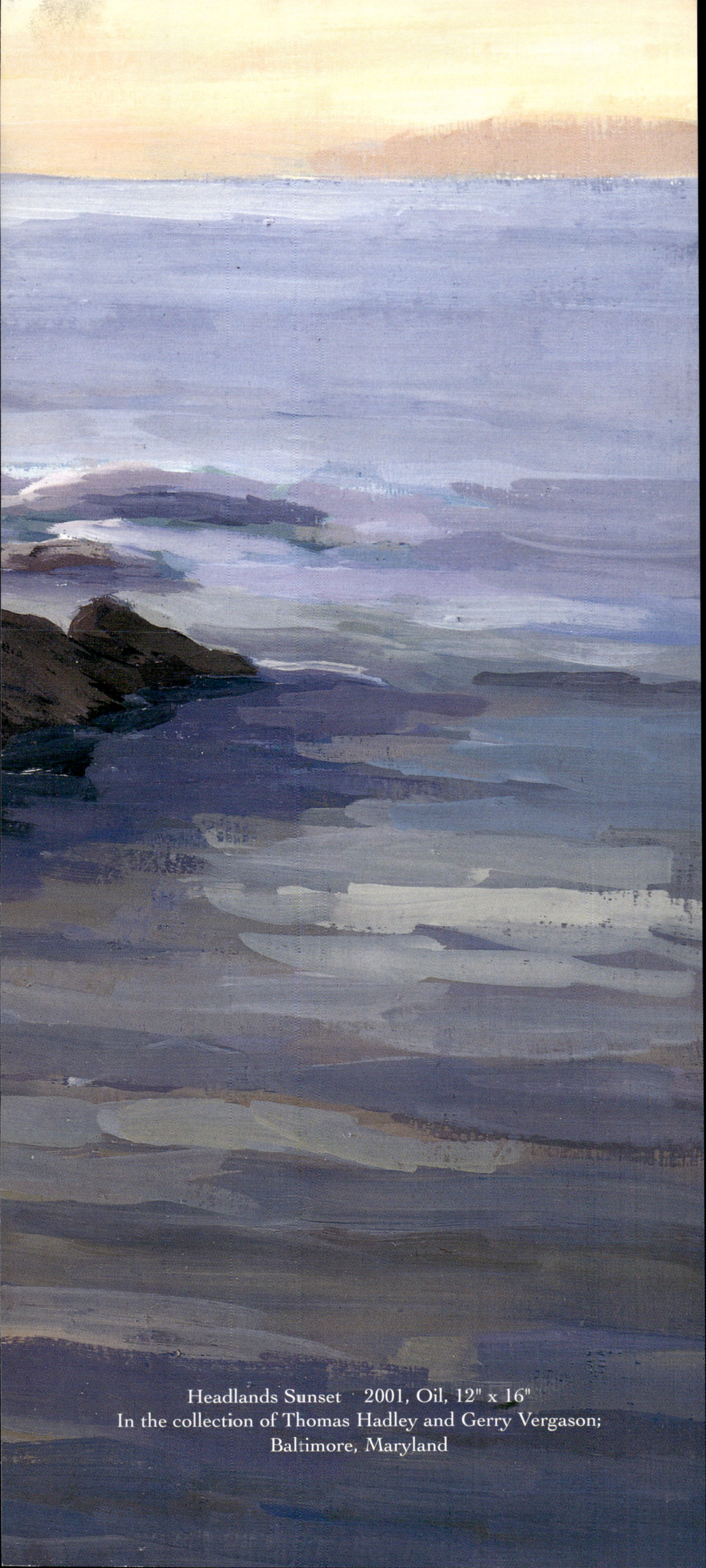

Headlands Sunset 2001, Oil, 12" x 16"
In the collection of Thomas Hadley and Gerry Vergason;
Baltimore, Maryland

The Beginning & The End

by James K . Peirsol

Often, during those early Mendocino days, I'd lie awake at night telling myself long, wonderful stories, which carried me into the farthest corners of the world. Sometimes I'd watch a sunset on the ocean and wish I were out there traveling with that great red ball of fire down the backside of the world. At other times I'd feel the urge to just start heading out for the great unknown—anywhere—it made no difference so long as it took me away from my everyday surroundings. Although I'd never heard it, I could imagine very clearly the sound of the surf on tropical shores—the whisper of the night wind through the palms.

And then, three-quarters of a century later, after having actually experienced many of those youthful dreams, I dozed one evening in my easy chair, and I remembered.

I remembered the log-strewn beach where, on warm summer evenings, the gang would gather for crabbing parties. I remembered the huge bonfires we built and the fresh-caught crabs we tossed into the ten-gallon cans filled with boiling salt water. I remembered the clams we dug in the tidal sands at the river's edge, the abalones we pried from the ocean rocks at low tide and the times I'd gone trolling for salmon very early in the morning on Big River. I remembered the soda springs, and the tree house, and the hollow stump with its secret brush-covered entrance. And I remembered Skinny Anderson, and Benny Scanlon, and Andy Ramos, and Thelma, and Mary Lou and all the others who had shared with me those shining, youthful hours.

And finally, when some slight sound brought me back to reality, I knew for certain that at last I had come full circle in my search for the wonders and the glories that make life really worth living. My memories had taken me home again to Mendocino.

From James K. Peirsol's
My Boyhood in Mendocino, 1905-1917
Mendocino Historical Review
(Volume VII, Number 1) Winter, 1982

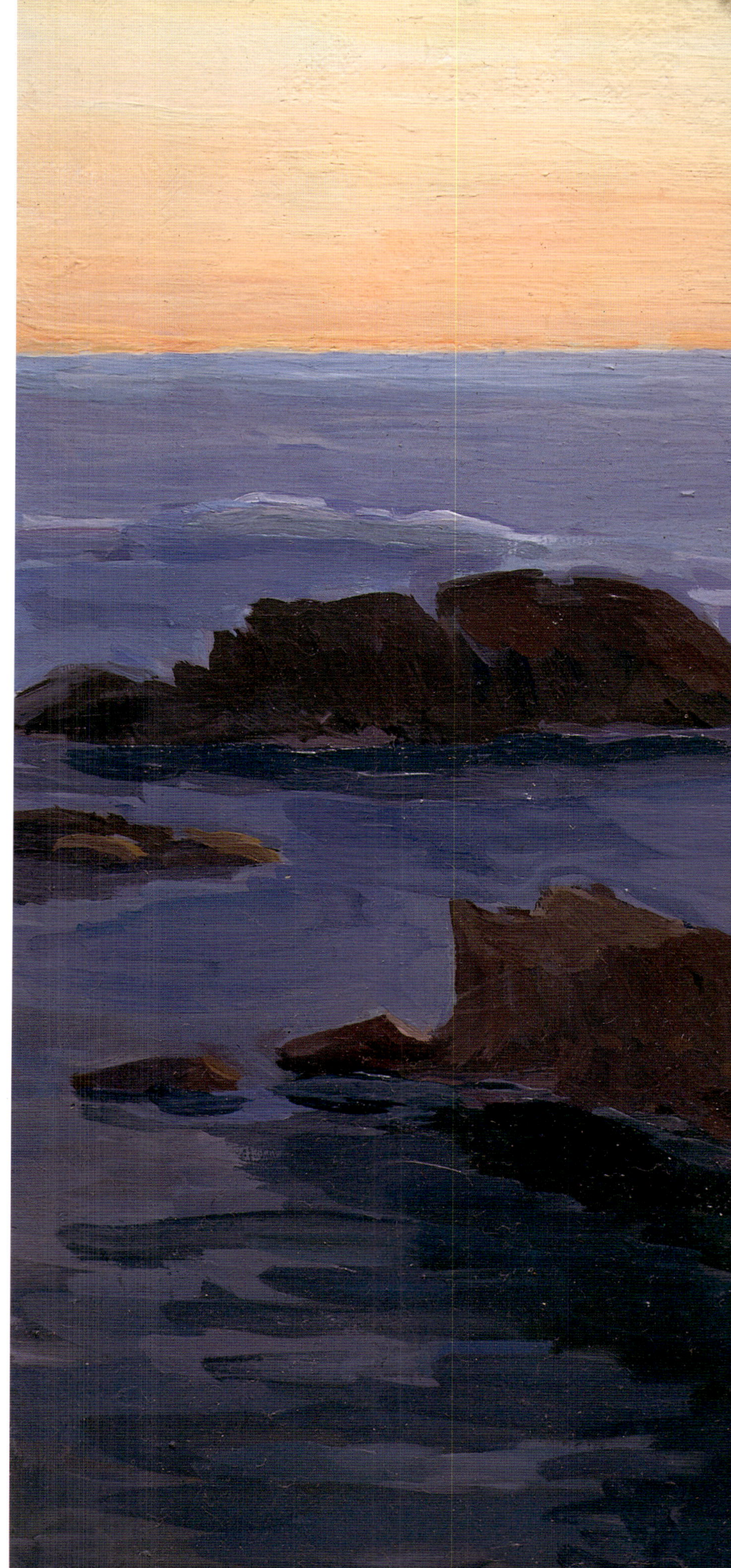

Headlands Sunset 2001, Oil, 9" x 12"
In the collection of William and Angela Young; Berkeley, California

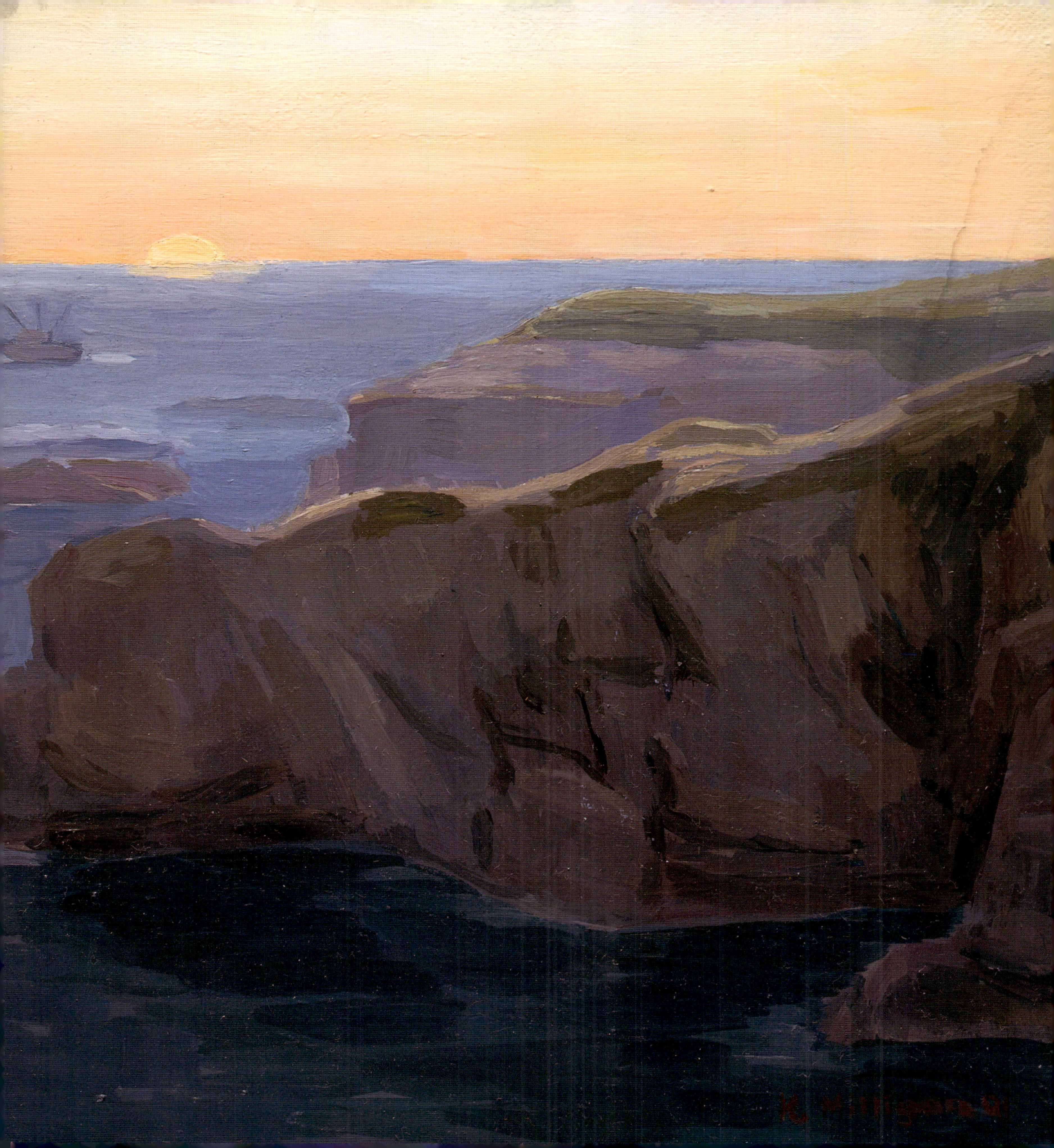

About Kevin Milligan

While growing up in St. Louis, Kevin Milligan painted scenes of the outlying countryside with his dad Guy Milligan, a professional designer and illustrator. Guy often brought home art supplies for Kevin to use, and his mom Jacquelyn encouraged him to keep practicing. Of the four Milligan children, Kevin is the only one to follow as the fourth generation in the arts — his grandfather was a stone artisan and his great-grandfather a cabinetmaker. Like his father, Kevin was a child artist, beginning to paint at age seven, and was greatly influenced not only by his dad's rural farm scenes, but also his midtown St. Louis cityscapes. Similar subjects have also been favorites of Kevin's. He's painted numerous views of the California countryside, and his cityscape "Oakland Skyline with the Grand Lake Theater," was selected for The 20th Century Urban Landscape Exhibition at the Oakland Museum.

Kevin's works are exhibited at regional and national levels where they have received awards and highly favorable reviews. In particular, *New York Times* critic David Shirey chose one of Kevin's landscapes for the 49th Annual Butler Midyear National Exhibition of American Art. And in 1992 Dr. Virginia Mecklenburg, Chief Curator, National Museum of Art, Smithsonian Institution, selected one of Kevin's oils for the Maryland Academy of Arts National Exhibition. Museum directors and curators from the San Francisco Museum of Modern Art, Los Angeles Municipal Gallery, Oakland Museum, and Cleveland Museum of Art have chosen Kevin's works for national and international shows in museums in Italy, North Carolina and California and for galleries in New York, Maryland, Ohio, Kansas and California.

Between 1975–77, he studied with acclaimed figurative painter Wilbur Niewald, Instructor, Chairman and Senior Painting Professor of the Painting Department at the Kansas City Art Institute (1953-92). Niewald received the 1988 College Art Association Distinguished Teaching of Art Award, and has written: "Kevin Milligan is an outstanding painter, approaching his work with intelligence and great determination."

In 1981, two years after earning his MFA at the University of North Carolina, Kevin moved to the San Francisco Bay Area in order to pursue his art and to work with his brother Kris, who has been a professional tennis coach for more than 20 years. Kevin still runs his own summer tennis camp at Cal State University Hayward and is an avid player near his home on the Mendocino Coast.

Kevin Milligan's training at the Kansas City Art Institute included study of the figure, still life and landscape. That collegiate training and the varied aspects of the landscape of California were a perfect match. The mountains, rugged coast, cityscapes, industrial views and vineyards of the "Golden State" have all provided subjects for Kevin's art. And now he is painting Mendocino, integrating its distinctive water towers, cottages and New England-style buildings set against a backdrop of golden fields, blooming greenery and the Pacific Ocean.

Presently Kevin lives in Mendocino. His Coastside Gallery may be found on the ground floor of a water tower built in the 1960s on the corner of historic Lansing Street and Calpella.

Coastside Gallery & Graphics P.O. Box 1538 – 10540 Lansing Street – Mendocino CA 95460

(707) 937-4960 coastsidegallery.com